BOOM! SPLAT!

Comics and Violence

Edited by Jim Coby and Joanna Davis-McElligatt

University Press of Mississippi / Jackson

The University Press of Mississippi is the scholarly publishing agency of the Mississippi Institutions of Higher Learning: Alcorn State University, Delta State University, Jackson State University, Mississippi State University, Mississippi University for Women, Mississippi Valley State University, University of Mississippi, and University of Southern Mississippi.

www.upress.state.ms.us

The University Press of Mississippi is a member of the Association of University Presses.

Copyright © 2024 by University Press of Mississippi
All rights reserved

∞

Co-funded by
the European Union

Library of Congress Cataloging-in-Publication Data

Names: Coby, Jim, editor. | Davis-McElligatt, Joanna, editor.
Title: Boom! Splat! : comics and violence / Jim Coby, Joanna Davis-McElligatt.
Description: Jackson : University Press of Mississippi, 2024. | Includes bibliographical references and index.
Identifiers: LCCN 2023034940 (print) | LCCN 2023034941 (ebook) | ISBN 9781496850034 (hardback) | ISBN 9781496850041 (trade paperback) | ISBN 9781496850058 (epub) | ISBN 9781496850065 (epub) | ISBN 9781496850072 (pdf) | ISBN 9781496850089 (pdf)
Subjects: LCSH: Violence in comics. | Comic books, strips, etc.—History and criticism. | Violence in literature. | Graphic novels—History and criticism. | Terror in literature. | Superheroes in comics.
Classification: LCC PN6714 .B6688 2024 (print) | LCC PN6714 (ebook) | DDC 741.5/3552—dc23/eng/20231019
LC record available at https://lccn.loc.gov/2023034940
LC ebook record available at https://lccn.loc.gov/2023034941

British Library Cataloging-in-Publication Data available

CONTENTS

Introduction: Here Is Violence Galore 3
JIM COBY AND JOANNA DAVIS-McELLIGATT

SECTION I. BANG! HISTORIES OF VIOLENCE

1. Hawk, Dove, Ditko, and Kant: Self-Defense for Superheroes 19
   SAM COWLING

2. Black and White Death: Graphics of Violence from the Great War 32
   CHRISTINA M. KNOPF

3. A Tale of Two Cuban Cartoonists 44
   DIANA ÁLVAREZ AMELL

4. Archiving the Past, Drawing the Present, and Preserving Displaced Histories of Violence in Nonfictional Graphic Novels 56
   NATALJA CHESTOPALOVA

SECTION II. ZZAP! FORMS OF VIOLENCE

5. *Calvin and Hobbes*: A Case Study of the Cartoon Fight Cloud 71
   JACOB MUREL

6. White Black Men and Black White Men: Reading Race as Violence in Mat Johnson and Warren Pleece's *Incognegro: A Graphic Mystery* 83
   JOANNA DAVIS-MCELLIGATT

7. Violence Trying *Patience*: Daniel Clowes, Gender, Semiotics, and the Duo-Parallel-Critical Alternative to McCloud's World-Image Typology in Comics . . . 100
   STEVEN S. VROOMAN

SECTION III. AARRGH! INTERPERSONAL AND COLLECTIVE VIOLENCE

8. Gender-Bending Aggression: A Comparative Study of Superheroine Aggression in *Hulk* (2016), *Captain Marvel* (2017), and *The New Wolverine* (2017) 117
   KIERA M. GASWINT

9. Male Authority against Female Bodies: Gender, Sexuality, and Violence in Comics 132
   ELISABETTA DI MINICO

10. "It's Football, Sir. It's Worth the Blood": Football and "The Violence That Finds Us" in Aaron and Latour's *Southern Bastards* 150
    JIM COBY

11. Complex Comics, Complex Trauma: Registration of Traumatized Childhood in the "Autographics" of Phoebe Gloeckner 161
    PARTHA BHATTACHARJEE AND PRIYANKA TRIPATHI

SECTION IV. THUNK! POLITICAL AND SOCIAL VIOLENCE

12. #BlackLivesMatter and Cartooning Racial Violence 173
    VINCENT HADDAD

13. Radical Empathy in *March* 185
    LEAH MILNE

14. "Peace Be with You": *The Sheriff of Babylon* and Violence in the "War on Terror" . . . 196
    LAWRENCE ABRAMS AND KALEB KNOBLAUCH

15. Violence for the Cause: Social Justice and the Need for Representations of Violence 212
    RITA COSTELLO

Acknowledgments. 227
About the Contributors 229
Index 235

BOOM! SPLAT!

Introduction

HERE IS VIOLENCE GALORE

JIM COBY AND JOANNA DAVIS-McELLIGATT

Discussions of cartoon violence have been typically concerned with representations of physical violence. Forms of physical violence run the gamut in comics, from the comedic slapstick typifying Sunday funnies and Rodolphe Töpffer's early strips, to the gruesome and macabre horror comics of the 1950s at which Fredric Wertham took such umbrage, to the more common and recently cinematic brutalization of nemeses and urban spaces driving any given issue or film fronted by a Marvel or DC superhero. These spectacles and scenes of violence have traditionally relied on the collision of bodies, things, objects, and environments, made manifest in the onomatopoeic language reflected in our title: BOOM! SPLAT! SNIKT! POW! Though physical violence is perhaps the most immediately recognizable of the violences we explore in this collection, it is far from the only type under consideration here. To that end, we must immediately define what we mean when we deploy the fraught and sweeping term "violence." Philip Dwyer notes that "the World Health Organization ... broadly defines violence as 'the intentional use of physical force or power, threatened or actual, against oneself, another person, or against a group or community, that either results in or has a high likelihood of resulting in injury, death, psychological harm, maldevelopment, or deprivation'" (3). The WHO importantly extends the definition of violence beyond the physical to include the psychological, emotional, cultural, and environmental effects of violence on people and their worlds. Dwyer himself locates violence as a matter of intention, as "acts born of a conscious desire to intentionally harm another person, group, or community, resulting in either physical injury or death" (5). For both the WHO and Dwyer, the matter of intention—an individual or collective design to cause deliberate harm—is essential to qualifying and classifying violence. However, Dwyer notes that scholars have been at work to expand the definition of violence to take into account structural and ideological violences, including systems that maintain people in coercive, exploitative relationships, such as slavery and forced labour; human trafficking in people and body parts; the slow and utterly unspectacular grind of poverty that can lead to disease and premature death; and the overexploitation and degradation of the environment. Broader categories such as racism, incarceration (along with the physical and mental violence that can entail), death from preventable accidents or disease, abuse, and cruelty towards animals, the industrialized killing of animals for consumption, as well as bullying, humiliation, and verbal abuse (especially if it results in self-harm or suicide), are also now regarded as forms of violence by some scholars. These broader categories of violence question the notion of intent, that is, scholars who adopt a broad definition of violence often argue that it cannot be reduced to a corporal experience and that the outcomes produced by a violent action are often unintentional (Dwyer 5–6).

Many of these forms of violence are not necessarily driven by individual or collective intention to cause harm, even though they often result in injury or death. Rob Nixon, for example, defines "slow violence" as "a violence that occurs gradually and out of sight, a violence of delayed destruction that is dispersed across time and space, an attritional violence that is typically not viewed as violence at all" (2). Climate change, global conflicts, industrialization, toxic waste dumping, fracking, deforestation, and poisoned rivers and oceans bring about "long dyings—the staggered and staggeringly discounted casualties, both human and ecological, that result from war's toxic aftermaths or climate change" (2–3). Nixon's definition of violence as both immediate and attritional, alternatively interpersonal and impersonal, on scales both local and planetary, and always involving interconnections between animals, people, places, and things opens up critical space for considering how comics creators engage with the capacious nature of violence.

Violence, even between people, is very rarely a single occurrence or phenomena; rather, our experiences of violence are felt at multiple intersecting nodes of our identities. Kimberlé Crenshaw's Black feminist definition of intersectionality, the theory of identity that argues we experience our identities multiply and in intersecting ways, is predicated on extensive examinations of violence against women of color. For Crenshaw, violence against Black women and other women of color is a dimension of both gendered and racial violence, but can include violence at the axis of, say, economic status, ability, marital status, educational attainment, religion, nation of origin, in addition to many other categories of identity. Crenshaw suggests that recognizing these critical intersections as formative to our experiences of life—and therefore our experiences of violence—are crucial for enabling structures of justice that attend to the whole of a person and their world, rather than only bits and pieces of them. Crenshaw notes that "intersectional subordination need not be intentionally produced; in fact, it is frequently the consequence of the imposition of one burden that interacts with preexisting vulnerabilities to create yet another dimension of disempowerment" (1249). Crenshaw's theory of intersectionality reminds us yet again that violence need not be intentionally designed for harm to result. At the same time, intersectional approaches to people enable us to better comprehend and confront the structures and systems that work to oppress individuals at multiple axes of their bodies and beings.

We contend that the exclusion of complex and varied modes, forms, and histories of violence neglects the complex function of violence in the comics language, which is all at once narrative, visual, and formal. Indeed, as Mary Louise Pratt explains, "Violence has scenarios . . . it has nodes" ("Violence and Language")—which is to say that violence is by no means as simple or clean-cut as traditional definitions have suggested. For the purposes of this collection, we define violence as any sort of action, interpersonal or collective, regardless of deliberateness or intentionality, that results in any degree of harm against or between people and their collective environments. In *BOOM! SPLAT!*, in addition to traditional modes of physical violence enacted between persons and their environments, we examine the forms and structures of violence embedded in the comics language itself, representations of historical violence, ways of reading and seeing violence, affects effected by and ideas about violence, aesthetics of violence, and systems of ephemeral, psychological, and ideological violence.

The last of these forms of violence have garnered increasing attention in the past decade, given that language and the policing of affect can often operate as forms of abstract violence. In strict opposition to the maxim that "words can never hurt me," studies now show that adverse language directed at a person can cause physiological damage not unlike the long-term effects of physical violence. As Lisa Feldmen Barrett explains, "Words can have a powerful affect on your nervous system. Certain types of adversity, even those involving no physical contact, can make you sick, alter your brain—even kill neurons—and shorten your life" ("When Is Speech Violence?"). When words are deployed as violence, the stress response can become physically catalyzed both cognitively and bodily: "If words can cause stress, and if prolonged stress can cause physical harm, then it seems that speech—at least certain types of speech—can be a form of violence" ("When Is Speech

Violence?"). And in this way, comics exists as an artform uniquely situated to address violence. Physical violence quite often concatenates to linguistic violence. As Mary Louise Pratt notes, "In our common sense, we often speak as if violence and language were mutually exclusive. . . . We also think of violence as often that which is beyond language. People often describe war as being beyond words. But violence actually is almost always accompanied by language" ("Language and Violence").

The consequences of harm done—from concretely observed physical injury or death to intangible emotional or psychological stress or trauma—are unevenly dealt and unequally experienced. Elaine Scarry has observed that pain is fundamentally inexpressible and singular to the experiencer. If there are multiple languages of violence, "there is no language for pain, . . . it (more than any other phenomenon) resists verbal objectification" (12). In fact, Scarry argues, physical pain, in particular, is "so nearly impossible to express, so flatly invisible, that the problem goes beyond the possibility that almost any other phenomenon occupying the same environment will distract attention from it. Indeed, even where it is virtually the only content in a given environment, it would be possible to describe that environment as though the pain were not there" (12). Given the dynamic ways comics syntax operates in a liminal space where word and image meet, cartoon language is a particularly dynamic way of representing not only violence, but the affectual, psychological, and emotional aftershocks of harm done. The combination of word and image enables creators to work within and against the limitations of nonrepresentational language in order to more clearly examine what violence looks like, how it happens, and whose pain matters in the end. By externalizing the internal, cartoons can stage a critical dialectic between the function of power, between those harmed and those causing harm, and between the reader and the creator's universe.

Sara Ahmed reminds us that just because we cannot feel or truly know another's pain does not mean that we have no responsibility to others in their moments of suffering. In fact, for Ahmed the inexpressibility of pain is precisely the catalyst for the alleviating of suffering: "The impossibility of feeling the pain of others does not mean that the pain is simply theirs, or that their pain has nothing to do with me. I want to suggest . . . that an ethics of responding to pain involves being open to being affected by that which one cannot know, or feel. . . . Insofar as an ethics of pain begins here . . . then the ethical demand is that I must act about that which I cannot know, rather than act insofar as I know" (30). Ahmed suggests that our paying attention to the pain of others—a pain we cannot feel ourselves, a pain to which we will always remain a distant party—has the potential to create new conditions of mutual understanding; by rejecting the conditions of empathy that suggest we learn to care deeply for others because we understand their pain, Ahmed suggests that we instead bear witness to the pain of another knowing full well we cannot experience it. All narrative has the potential to enable readers to bear witness to the pain of others in this way—we argue that comics are uniquely equipped to do this work given the way both representational and abstract language operate together on the page. As a consequence, readers are uniquely able to confront violence in multiple modes simultaneously on the comics page.

Comics scholars have long grappled with the signification of violence—how to best represent violence, and in what precise aesthetic form? In *Comics and Sequential Art*, Will Eisner explains how the literal framing of a comics character's words or thoughts can reveal malice, animosity, or the intent of violence; for example, a "jagged outline implies an emotionally explosive action. It conveys a state of tension" (46). Significantly, Eisner does not explicitly note here that the action itself is violent, but rather that it is on the precipice of violence. The *almost violence* of the jagged speech bubble then suggests that the harm lies not within the immediate words or thoughts, but within their intent for long term destruction. Eisner's observation about the capacity of signs to be transliterated into violence makes a strong case that words do have the potential to both represent and enact violence, and calls to mind arguments about the importance of linguistic and narrative representations of violence in comics.

Representations of violence in cartoons have tended to be taken for granted as endemic to the form. Cartoon images of violence, however, in all its manifestations—physical, psychological, ideological, systemic, material, and invisible—bolsters much of the visual, narrative, and structural content of the form. In spite of the ubiquity of violence in the cartoon language, acts of violence have long existed without much commentary. Perhaps this is because scholars intuitively understand that, yes, of course, violence should be present in comics—why should we remark on it? As Nina Mickwitz, Ian Horton, and Ian Hague have recently noted, "The presence of violence in the comics form is now so prevalent and accepted that it tends to go unremarked" (1). In short, we have not yet been able to see the violence of the forest for the laser-shooting, kickboxing, BAM!-inciting trees. Our collection seeks to fill in these critical gaps by offering sustained explorations of the function of manifold violences in the comics language, from those you can see to those you can feel, to those you can think, to those you can say, to those you can do.

The culture, distribution, and content of comics changed forever in 1954—indeed, we feel the impacts even now. Long a mainstay of America's reading diet, comic books began to fall under the scrutiny of parent groups, church leaders, and politicians alike. The bright colors and cheaply printed pulp pages of comic books that had once provided an escape for readers—both children and adults—suddenly were presumed to house something lascivious, insidious, and morally corrosive. Chief among the critics who condemned comics and the comics industry was the German-born psychologist Fredric Wertham. In the introduction to his landmark work *Seduction of the Innocent*, Wertham suggested that "chronic stimulation, temptation and seduction by comic books . . . are contributing factors to many children's maladjustment" (10). Anxious that children would be forever corrupted by the content of comics—the ghastly macabre of horror comics, the buxom and muscled characters of romance comics, the cartoonish slapstick and distaste for authority evinced across funny animal comics—Wertham's criticisms were leveled squarely at the creators and readers of comics. In addition to citing his own adolescent patients whose transgressive behavior he attributed to comics reading, Wertham provided close readings of several specific comics narratives he deemed particularly offensive. Chief among Wertham's complaints was that comics narratives were intrinsically violent, and that repeated exposure to acts of brutality would permanently malform the minds and overdetermine the actions of his impressionable young clients. "Here is violence galore," Wertham writes. "Violence in the beginning, in the middle, and at the end" (8). Though often portrayed as the primary instigator of public backlash to comics, Wertham was far from alone in mounting these criticisms of cartoons. In his comprehensive study of midcentury comics culture, David Hajdu references a number of influential naysayers who aimed their vitriol at the comics industry; the professor Gershon Legman, for example, "spat purple venom" (Hajdu 231) at the comics industry: "Garnishing presented in clashing colors, and cheaply printed in forty-eight pages of paper-bound pulp with even more garish covers, what recourse there is in comic-books to the printed world is, totally, language violence" (quoted in Hajdu 231).

In both Legman's and Wertham's demonstrative critiques, anxieties about the violence of cartoons repeatedly bubble to the surface. More specifically, anticartoon critics worried about the potential effects of reading about and witnessing acts of violence and expressed concern that young people might enact their own violences based on what they witnessed and perceived in the comic books readily available to them. The effects were widespread. Carol L. Tilley notes that Wertham's work spurred an already galvanized public to agitate successfully for changes in the editorial and advertising content of comic books. The CMAA's [Comics Magazine Association of America] resulting code, in turn, crippled the successful comics industry by ensuring that comics that carried its imprimatur were free of offensive content such as poor grammar, excessive violence, and supernatural beings. (385)

It was only in 2011, with the dissolution of the Comics Code Authority, that popular comics fully and freely abandoned the last of the strictures which had been in place since the mid-1950s. And while anxieties about representations of violence in comics have largely fallen to the wayside since the moral panic of the 1950s, displaced onto moral panics about the Beatles, science fiction, horror films, *Grand Theft Auto*, YouTube, and so on (and so on and so on), violence remains every bit as ubiquitous in comics as it ever was. For all the posturing and outrage leveled against the comics industry, the content creators remain steadfast in their employment of symbolic and visual violence as a narrative technique. Indeed, representations of violence have been integral to the comics language and, therefore, of deep concern to scholars of comics studies.

The earliest pieces of art typically classified as comics, such as Rodolphe Töpffer's "Historie d'Albert," prominently revolve around the ne'er-do-well titular character consistently (and rewardingly) receiving firm kicks on his backside for upsetting social mores. The cover of Action Comics #1 features Superman lifting a demolished car above his head, while terrified people flee from the center of destruction. Perhaps the most singularly famous cover of an American comic book showcases Captain America delivering a devastating punch to Adolf Hitler, and, as this was the first issue of his series, metaphorically punching his way into the American consciousness. While his popular scholarship has somewhat fallen out of favor in recent years, even Scott McCloud's otherwise placid *Understanding Comics* relies on a horrific, if unseen, act of violence in order to demonstrate the idea of closure within the field of comics. By constructing narratives between the gaps readers take on an added responsibility and weight—they become active participants in creation of the story; central to the act of closure, McCloud argues, is the likelihood that readers will cede to their worst impulses when filling in gaps of cartoon narratives. McCloud's choice of panels includes an axe-wielding maniac chasing a man, followed by an exterior shot of a skyline with a speech bubble indicating a scream of panic that reads "Eeya!" (68). "To kill a man between the panels," McCloud notes, "is to condemn him to a thousand deaths" (69). Even so, comics scholars have only recently begun to seriously interrogate the idea with any sustained vigor. Part of this, no doubt, stems from academia's continued reluctance to accept comics studies scholarship. Nevertheless, "There is little question that it is an exciting moment in which to read, study, teach, and write about graphic narratives" (Stamant 1). Scholars of comics studies continue to find themselves all too frequently beyond the pale of legitimacy. And though, admittedly, there has been much progress since Thierry Groensteen charged in 2000 that "it is curious that the legitimizing authorities (universities, museums, the media) still regularly charge [comics] with being infantile, vulgar, or insignificant" (3), it is likewise true that challenges about the "worthiness" or "literariness" of comics remain manifold. We will not delve further into the history of academia's reluctant acceptance of comics into its hallowed halls, but the fact that we were each the first faculty members to teach classes dedicated to comics studies at our previous universities signals that, much as we might like to believe otherwise, the field still has much progress to make. We aim for this collection of scholarship to help pave that road of progress. Violence is inherently vast, multiplicitous, and widespread. As such, the scholarship included in this collection addresses widely varied, often-contradictory methodologies and manifestations of violence in comics.

BOOM! SPLAT! Comics and Violence is composed of fifteen essays, organized thematically in four sections. Section I: Bang! Histories of Violence, explores how cartoon violence has shaped and been shaped by particular historical contexts. The essays in this section consider how representations of violence are dependent on historical conditions that determine the modes of visual-narrative and structural storytelling in the comics language. In chapter one, "Hawk, Dove, Ditko, and Kant: Self-Defense for Superheroes," Sam Cowling argues that the series *The Hawk and the Dove* (1968), by placing a nominally pacifist character at the heart of the action, is a peculiar experiment in the superhero genre. Pitting two superpowered brothers at loggerheads over the ethics of violence, this series (and its precursor in which the titular characters debut) marks a distinctive period in Steve Ditko's exploration of violence and morality within the superhero genre at a crucial time in US history. Along with its striking critique of the ethics of nonviolence, Cowling argues that Ditko's brief run with these characters is marked by an engagement with the nature of moral knowledge. In chapter two, "Black and White Death: Graphics of Violence from the Great War," Christina M. Knopf reads hermeneutic images and visual motifs of violence and death in comics from and about World War I. Focusing on graphic narratives from the United Kingdom and British Commonwealth, Knopf examines primary graphic accounts created by soldiers during the Great War, secondary graphic accounts created through interpretations of historical research, and tertiary accounts that blend primary narratives with reimagined visuals premised on secondary sources. Knopf's study builds on distinctions of memory and postmemory of the war, as she considers how different proximities to its violence shape portrayals of its violence, particularly given that changing motifs over time highlight the process of memory and memorializing.

In chapter three, "A Tale of Two Cuban Cartoonists," Diana Álvarez Amell compares the lives and comic art of two Cuban cartoonists, Antonio Prohías and Santiago Armada, who both published under the pen name Chago. Though Prohías left Cuba for the US early in the 1960s and Chago stayed, Álvarez Amell examines how both artists experienced painful entanglements with their country's politics. Prohías was able to cross the cultural divide by successfully transforming his Cuban Sinister Man into the American phenomenon of the transnational wacky sinister spies in *Spy vs. Spy*, popularized in *Mad Magazine*. Chago's revolutionary commitment led him at first to design cheerful and politically engaged cartoons, which were eventually abandoned for an enigmatic and morose *Salomón*, a series that was banned in Cuba. Over time, Prohías and Armada's graphic work in a popular medium has acquired testimonial value as symbolic representations of their historical time. In chapter four, "Archiving the Past, Drawing the Present, and Preserving Displaced Histories of Violence in Nonfictional Graphic Novels," Natalja Chestopalova argues that portrayals of violence and trauma in comics have evolved far beyond the genres of superhero and autobiography into modalities that resist immediate identification because they embody the changing flow of cultural memory and its activist capital. This pivotal shift positions comics as a decolonizing medium with the potential to create new counterhegemonic narrative-archives outside of institutionalized spaces and practices. In Chestopalova's exploration of Joe Sacco's *Palestine* (2001) and *Footnotes in Gaza* (2009), as well as more recent works, such as Jeff Lemire and Gord Downie's *Secret Path* (2016) and Kate Evans's *Threads: From the Refugee Crisis* (2017), she argues that cartoons can function as part of the unofficial multimodal archive that exists on the periphery of institutionalized memory. These graphic novels challenge conceptions of local and global spaces and shift the perception of the physical and emotional distance that occurs between the reader and sites of individual suffering, generational violence, and community trauma. Whether addressing the violent past of Canadian residential schools or the violence perforating refugees' lives, the narrative effects force the reader to view the sites of trauma from a variety of angles and experience multiple spatial and emotional relationships, from global to local to intersubjective.

Section II: Zzap! Forms of Violence examines how violence is made manifest at the level of the icon, sign, and symbol, and as a structural and formal aspect endemic to the comics language. Central to this section is considerations of how these forms and structures of violence are interpreted and given meaning by readers, and how they are designed and brought to bear by creators. In chapter five, "*Calvin and Hobbes*: A Case Study of the Cartoon Fight Cloud," Jacob Murel turns his attention toward the ever-ubiquitous dust-devil from Sunday morning comic strips: the "Cartoon Fight Cloud." This amorphous yet instantly recognizable cloud of stars, lines, fists, and symbolia appears in countless comic strips. Through a close reading of several *Calvin and Hobbes* strips, Murel argues that by eschewing actual drawn violence, and instead obfuscating the acts beneath an impenetrable fog, Watterson requires the reader to actively participate in the comic strip's violence and to become complicit in the acts they imagine, but do not quite witness. In chapter six, "White Black Men and Black White Men: Reading Race as Violence in Mat Johnson and Warren Pleece's *Incognegro: A Graphic Mystery*," Joanna Davis-McElligatt examines the function of physiognmy and phenotypicality in the two editions of *Incognegro*—the 2008 edition, in which all characters are represented in stark black-and-white outlines, and the 2018 edition, which adds additional gray and black shading to every figure. Davis-McElligatt argues that the discrepancies between the 2008 and 2018 editions of *Incognegro* help to elucidate the process of reading race and inscribing its meaning on Black bodies, complicating readers' attempts to arrive at comfortable conclusions about a subject's race or ethnicity based on either phenotype or skin tone alone. The function of reading race in comics, Davis-McElligatt contends, is central to the processes of meaning-making in the form. Finally, in chapter seven, "Violence Trying *Patience*: Daniel Clowes, Gender, Semiotics, and the Duo-Parallel-Critical Alternative to McCloud's World-Image Typology in Comics," an essay workshopped extensively with insight from students, Steven S. Vrooman examines the myriad forms of violence in Daniel Clowes's recent work *Patience*. Vrooman argues that the critical vocabulary for discussing violence in comics has been woefully stunted by an overreliance on Scott McCloud's principal axioms in *Understanding Comics*; as a consequence, Vrooman posits new lines of discourse to help both authors and readers to better understand and catalog how violence—both the physical form and the more imbedded forms—might be better read.

Section III: Aarrgh! Interpersonal and Collective Violence examines modes and systems of violence between people, between people and their community, and between people and their environment. Though these systems and structures of interpersonal and collective violence are produced out of gender dynamics, cultural norms, and the autobiographical impulse to document trauma, each essay takes as its central critical locus the ways in which trauma impact the person and their immediate surroundings. In chapter eight, "Gender-Bending Aggression: A Comparative Study of Superheroine Aggression in *Hulk* (2016), *Captain Marvel* (2017), and *The New Wolverine* (2017)," Kiera M. Gaswint analyzes three of the most well-known gender-bending Marvel characters—She-Hulk, X23, and Captain Marvel—in an attempt to understand how readers perceive aggression when a title is passed between differently gendered bodies, and how expressions of violence change as a consequence of those bodies. Gaswint explores how the experience of aggressive female characters is tied to their original male counterparts, despite the fact that the aggressive female experience is critically different from the male experience. In chapter nine, "Male Authority Against Female Bodies: Gender, Sexuality, and Violence in Comics," Elisabetta Di Minico argues that the depiction of women in comics is necessarily complicated because the representation of female characters is not univocal and fixed, neither temporally nor geographically, neither physically nor conceptually. Women can be as strong and indomitable as they are hypersexualized, relegated into domesticity and dreaming of a perfect married life, or occupying positions of power. Because women can be damsels in distress, sidekicks, superheroines, girlfriends, wives, lovers, slaves, mistresses, and villainesses, DiMinico examines how violence against women, toxic masculinity, objectification, and disempowering and depreciation are presented and received in selected comics from Marvel and DC.

In chapter ten, "'It's Football, Sir. It's Worth the Blood': Football and 'The Violence That Finds Us' in Aaron and Latour's *Southern Bastards*," Jim Coby takes readers to the Deep South in the fictional locale of Craw County, Alabama where violence, football, and the violence concomitant to football are a way of life. Euless Boss, a fearsome and ferocious football coach of the Craw County Runnin' Rebs football team, is willing to employ physical and psychological violence against anyone who crosses him or his interests. Coby explores Boss's pathology and his unique willingness to put himself and others in harm's way as a manifestation of the ideals proposed in Harry Crews's facetious essay "The Violence That Finds Us." In the end, Coby claims that Boss's disposition can reveal much about legacies of trauma and the willingness to pursue violence in the poor, white South. Lastly, in chapter eleven, "Complex Comics, Complex Trauma: Registration of Traumatized Childhood in the 'Autographics' of Phoebe Gloeckner," Partha Bhattacharjee and Priyanka Tripathi argue that one of the most frequently cited reasons for complex trauma is childhood abuse, which has been directly linked to disruptions in cultural as well as personal memory. Bhattcharjee and Tripathi analyze Phoebe Gloeckner's *A Child's Life and Other Stories* (1999, 2000) and *Diary of a Teenage Girl: An Account in Words and Pictures* (2002, 2015) and discuss how graphic narratives can represent complex trauma and the work of postmemory following the violence of childhood abuse are no exception to it.

The final, and arguably most urgent, Section IV: Thunk! Political and Social Violence, investigates violence in comics as an inherently political mechanism. The essays in this section consider how contemporary cartoon narratives explore racial violence in and as perpetrated by the US and its citizens, and make the case that comics art, even when depicting our most abhorrent moments of violence, provides an inroad for exploring and grappling with monumental issues of social justice. In chapter twelve, "#BlackLivesMatter and Cartooning Racial Violence," Vincent Haddad examines a series of comics in order to ascertain the function of racial violence in the comics medium through a consideration of style, narrative, and aesthetics. Haddad suggests that there is certainly political potential in representations of racial violence, and that superhero comics offer a unique opportunity to examine who is considered to be the right recipient of retributive violence, and who is constructed as a victim of violence. However, Haddad concludes that images of racial violence do not always or only produce empathic responses in readers—in many instances, they may do just the opposite; racial violence, Haddad argues, must be coupled with narrative structures that support and contextualize them, and that provide readers with an opportunity to scaffold their complex of responses to them. In chapter thirteen, "Radical Empathy in *March*," Leah Milne focuses on John Lewis, Andrew Aydin, and Nate Powell's graphic memoir trilogy, and analyzes how the texts' visual engagement with the intersections between violence and empathy. More specifically, Milne argues that because Lewis was a major proponent of practicing nonviolence, even in the face of the discrimination and relentless assault that he and others faced during the civil rights movement, the visual elements in the graphic novels speak to the challenges and limits that this nonviolence has for those suffering from racial oppression. Milne examines how similarity bias, or the inclination to prefer and be more empathetic towards those who look like you, has a particular resonance in graphic novels and in Lewis's trilogy in particular, whose artistic style—crafted by artist Nate Powell—aims for near photo realism; Milne suggests that *March* deliberately confronts readers about this bias through sprawling black-and-white images that often travel beyond the comic's panels, thereby challenging readers' understanding of empathy and its limitations in the face of violence.

In chapter fourteen, "'Peace Be with You': *The Sheriff of Babylon* and Violence in the 'War on Terror,'" Lawrence Abrams and Kaleb Knoblauch examine depictions and typologies of violence in Tom King and Mitch Gerad's *The Sheriff of Babylon* (2015). Abrams and Knoblauch establish a typology of violence, arguing that *The Sheriff of Babylon* depicts violence in several significant ways: by hiding key violent acts behind all-black panels or disorienting clouds of dust and debris, by racializing and gendering overt displays of violence, and by grappling with ineffective violence, which can lead readers to question the efficacy of America's so-called "War on Terror" and the moral legitimacy of American hegemony. In closing, in chapter fifteen, "Violence for the Cause: Social Justice and the Need for Representations of Violence," Rita Costello, in a sweeping and authoritative chapter, reckons with the myriad permutations and manifestations of violence in comics cultures. Beginning with the Comics Code Authority and moving toward contemporary comics, Costello explores how some of the most highly regarded authors, such as Stan Lee and Alan Moore, and canonical texts, such as Art Spiegelman's *Maus* and Marjane Satrapi's *Persepolis*, have incorporated violence not for violence's sake, but as a means to make overarching cultural and critical interjections. Whether in government-supported calls to address drug problems in Lee's Spider-Man, or in challenging readers' basic conceptualizations of precisely with whom and how we empathize with human and animal life alike in Spiegelman's *Maus*, Costello argues that representations of violence can effectively provoke readers to confront matters of social justice lying beneath the surface of texts.

As Hillary Chute has argued, "Comics can be so powerful because it presents the texture of real-life disaster and war without sensationalizing the violence—and yet without turning away from it" (37). We hope that, as Chute suggests, in our refusal to turn away from violence, *BOOM! SPLAT! Comics and Violence* will serve as a resource for scholars and comics enthusiasts who wish to contemplate and confront the permutations, forms, structures, and discourses of violence that have always animated cartoons. By providing contexts and analysis at multiple axes of violent representation—both formal, narrative, and visual—the essays in this collection are critically necessary for understanding the role that violence has played historically and in our current moment, and to better understand how cartooning imbricates, resists, and expands on our thinking and experience of violence in all its manifestations.

Works Cited

Ahmed, Sara. *The Cultural Politics of Emotion*. New York: Routledge, 2015.

Barrett, Lisa Feldman. "When Is Speech Violence?" *New York Times*, July 14, 2017. https://www.nytimes.com/2017/07/14/opinion/sunday/when-is-speech-violence.html. Accessed June 12, 2020.

Chute, Hillary. *Why Comics? From Underground to Everywhere*. New York: HarperCollins, 2017.

Crenshaw, Kimberlé. "Mapping the Margins: Intersectionality, Identity Politics, and Violence Against Women of Color." *Stanford Law Review* 43, no. 6 (1993): 1241–99.

Dwyer, Philp. *Violence: A Very Short Introduction*. Oxford: Oxford University Press, 2022.

Eisner, Will. *Comics and Sequential Art*. New York: Poorhouse Press, 1985.

Groensteen, Thierry. "Why Are Comics Still in Search of Cultural Legitimization?" In *A Comic Studies Reader*, edited by Jeet Heer and Kent Worcester, 3–12. Jackson: University Press of Mississippi, 2009.

Hajdu, David. *The Ten-Cent Plague: The Great Comic Book Scare and How It Changed America*. New York: Farrar, Straus and Giroux, 2008.

McCloud, Scott. *Understanding Comics*. New York: HarperPerennial, 1994.

Mickwitz, Nina, Ian Horton, and Ian Hague, eds. *Representing Acts of Violence in Comics*. New York: Routledge, 2020.

Nixon, Rob. *Slow Violence and the Environmentalism of the Poor*. Cambridge, MA: Harvard University Press, 2011.

Pratt, Mary Louise. "Violence and Language," *Social Text Online*, May 21, 2011. https://socialtextjournal.org/periscope_article/violence_and_language_-_mary_louise_pratt/. Accessed Nov. 15, 2022.

Probyn, Elspeth. *Blush: Faces of Shame*. Minneapolis: University of Minnesota Press, 2005.

Scarry, Elaine. *The Body in Pain: The Making and Unmaking of the World*. New York: Oxford University Press, 1985.

Stamant, Nicole. "Graphic Narrative: An Introduction," *South Central Review* 32, no. 3 (2015): 1–7.

Tilley, Carol L. "Seducing the Innocent: Frederic Wertham and the Falsifications That Helped Condemn Comics," *Information & Culture: A Journal of History* 47, no. 4 (2012): 383–413.

Section I

BANG! HISTORIES OF VIOLENCE

1

HAWK, DOVE, DITKO, AND KANT
Self-Defense for Superheroes

SAM COWLING

INTRODUCTION

Superhero comics are burdened with certain narrative expectations. Chief among them is a violent confrontation between hero and villain or, in all-too-familiar cases of manipulation and misunderstanding, violent confrontation between hero and hero.[1] Unsurprisingly, then, superhero comics offer a staggering number of ways in which expectations of violent confrontation can be met. Superpowers vary wildly but usually in ways that serve to magnify the intensity of violent conflict. Settings are altered but often to embed characters in increasingly dangerous surroundings. Superhero teams are constituted and reconstituted but usually in ways that deliver novel permutations of previous violent confrontations. Rendering these confrontations in novel and jaw-dropping detail is among the central artistic aims in many superhero comics. But, as with any other genre, authors and artists have sought out ways to challenge, invert, or otherwise frustrate the narrative expectations of superhero comics. While strategies for defying the norms of violence in superhero comics come in a variety of forms, one strategy for thwarting the narrative expectation of violence remains exceptionally rare: the presentation of a pacifist or putatively nonviolent superhero.

Perhaps the most famous effort of this kind is found in Steve Ditko and Steve Skeates's 1968 series *The Hawk and the Dove*, which stands out as an unusual exercise in upending the expectations of violence that underpin superhero comics. The peculiarity of this series stems from the genre-defying characterization of one of its two focal heroes, Dove. While Dove's counterpoint, Hawk, is preternaturally eager to fight, Dove is the picture of servility, stricken with an anxiety to avoid conflict at apparently any cost. And, while craven characters are familiar enough in superhero books, they are almost never heroes, much less titular characters.

The central narrative conceit of *The Hawk and the Dove* has its origin in the political conflict regarding America's military involvement in Vietnam. In early 1968, DC editor Carmine Infantino seized on the largely derisive terms "hawk" and "dove," popularized in public debate over the war. Infantino then tasked Ditko, with editorial support from Dick Giordano, to draw and plot a comic reflecting these labels. Later, with Skeates scripting dialogue, the book would emerge as one of the stranger sixties spins on superhero comics due to its efforts to explore the tension between these exaggerated, stereotypical views regarding violence. The awkward central conceit of the book, when coupled with Ditko's peculiar style and plotting, presents a frequently exhausting and perpetually anxious view of civil society under political stress and emotional strain.

Although the impetus for Hawk and Dove's creation was the Vietnam War, the narratives that run throughout the series steer conspicuously wide of direct engagement with the war itself. And, while superheroes featured in war comics usually embody or typify patriotic values, Hawk and Dove are "war characters" of an attenuated and especially strange sort. They are not intended to serve as heroic personifications of national ideals, but rather as embodiments of the derisive stereotypes that arise in political debates regarding military violence in Vietnam and elsewhere. While personifications of national and moral ideals are quite familiar in both war and superhero comics, Hawk and Dove stand out for being heroic personifications of negative stereotypes drawn from the political metacommentary surrounding war. (The figurative association of doves with peace is longstanding; however, the use of "hawk" and "dove" as polarizing terms regarding military violence is often traced to the Cuban Missile Crisis.[2])

Given the odd circumstances of their conception, it is unsurprising that Hawk and Dove begin their narrative lives with little characterization beyond their stereotypical attitudes towards violence. Since these attitudes are, by design, incompatible with each other, the stories featuring Hawk and Dove are marked by rapid and overwrought debates over the permissibility of violent intervention. As a result, Ditko and Skeates's *The Hawk and the Dove* functions largely as an experiment concerning the boundaries of superhero comics and the norms of violence that inform them. Repeatedly, the reader finds herself engaged with a narrative thought experiment that plays out on the page: what happens when a superhero engages crime without the possibility of deploying violence? More generally, can a character opposed to violence *really* be a superhero?

Because of its unusual lead characters, *The Hawk and The Dove* affords us a helpful tool for uncovering some of the implicit moral presuppositions of superhero comics, especially as they concern the ethics of violence.

THE HAWK AND THE DOVE

Hawk and Dove's debut in DC's *Showcase* #75 (cover date: June 1968) sets out the characters' origin and concludes with an advertisement for a continuing *The Hawk and the Dove* series, which would run for only six issues before its cancellation in June 1969. In a somewhat ironic turn, the political opposition that undergirded the rhetorical conceit of the book also played out among Hawk and Dove's cocreators. Ditko, a staunch conservative, and Skeates, a self-described "hippie," were immediately at loggerheads about the characterization of Dove. As Skeates would describe it,

> A lot of changes would happen after I turned in a script. Quite often, my idea of what to do with the Dove was have him do brave stuff—and then it would be changed by either Dick or Steve into the Hawk doing that stuff. They'd say it was out of character for the Dove. They seemed to be equating Dove with wimp, wuss, coward or whatever. (Skeates 72)

Perhaps for this reason, the production of the series was notably unstable with Ditko leaving after only three issues and Skeates leaving after issue four. Gil Kane took over primary art duties with issue four and both writing and art duties in issues five and six. Much of the discussion below focuses on the internal character dynamics first set by Ditko and Skeates, with the aid of Infantino and Giordano, though Kane's contributions prove significant in working through the initial conditions established in this first *Showcase* issue. Additionally, in light of Skeates's remarks about the editorial process and the frequent revision of his scripting by Ditko and Giordano, there is reason to believe that Ditko had a primary role in establishing certain characterizations and narrative dynamics.

In keeping with their typical dialogue throughout the continuing series, the alter egos of Hawk and Dove, Hank and Don Hall, are introduced mid-argument. The brothers' roles as exemplars are made immediately manifest: they are positioned near opposed groups of protesters on a college campus. One group, aligned with Don, decry a conspicuously unnamed war, and the other group, aligned with Hank, protest in favor of the generic war with signs that read "Keep up the bombing" (Ditko et al. 1). Don, the slight blonde, is bow-tied and cardigan-clad, while Hank—red-haired and sneering—is balled up in a state of angst and frustration. The protests quickly erupt into violence, although no indication of what triggers this escalation is given, nor is any resolution of the brawl shown. Instead, the scene immediately shifts to a courtroom where the boys' father, Judge Irwin Hall, is handing down a maximum sentence to a recently convicted criminal.

The didactic role of Judge Hall is swiftly established with Ditko and Skeates directly positioning him as the counterpoint to the pair of brothers. Where the reader is invited to see both Don and Hank as foolhardy and hostage to their emotions, Judge Hall offers unvarnished albeit frustratingly opaque appeals to "reason" and "logic" as the proper arbiter of moral issues regarding violence. Judge Hall intervenes in Hank and Don's squabbling as follows:

> Oh, and you think you're right! Well then, suppose you explain to me just what it is that makes YOU right and THEM wrong! Time and again I've asked you and Don to explain your beliefs to me! But neither of you seem able to do so! As far as I can see, neither of you have thought this thing out! That means you're BOTH wrong! As I've said before, it's not enough to repeat slogans! You have to have more REASONING behind your beliefs! (Ditko et al. 11–12)

Later, Judge Hall adds,

> Sometimes it surprises me that MY two sons could act so irrationally! You're always arguing, but neither of you know what you're talking about! You've got to learn—the ONLY way to solve problems is through logic! (Ditko et al. 12)

For all its didacticism regarding the ethics of violence, the moral undergirding of *The Hawk and the Dove* remains woefully unclear. Evidently, Ditko and Skeates envision Judge Hall and his interaction with Hank and Don to be saying *something* about the ethics of violence, but what exactly? Is it merely a means for demonstrating the untenability of any middle ground regarding the ethics of violence? If so, it would seem to anticipate the uncompromisingly brutal ethics made explicit in Ditko's later work.

A natural place to look for interpretive guidance is moral philosophy, but, even here, importantly different readings of Hawk and Dove suggest themselves, several of which push us in a notably different direction than familiar gestures towards Rand's influence on Ditko. The most straightforward of these invites a reading that hinges on the virtue ethics espoused by Aristotle.[3] Such a reading enjoys some support from Ditko's engagement with Aristotelian themes and ideas, though these were invariably refracted through Ditko's urgent preoccupation with Randian Objectivism. For example, Ditko repeatedly appeals to "A=A," which Rand alleges is a distinctively Aristotelian thesis, in characterizing the Randian exemplar, Mr. A. (see Bell 2008: 111). While Ditko seems to think this captures the law of identity and the essence of Aristotle's philosophy, most philosophers would find this a highly idiosyncratic reading of Aristotle (or the content of a tautology). In similar homage, Vic Sage's confidant in *The Question* stories was pointedly named "Aristotle."[4] But, when read along these lines, Judge Hall is naturally positioned as an embodiment of an Aristotelian conception of virtue, which distinguishes virtuous moral traits by situating them as "the golden mean" on a spectrum between vicious extremes. (By way of example, the virtue of courage falls between the vicious traits of recklessness and cowardice.) So interpreted, Judge Hall's putatively moderate views on violence would emerge as virtuous precisely because of their intermediary position between the polarizing vices of Don's servility and Hank's irascibility.[5] When cast against this Aristotelian backdrop, the extreme nature of Hawk and Dove's stances immediately presents the two as vicious and morally problematic. It seems, however, that while Ditko and Skeates find fault with Hank and Don there is a sustained effort to cast them in a broadly heroic light. In addition, a broadly Aristotelian reading fails to account for what is perhaps the most striking feature of the series' frequent moralizing: Judge Hall's labored and peculiar insistence that moral justification issue from "logic" alone.

Judge Hall's remarks regarding violence and ethics are puzzling in both their prominence and their opacity. Don and Hank plainly attempt at various points to provide justification for their preferred stances—though, admittedly, neither offer any very compelling grounds. But Judge Hall swiftly dismisses each of them for failing to rely on logic or reason. It seems, then, that if Judge Hall is to insist that moral beliefs be grounded in "logic," the intended sense of "logic" must be of an especially substantial sort. Presumably, it must be a conception of reason or logic that ensures a robust link between logic or reason and moral value; in particular, it must be an epistemic link that ensures moral principles are discoverable through purely logical or rational reflection. There is, to be sure, a Randian source for Ditko's interest in such a view as evidenced directly in Judge Hall's dialogue: "Right and wrong cannot be a matter of convenience! A society must be governed by objective laws—and man by objective principles! Think about it and let me know what guides you two!" (Ditko et al. 40) Here, our interest is looking further back and philosophically deeper than the limited attention to moral epistemology Rand provides.

Accounts of our moral knowledge that hold reason or logic to play a foundational role in our knowledge of moral facts are not uncommon in the history of ethics. Such views—usually labelled as instances of *moral rationalism*—often draw an analogy between our knowledge of logic or mathematics and our moral knowledge insofar as each body of knowledge is discoverable via reason alone rather than sentiment or experience.[6] As Samuel Clarke, the eighteenth-century English philosopher, vividly describes the connection between reason and moral objectivity,

> There are therefore certain necessary and eternal differences of things; and certain consequent fitnesses or unfitnesses of the application of different things or different relations one to another; not depending on any positive constitutions, but founded unchangeably in the nature and reason of things, and unavoidably arising from the differences of the things themselves. (Clarke 38)[7]

Clarke later maps out the tie between reason and moral judgment:

> Thus it appears in general, that the mind of Man cannot avoid giving its Assent to the eternal Law of Righteousness; that is, cannot but acknowledge the reasonableness and fitness of Men's governing all their Actions by the Rule of Right or Equity: And also that this Assent is a formal Obligation upon every Man, actually and constantly to conform himself to that Rule. (Clarke 190)

Viewed through the lens of moral rationalism, Judge Hall's critique can be read straightforwardly, since Don and Hank's moral beliefs are grounded exclusively in sentiment and emotion, which affords no prospect of moral knowledge. *Moral sentimentalism*—roughly, the view that our moral knowledge is grounded in our affective states such as anger or sympathy—is caricatured as cartoonishly implausible, delivering either Hank's brutish hostility or Don's unprincipled timidity. In neither case does Ditko leave space for the idea that our affective sympathies might ground our knowledge of right and wrong. Judge Hall gives clearest voice to this strain of moral rationalism, while admonishing a criminal midsentencing: "Sir, this is a court of law! Law is based on facts, on logic . . . Not on emotion! You're here to answer for what you DID! How you feel about it NOW is irrelevant!" (Ditko et al. 61).

The dynamic between Don, Hank, and Judge Hall points the reader to a striking but historically influential view of morality in which the world admits of an intrinsic moral order discoverable via reason alone. The idea that moral demands are stitched directly into the fabric of reality is echoed in remarkable fashion when Don and Hank are gifted their powers. With Judge Hall in danger, a mysterious voice emerges seemingly unbidden and without explanation, in order to provide Hank and Don the power necessary to save their father.[8] The voice instantly imbues Hank and Don with powers carefully tailored to address exclusively imminent threat. While these powers can be summoned by uttering "Hawk" and "Dove" respectively, they cannot be activated without the presence of wrongdoing and, upon conclusion of conflict, Hawk and Dove revert to their ordinary state. Rather strikingly, the voice ensures a perfect proportionality of Hawk and Dove's powers as means for redressing evil, not through the aptness of Hank or Don's emotional sentiments, but by an unexplained, infallible kind of moral dynamics. In this way, the mysterious voice serves as a narrative embodiment of the moral rationalist presupposition that there is an exacting moral structure to the world that places precise and objective demands on agents. More striking still, we might hope to find ourselves in something like Hank and Don's position, where the world's basic moral principles could be spoken to us, directly and unambiguously, so long as we "listen" with reason and logic rather than relying on our inconstant emotions and sympathies.

VIOLENCE'S LIMITS

The Hawk and the Dove presents a species of moral rationalism according to which reason is the ultimate source of and sole means for discovering ethical principles. And while it is notable for its vivid treatment of the *epistemology* of morality, it remains an open question what the series implicates regarding the *content* of morality and, specifically, which ethical principles govern or bear on the morality of violence.[9] Extracting a verdict on what, if any, kinds of violence are morally permissible in the narrative world of Hawk and Dove therefore requires especially close attention to their respective characterization and the narrative mechanics of the series.

The Hawk and the Dove is both an eerily dismissive engagement with pacifism and an insubstantial investigation into the harms of unreflective violence. Note that while Hawk is consistently chastised by Dove for attacking people without hesitation or reflection, Hawk's predilection for violence never leads him to assault bystanders or gravely harm innocents, and neither do Hawk's attacks on those unambiguously singled out as criminals lead to grievous injury. So, if there is any remotely substantial critique of Hawk's attitude towards violence, it is not by way of the most direct and perhaps familiar concerns about violence, that it endangers innocent parties or typically transforms proportionate responses into acts of brutality. To the contrary, Hawk's tendency towards violence is portrayed negatively only in virtue of leading to strategic unpredictability or generating emotional conflict with Dove. Given Skeates's remarks about the views of Ditko, Infantino, and Giordano regarding violence, it is perhaps unsurprising that Hawk's affinity for violence is portrayed as a mere strategic miscalculation rather than as grounds for serious moral condemnation.

While Hawk's stance on violence receives at best a modest reprimand in the series, Dove's resistance to violence is portrayed far less favorably. At various points, his hesitancy to engage in violence permits criminals to escape, results in considerable injury to himself and Hawk, and, in one rather harrowing turn, leads police to shoot and kill a criminal who might have otherwise been nonfatally subdued. Throughout the series, Dove's avowal of nonviolence is presented as inseparable from his cowardice and thereby amplifies the standard and derisive associations of the "dove" epithet. Dove's narrative arc provides no inkling whatsoever that a resistance to violence might issue from a principled moral commitment or reflect any sort of inner moral rectitude. If anything, Dove's reluctance to engage in violence is consistently marked by two salient features: a manifest incoherence and a bizarrely facile view about the nature of violence.

The futility of Dove's brand of nonviolence is made clearest when, in *The Hawk and the Dove* #2, we witness him subdue a criminal almost exclusively by weathering enough blows to exhaust his opponent. Here and in other instances where Dove refrains from striking criminals, the incoherence of his attitudes emerges as he merely shifts the task of engaging violence to Hawk. In other cases, where Dove's physical powers permit the opportunity to physically subdue his attackers with minimal harm, his efforts to avoid violence merely abet Hawk's subsequent brutality. Repeatedly, Dove is presented as merely forestalling or redirecting violence, but never genuinely preventing it from taking place. Worse still, at various points his remarks suggest a flatly incoherent conception of nonviolence, as we see when Dove claims, "I'll fight them my way!" (Ditko et al. 53). Notably, this incoherence is eventually acknowledged but only after the cancellation of the original series in the 1970s *Teen Titans* #29, written by Skeates, who returned to the character without Ditko. While attempting to place a criminal in a wrestling hold, Dove thinks,

Gotta hold onto this guy till Hank finishes with Ocean Master! Then Hank'll be able to take care of this one, and I'll ... Wait a minute! I'm counting on Hank's methods to pull us through—? How can I be a Dove? If I count on Hank's violence, then I'm no better than he is! (Skeates et al. 16)

Along with the dubious coherence of Dove's views regarding violence in the initial series, Dove's remarks regularly present a bizarre view of the nature of violence and what might distinguish it from nonviolent intervention. Not only is it unclear what Dove views as genuinely violent behavior, it remains entirely unexplained why he might view violence as morally impermissible. At some points, Dove seems to merely reject brutality rather than violence per se, remarking to Hawk, "No! I still don't think excessive violence is necessary! Or justifiable!" (Ditko et al. 130). Stranger still, Dove places characters in locks or holds, strikes hands in order to dislodge weapons, and trips or binds attackers. Upon forcibly restraining one assailant, Dove congratulates himself: "I DID it! I proved that I could beat him WITHOUT violence! I ... I proved it!" (Ditko et al. 79). Such remarks suggest not a coherent form of pacifism, but a moral code that fetishizes actions such as punching or kicking as the salient moral divide between violence and nonviolence.

Viewed through the lens of any familiar ethical theory, Dove's characterization relies upon an exceptionally strange point at which to draw any ethically significant distinction. Although there is precious little agreement in ethics regarding what is permissible, there is near consensus that proportionate response for the sake of self-defense is morally permissible. Indeed, as Uniacke (1994: 1) notes, "self-defence is widely regarded and cite as a paradigm of morally permissible private homicide." We are not, it seems, acting wrongly when we respond with violence in an effort to save ourselves from manifestly lethal assault. For this reason, there is nothing *intrinsically* immoral about certain sorts of physical actions—e.g., Dove's punches, trips, and holds. Instead, their moral status is determined by contextual matters—namely, whether they are responses to unjust assault, reflect illicit attitudes, or generate harmful consequences.

The oddity of Dove's attitudes is further compounded by the conspicuous absence of any clear grounds for his eschewing violence. While there are different rationales for nonviolence or pacifism, the most compelling of these stems from a prohibition against doing harm to others. Puzzlingly, Dove is stricken with fear of engaging in violence, but expresses remarkably little concern about harm itself or the aim of preventing it. When engaging with a criminal, Dove is primarily focused on whether his own conduct might be described as violent and only secondarily concerned with whether others are being harmed. In this way, his commitment to nonviolence is portrayed in a manner that renders its motivations, not as commendable albeit extreme, but instead as alien, implausible, or otherwise wrong-headed. Indeed, the dramatic watermark of the series comes in the fifth issue where Dove's commitment to nonviolence collapses in spectacular and disturbing fashion. Fearing that a gunman has slain Hawk, Dove stalks and pummels the shooter while ranting "KILLER! KILLER! FILTHY, ROTTEN KILLER!" (Ditko et al. 153). Later, he confesses to a convalescing Hank: "I don't know what's real anymore!" (Ditko et al. 157). Although it is tempting to read Dove's breakdown as an effort to bring the character in line with the standard features of the superhero genre (or to address lagging sales), the central effect is to paint Dove as deeply unstable and, by doing so, retrospectively undermine any sense that his prior commitment to nonviolence owes to moral principle rather than psychological instability. As a short-lived experiment in a narrative of a nonviolent hero, Dove's arc ends in what seems to be an even less intellectually and psychologically stable position than it began.

UNREASONABLE SELF-DEFENSE?

Up to this point, my efforts have focused on understanding the views regarding moral knowledge and the ethics of violence that emerge from *The Hawk and the Dove*. With all its peculiarities in view, I now turn to the question of what this narrative experiment might tell us about the broader norms of violence within the superhero genre. To this end, we are best served by considering what are surely the strangest moments in the series: the points at which, given Dove's extreme views regarding violence, he seemingly abides physical assault without asserting his apparent right of self-defense.

For critics of pacifism, Dove's actions mark the hinge-point at which the ethical requirements of stereotypical pacifism lapse into manifest implausibility. After all, even those philosophers who offer famously strict prescriptions about what might permissibly be done in defense of self or others have typically endorsed the permissibility of proportionate use of force in self-defense. Notice, however, that Ditko's wildly unsympathetic portrayal of Dove's pacifism relies upon a critical assumption that he is foolishly neglecting to assert his right to self-defense. As I will now suggest, this assumption turns on a conception of self-defense and the permissibility of violence that, while widespread in the superhero genre, eventually collapses under closer scrutiny.

Appeals to one's right to self-defense in justifying violence can be undermined for two familiar reasons. First, if you are, in fact, immune to significant harm, it is prima facie impermissible for you to use violence in the cause of self-defense. When, for example, a small child sets out to clobber me with a balloon, I have no plausible claim to permissibly shove her to the ground, provided I am aware of the circumstances.[10] Second, if you have knowingly thrust yourself in harm's way without complicating considerations, it is similarly impermissible for you to employ violence for the sake of self-defense. Suppose, for example, you decided to jump onto a bobsled track midrace. Had some fiendish bobsledders conspired to assault you on a sidewalk without your knowledge, your right to self-defense would permit proportionate response. But, if you have simply thrust yourself in harm's way while well aware of impending danger, you have seemingly forfeited your right to, say, blow up the bobsled track to save yourself.

In light of the just-noted considerations, asserting one's right to self-defense proves a nuanced and morally fragile matter.[11] If immunity to significant harm and actively generating the potential harm one faces can undermine a claim to rightful self-defense, the assumption that pervades Dove's characterization proves mistaken, since using violence against criminals would not be justified by way of self-defense. Dove, like Hawk, is a superpowered individual and notably impervious to injury. Moreover, Dove's encounters with violence are almost entirely the product of tossing himself headfirst into imminent danger. So, while we might be initially inclined to think that Dove's use of violence while fighting back against criminals would be morally permissible by virtue of constituting self-defense, it is far from obvious that this constitutes self-defense in any uncontroversial sense.

This point generalizes beyond the case of Hawk and Dove and draws out the fact that our ordinary conception of self-defense can only rarely justify the typical violence undertaken by superheroes. After all, superheroes are plausibly viewed as both typically immune to harm and as intervening with full knowledge of risk. To be sure, the prospect of potential harm is made salient through the craft of storytelling, but again and again superheroes exhibit a remarkable immunity and at each turn they appear to seek out risk and danger albeit for sympathetic reasons. Although the pervasive violence in superhero comics is only rarely justified by appeal to self-defense, this does not, on its own, show such violence to be unjustified. But unless the ethics of violence in superhero comics involves a radical suspension of our ordinary moral beliefs such that standing moral principles are abandoned, readers' apparent belief that superhero violence is permissible or even praiseworthy still calls for some principled moral explanation.

If self-defense is insufficient to explain our moral approbation of superhero violence, then we must presumably appeal to some sort of broadly consequentialist principle. Such a principle will ratify violence precisely because superheroes, unlike mere normal individuals, are uniquely and specially equipped and entitled to protect the innocent. Indeed, it looks as though this principle emerges as a necessary ethical commitment of the genre. But if this moral commitment is what allows readers to stomach violence in superhero comics, we can see why the aesthetic experiment with Dove leaves only a sour taste in the mouth of readers. At every turn, his reluctance to undertake violence runs directly contrary to what the ethical norms and moral expectations that the superhero genre is steeped in and depends upon. While draped in all the trappings of a typical superhero, Dove refuses to play along with a foundational commitment of the genre: that violence by superheroes is somehow morally unproblematic. By rejecting violence, he forces the reader to attend to questions about the complex and concerning ethics of violence that the superhero genre crucially relies upon its readers to deftly and seamlessly ignore.

Notes

1. On violence and its typical modes in superhero comics, see Gavaler (24–28). On pacifism in superhero comics, see Wanner.

2. See Alsop and Bartlett.

3. The watershed in virtue ethics is Aristotle's *Nichomachean Ethics*, though myriad views regarding the structural relations between virtues and vices have been subsequently developed. On virtue ethics in its contemporary guise, see Hursthouse.

4. On Ditko's intellectual ties to Rand, see Bell and Brühwiler.

5. Such a reading is complicated by but conforms with the requirements of the Comics Code Authority, which mandate that a figure of authority like Judge Hall "never be presented in such a way as to create disrespect." On the CCA, see Nyberg.

6. On moral rationalism and its contrast with sentimentalism, see Gill.

7. Cf. Kant on moral rationalism: "The ground of obligation here must not be sought in the nature of the human being or in the circumstances of the world in which he is placed, but a priori simply in concepts of pure reason" (Kant 3).

8. The panels in which the mysterious voice emerges not only collapse our conventions regarding text and image in a manner that prefigures Ditko's much later work, especially his *Witzend* work and subsequent Mr. A comics, where the visual space of the panel is replete with text as physical space.

9. The distinction here is one between the first-order epistemology of ethics, which concerns the source of our justification regarding moral beliefs, and normative ethics, which (roughly) concerns which, if any, ethical claims are true. Moral rationalism is, strictly speaking, silent on matters regarding normative ethics.

10. Concerns about proportionality are the critical axis of complexity concerning accounts of self-defense. See Uniacke and Ryan.

11. It is difficult to understate the complexity of variation among extant accounts of self-defense. Numerous complications are elided here. See Thomson and Doggett.

Works Cited

Bell, Blake. *Strange and Stranger: The World of Steve Ditko*. Seattle: Fantagraphics, 2008.

Brühwiler, Claudia. "'A Is A': Spider-Man, Ayn Rand, and What Man Ought to Be." *PS: Political Science and Politics* 47, no. 1 (2014): 90–93.

Clarke, Samuel. *A Discourse Cncerning the Unchangeable Obligations of Natural Religion, and the Truth and Certainty of the Christian Revelation*. London: John and Paul Knapton, 1738.

Ditko, Steve, Steve Skeates, Gil Kane (w.), and Neal Adams (p.). *The Hawk and the Dove: The Silver Age*. Burbank: DC Comics, 2017.

Doggett, Tyler. "Recent Work on the Ethics of Self-Defense." *Philosophy Compass* 6, no. 4 (2011): 220–33.

Gavaler, Chris. *Superheroes*. London: Bloomsbury Academic, 2018.

Gill, Michael. "Moral Rationalism Vs. Moral Sentimentalism: Is Morality More Like Math or Beauty?" *Philosophy Compass* 2, no. 1 (2007): 16–30.

Hursthouse, Rosalind. *On Virtue Ethics*. Oxford: Oxford University Press, 1999.

Kant, Immanuel. *Groundwork of the Metaphysics of Morals*. Cambridge, UK: Cambridge University Press, 1998.

Nyberg, Amy Kiste. *Seal of Approval: The History of the Comics Code*. Jackson: University Press of Mississippi, 1994.

Ryan, Cheyney. "Self-Defense, Pacifism, and the Possibility of Killing." *Ethics* 93, no. 2 (1983): 508–24.

Skeates, Steve (w.), and Nick Cardy (p.). *Team Titans #29* (September–October). Edited by Dick Giordano, 1970.

Skeates, Steve. Interview by Jon B. Cooke. *Comic Book Artist Magazine* 5. Raleigh, NC: TwoMorrows, 1999: 71–72.

Thomas, Judith Jarvis. "Self-Defense." *Philosophy and Public Affairs* 20, no. 4 (1991): 283–310.

Uniacke, Suzanne. *Permissible Killing*. Cambridge, UK: Cambridge University Press, 1994.

Wanner, Kevin. "In a World of Super-Violence, Can Pacifism Pack a Punch?: Nonviolent Superheroes and their Implications." *Journal of American Culture* 39, no. 2 (2016): 177–92.

2

BLACK AND WHITE DEATH
Graphics of Violence from the Great War

CHRISTINA M. KNOPF

War comics may present stories of patriotism and heroism, of bigotry and hatred, of the gory or the glorious, of sacrifice or survival. The genre is "obsessed with violence" (MacCallum-Stewart, "First World War," 1), but it also "has the potential to both commemorate and to interpret the violence of war in ways" that other aesthetic forms cannot (Wurtz, 206). Of comics and imagery of the Great War, Maaheen Ahmed noted that while certain "evocative stock images persist . . . : gas, filth, decay, dismembered bodies and, of course, blood" (3), comic imagery of the 1910s were more likely to draw from propaganda and entertainment or to be more sensorial (2–4), while comics from the 1970s onward accompanied "playful" graphics with "historically accurate details" to offer "increasingly fantastic renditions of the war" (3). Some narrative accounts in the decades immediately following the war were positive, such as those in children's literature, portraying the conflict as a great adventure of heroism and sacrifice (Flothow 147). As years passed, images of muddy trenches, lice-infested clothes, rat-gnawed bodies, and heavy bombing were more likely to dominate perceptions of soldiering during the Great War (Corrigan, loc. 1220). This study builds on distinctions of memory and postmemory of the war, considering how different proximities to its violence shaped portrayals. Both positive and negative depictions deal in the violence of war, but that violence takes different forms. Changes over time may be explained, in part, through the ways the Great War has been "remembered, conventionalized, and mythologized" (Fussell ix). For those who recorded it as a matter of memory, the conflict was "a part of their own experience" (Sokołowska-Paryż and Löschnigg 1). For those for whom the war was "a historical event located in a distant past," it may be understood as "post-memory" (Sokołowska-Paryż and Löschnigg 1), a memorialization of the war "as a historical experience with conspicuous imaginative and artistic meaning" (Fussell ix). We might add "collective memory" as another layer to this process, as a means of communal mythmaking (Campana 43–44) in which political actors and group members make sense of "significant pasts" and "meaningful presents" and "how those moments manifest themselves or are invoked differently in subsequent contexts" (Olick and Levy 923). This study divides graphic narratives of the war into primary accounts created by soldiers of the war (memory); secondary accounts created through creative interpretations of historical research (postmemory); and tertiary accounts that blend primary source material with secondary visuals (collective memory).

Image function analysis parses the ways in which each of these three approaches represent the violence of the Great War. Randy Duncan defines this method as "an approach for understanding the various functions of images in a comic book or graphic novel" that "examines how those functions can communicate a particular meaning to a reader" (43). Images in comics both show/tell the story and provide commentary/insight *about* the story. "Sensory diegetic images" are storytellers revealing the physical reality of the story world (Duncan 44). They represent the external, sensory, reality of the characters. The internal reality for the characters is represented through "non-sensory diegetic images" depicting the "thoughts, emotions, and attitudes" experienced by the characters (Duncan 45). Images that are outside of the story world, which are not part of the physical, mental, or emotional reality of the characters, are "hermeneutic images" (Duncan 45). These images might involve certain color choices or ways of framing; they might appear as "visual motifs" or images that appear repeatedly or occur at "pivotal moments" in the narrative (Duncan 47). They are the creator's commentary on the story, often attempting to influence reader interpretation. The three image functions work in consort to communicate to the reader, and image function analysis thus reads a comic for its story, then for its hermeneutics or motifs, and then to consider how the hermeneutics shape the story (Duncan 47). The discussion here follows a similar format in describing the diegetic scenes and then identifying and exploring the hermeneutic images and visual motifs.

The comics selected for analysis meet three criteria. The focus of the comic is explicitly World War I; at least one creator of the comic and/or original source material is a native of the United Kingdom or British Commonwealth, and, for primary accounts, is connected to the military. The comics were published, either during or after the war, in a periodical, book, or anthology. Primary accounts that met these criteria and were accessible include six books and anthology collections[1] and assorted issues and excerpts from seven archived or reprinted trench newspapers[2] from England, Canada, Australia, and New Zealand. The secondary accounts include one comic series, one graphic novel, and one anthology.[3] The tertiary accounts include one short story and one anthology.[4]

MEMORIES OF VIOLENCE IN PRIMARY COMIC ACCOUNTS

Comics drawn by soldiers of the Great War were created during the war for trench publications, such as battalion newspapers. Trench newspapers were common among all troops on both sides of WWI. Single- to multi-page leaflets offered an alternative to the official presentation of the war with a "bottom-up" (Chapman and Ellin, "Dominion Cartoon," 175) social perspective with insight to the beliefs, concerns, desires, and daily activities of the common soldier (Nelson, 167; Daughton, loc. 786). Dominion trench cartoons tended to feature themes common throughout soldier humor, regardless of nationality: complaints about officers and regulations, food, and medical service, reflections on cultural differences of local populations, and the celebration of the ordinariness of the citizen soldier (Chapman and Ellin, "Multi-Panel," 120; Chapman and Ellin, "Dominion Cartoon," 175, 185). Nonetheless, the duration of the British Empire's involvement in the war meant that the comics of British and Australian artists tended toward realistic images "that traded in war's brutality and insanity" (Casey 07.4). Combat and its costs were prominent in the cartoons of England's trench paper *Blighty*; not only were there repeated scenes of men firing over the top of trenches, but also men pinned under vehicles and buttresses by explosions. Soldiers with bandages, wheelchairs, and crutches were prominent visual themes—appropriate given that "a Blighty" was an injury that could get one sent home to Blighty/England. The most common depiction of combat violence, however, was captured by the visual of shells: soaring across frames, hovering midair, littering the ground, poised to drop straight from above, being ridden by enemy soldiers, exploding in peaceful moments, and occasionally landing on enemy targets.

England's Captain Bruce Bairnsfather was the most famous cartoonist of the Great War. He served on the front with the 1st Battalion, Royal Warwickshire Regiment, and was injured by the burst of a sixteen-inch shell in 1915, resulting in a diagnosis of "shellshock" (Youde, para. 6). His ironic strips demonstrated humor through every hardship of war. He explained, "The whole of the thing made me laugh. I could not refrain from smiling at the absurdity, the stark, fearful predicament" (Bairnsfather, *Carry On*, 31). Bairnsfather's artwork appeared throughout trench newspapers of the allied forces and in many published books, with cartoons about and relatable to the common soldier, with panels dominated by images of rain, mud, and, especially, shells. Even in his postwar volume *Old Bill Looks at Europe* (1935), an illustration features a shell spiraling its way over Old Bill's head, captioned, "Everything should be done to prevent scenes like this from occurring in Europe again" (Bairnsfather, *Old Bill*, 26). As many as sixteen shells can be seen flying over the heads of Bairnsfather's soldiers. Most of the time, the presence of a shell, as with other weapons of violence and destruction, is met with wry acceptance and dry wit by the characters: a rain of shells may go completely ignored, a dud may be used as a chair, grenades are juggled, and swords are used for cooking. In this way, depictions of shelling serve as a phenomenology of trauma, recording both the destructive power of the shell and the life or hope that was not destroyed (see Chute, *Disaster Drawn*, 137).

Corporal Cecil L. Hartt served in the 18th Battalion of the New South Wales Contingent of the Australian Imperial Force and was wounded at Gallipoli. While recovering, he drew amusing cartoons that were published under the title *Humorosities*, hinting at his efforts to find humor in the atrocities of war. Frank Dunne's *Digger Days: Laughing through the Great War*, dedicated to the memory of Hartt in 1919, was similarly an attempt to "sieve the happier moments from the painful memories of the muddling through of 1914–1918" (Dunne 1). *The Anzac Book* was a collection of journalistic observations in various verbal and visual forms offering insight into life at Gallipoli, published as a commemorative souvenir. *Shell Shocks*, too, is a multicreator production described as "typical of life at the Front . . . within reach of the enemy's guns," demonstrating the stoic good humor of the troops under strenuous conditions (Godley 4). Accordingly, many of the cartoons satirized elements of danger and of discomfort, treating the falling of shells with the same aplomb as the fall of rain. The accoutrements of their profession, such as guns, picks, shovels, and tin helmets, were found in most scenes, as well. These tools of death, destruction, and protection hinted at a life of violence and danger, especially when paired with shells and explosions that were similarly common scenic elements.

Shells are sensory diegetic images in that they are part of the physical world that the comics represent, but they also serve a very significant hermeneutic purpose in helping readers to interpret the creators' experiences. The visual of the shell, usually impossibly large, not only represents the real conditions of war of being under fire, but also suggests to readers how to understand those conditions: the ubiquitous presence of shells represents the ubiquitous presence of violence and death. The exaggerated size is not just comedic but representative of the prominence of the shell in the lives of soldiers and the extent of its emotional and mental presence in their memories of the war. And yet, the visual results of the formidable shells are often comical, eliciting hilarity rather than horror. Writing of humor in war literature, Joseph J. Waldmeir notes "the peculiar relationship between humor and pain" (15). Finding comedy in the violence of shells is the epitome of gallows humor—the purposeful mockery of death or danger to defy grim realities (Obrdlik 709).

POSTMEMORIES OF VIOLENCE IN SECONDARY COMIC ACCOUNTS

Many comics and graphic novels "'do' history, in a wide variety of ways" (Marshall 26): biography, historical nonfiction and fiction, narration and documentation. One of the earliest comics to "'do' history" of the Great War was *Commando* in the 1940s–1950s. While other war comics were focused on World War II, *Commando* embraced "compelling storylines in diverse historical settings," such as the Gallipoli Campaign of World War I (Patrick, para. 15). Few other comics tackled the conflict until the changing sociopolitical landscape of the 1970s opened up space for war comics, which had previously emphasized themes of patriotism and heroism, to discuss the chaos and futility of war, consistent with the popular memory of WWI (Scott 650–51; MacCallum-Stewart, "First World War," 6).

One notable comic that "took an unflinching look" at "the brutal nature of war and the senselessness of war on the whole" is *Charley's War* (Scott 651). Written by Pat Mills and illustrated by Joe Colquhoun—a World War II veteran of the Royal Navy—it was originally published in *Battle-Action* between January 6, 1979, and October 4, 1986. Based on meticulous research of WWI and framed by social, political, and economic concerns of its day, especially in its attention to class warfare, *Charley's War* is celebrated for its ability "both to commemorate and to interpret the violence of war" in a way that gives precision and emotion to a war aesthetic that is not beautiful (Wurtz 206). The pen-and-ink illustrations are replete with all the violent action typical of the war comics genre that emphasize combat (Scott 650) with meticulous attention to historical accuracy (Edwards 185). But framing the pages of bullets and bursts, and gas and grenades, are pieces of imagined and recreated historic artifacts, such as letters, photographs, postcards, and cartoons. These touches of realism or documentation exist alongside more impressionistic artwork, such as people/bodies morphing into rows of white crosses. This mix makes the comic a site of constructed memory that melds the personal and private with the collective and public. The use of letter excerpts, appearing as torn pieces of handwritten pages, is a visual motif of *Charley's War*; the intimacy of correspondence establishes a connection with the audience, while the jagged edges surrounding the letters hint at the relationships and bodies that were ripped apart by the violence of war.

Robbie Morrison and Charlie Adlard's *White Death* is premised on extensive historical research to make the narrative as accurate and realistic as possible. As such, it aptly represents postmemory of the war as a historical experience, removed from one's own, of artistic significance. The story is set on the Italian Front, along the treacherous altitudes and frigid temperatures of the mountain ranges separating Italy and the Austro-Hungarian Empire. "White death" was the name bestowed on deadly avalanches that claimed thousands of lives in this lesser-known corner of the conflict (Spinney, para. 9). Morrison developed his story with the idea that the avalanche was a metaphor for war as an unstoppable force consuming everything in its path. Adlard's artwork, done in black charcoal and white chalk over gray paper, reinforced this with snow as the dominant visual motif—the only part of the images with any color. Violence is depicted through explosive emanata—thick black lines suggesting flying debris and shrapnel and thin lines indicating the deadly paths of bullets—and piles of white snow filling or falling into frames and obscuring the scenes, and billows of black and gray gas. Frames are filled with grenades, knives, rifles, and machine guns, and men's faces are contorted in pain and horror as they confront or succumb to battle.

The faces are more than mere sensory and nonsensory diegetic features that tell readers what the characters see and how they feel. The face, and particularly the skull, is a visual motif of *White Death*. The story opens with a panel-by-panel zoom-in on a skull. The imagery is echoed in the large eyes and gaping mouths of shocked or agonized soldiers and in uncanny visages of gas masks. Close-ups that make facial features too large push readers to lose themselves in the scene or the moment, to lose a sense of proportion and perspective and to intimately confront not only the character, but also the self—as if one is looking in a mirror. Indeed, the over-large eyes of the gas mask occasionally show the *reflection* of what they see, given that wide eyes suggest an unrelenting demand to look, to see, to reflect, and to remember (Hagener and Elsaesser 55–56, 58, 72, 82). The confrontational stare of a mutilated face is accusatory, and the loss of a nose represents betrayal (Bailey, para. 8–9). The ghoulish faces declare, "You—society—let this happen, made this possible." The absence of lips indicates that lies have been spoken (Bailey, para. 9); these may be the falsehoods of war-era propaganda about heroic soldiers (Chapman and Ellin, "Dominion Cartoon," 175), of postwar stories of grand adventure (Flothow, 150), or of modern mythologizing of the war as an unfathomable tragedy (Corrigan, loc. 72).

The 2015 Eisner Award–nominated anthology *To End All Wars* is a collection of vignettes that focus on lesser-known and more personal stories of or about the war. In its variety of stories and settings, explicit depictions of violence are intermittent. One of the most visually active combat scenes is the story of the sinking of the HMS Aboukir in 1914, scripted by Ian Douglas with art by SM. The story unfolds around the paths of the enemy torpedoes and their explosive contact points on ship: the running, jumping, and falling of sailors who have caught on fire and the smoldering remains of ship and sailors adrift in the sea at night. These moments of violence are followed by representations of the days of torment experienced by the traumatized U-Boat captain who ordered the attack. Page after page emphasize his wide, shocked, eyes, surrounded by the lines and circles of sleeplessness and stress. Similar images skulls, ghostly gas masks, disfigured heads, gaunt expressions of horror, and visages twisted in rage punctuate the story of poet Hedd Wyn, entitled "The Black Chair," by Jonathan Clode and illustrated by Catherine Pape.

The secondary graphic narratives examined here epitomize modern antiwar notions that focus on the horror, rather than the valor, of war. Their rich historical nuances and accuracy contribute to memory construction and convey a deep sense of the abject through their portrayal of emotional and physical violence and incomprehensible death. (Also see Fitzsimmons and Reynaud.) Their two key images—correspondence and death—encapsulate postmemory of the war, symbolic of the nostalgia and tragedy surrounding the pitiable figure of the miserable soldier that is echoed throughout the cultural mythology of the Great War (Roper 421–22). Incumbent in the tragic nostalgia is collective guilt—the disgust and disillusionment—that became a powerful postwar construction (Roper 421) as the wider community discovered the distance between the war's propaganda and its reality. The disfigurements of the two-dimensional death masks cast accusations of betrayal, deception, and willful negligence through the perfect hindsight of their sightless eyes, while the reminiscences of letters retrospectively suggest the gap between the comforts and love of home and the agonies and hatred of the war.

COLLECTIVE MEMORIES OF VIOLENCE IN TERTIARY COMIC ACCOUNTS

Collective memory can be understood as "ways in which social pasts interact with social presents," including a "relationship between remembered pasts and constructed presents" (Olick and Levy 934). Likewise, "tertiary" graphic narratives represent interactions between past creations and present creators, in which modern artists and writers use the past creative work of soldiers to create new art and literature. The blending of eye-witness interpretations, artistic reinterpretations, and the far-removed creation of the images from the words presents a unique moment of historical perspective and an example of the construction of collective memory as one means through which a group produces narratives of its past to support its identity in the present. This process often involves making sense of violence by transforming it into a model or lesson (Campana; Stone; King).

Coinciding with the centennial of the Great War in 2014, Chris Duffy published *Above the Dreamless Dead: World War I in Poetry and Comics*, in which an international array of artists interpreted trench poetry, a genre marked by its relationship to violence and descriptions of trauma deformity (Sychterz 137, 143, 145–46). Artist Phil Winslade set realistic chaotic battle scenes against a dispassionate, orderly retelling of Siegfried Sassoon's "The General." Wilfred Owen's ironic poem "Great Love" was set to ill-defined drawings of death and decay, which both ignored the poem's metaphors of love and muddied the imagery of killing and blood. George Pratt took a similar approach, setting Owen's "Soldier's Dream" to a sequence of four images—a gun, Christ, a decaying face, and the silhouetted feet of soldiers charging. Skulls and ghostly faces of death stare out from David Hitchcock's panels, illustrating an adaptation of Isaac Rosenberg's "Dead Man's Dump." Such fragmented imagery, Hillary Chute argues, "is a prominent feature of traumatic memory. The art of crafting words and pictures together into a narrative punctuated by pause or absence, as in comics, also mimics the procedure of memory" (*Graphic Women*, loc. 257). Moreover, throughout the assorted adaptations, readers encounter heavy black inks, paints, and chalks. There is little white space in most of the narratives, suggesting the filthy confines of the trenches, the depth of hopelessness, and the obscurity of death.

Published in December 2015 as an original comic by *Task and Purpose*, a news site produced by members of the American military community for American veterans, "The Legendary Story of the 1914 Christmas Truce" was a short eighteen-frame narrative developed by illustrator Matt J. Battaglia from diary entries featured in a 2011 *Smithsonian Magazine* article. The artwork is done entirely in a cold palette of blue and black, punctuated by white snow and a gray soccer ball. Though the colors suggest the peace of the holiday, violence is still present; the diegetic snow and hermeneutical blues convey the bite, even brutality, of the cold winter weather. Beneath the falling snow, the men sit in trenches, guns—the instruments of violence—at the ready. The fighting has stopped, but the conflict rages on through a soccer match, as the ball and the men's feet cause tiny eruptions of snow as they traverse the ground of No Man's Land, echoing the fragmentation from artillery rounds.

The artwork in tertiary graphic narratives is heavy in style and design with muted and dark color palettes dominating the pages, suggesting the artists' desired emotional mood and aesthetic atmosphere for readers. Their "monochromatic tonality" may suggest the "psycho-physiological effect of aging" (Gage 19); in this way, the subdued colors in these comics may be read as the dimming of memory through the passage of time, coinciding with the mortal loss of those who wrote the original accounts. Black, in Western traditions, and white, in Eastern traditions, are also colors associated with mourning and death. Here, the physical presence of the violence found in primary accounts, such as the flying shells, and the lingering artifacts of war's cost found in the secondary accounts, such as the letters, have faded. The personal, individual, memories, were "susceptible to re-interpretation in line with emergent collective accounts because memories exist only at the level of the imagination" (King 581).

As years passed, collective memory tended toward the trenches with their dirt and decay, mines and mortars, and blood and bodies as the persistent images of the Great War (Flothow; Corrigan). The sense of loss—the loss of innocence, the loss of life, the loss of humanity, and the loss of memory—is what remains among the cynically romantic collective memory about survival in the trenches.

CONCLUSION

The comics' dominant hues of black and white hide the bloodshed but not the violence of World War I. Soldiers are surrounded by trenches, wire, and explosions across all three narrative types. The jarring oppositions of the exaggerations of humor and irony in the imagery of the primary accounts and the pitifulness of death and nostalgia in the imagery of the secondary accounts are consistent with what historians have noted as the "two Western Fronts" (Badsey 113)—a mythic one of cultural representations and collective memory, constructed from the trench literature of disillusioned officers, and one based in historical facts, which acknowledges high morale among troops.

Falling between these two, with images of mirth as well as mutilation, are the tertiary accounts, shaped by both the experiences of the soldiers and by the rueful interpretations of those experiences nurtured in the memory of intervening generations. Each type of visualization challenges conventions of war depictions: war is not supposed to be funny or futile or faint, but daring, dutiful, and dauntless. These distinctions among visual motifs of the comics by soldiers, from historical accounts, and with the words of soldiers, highlight the process of memory and memorializing in the Great War: the details of the violence fade to impressions of the horror, which begin to decay with the dead.

Notes

1. *Fragments from France* (New York: G. P. Putnam's Sons, 1917) and *Carry On Sergeant!* (Indianapolis: Bobbs-Merrill, 1927) by Bruce Bairnsfather, Frank Dunne's *Digger Days!* (Sydney, AU: Smith's Weekly, 1919), Cecil L. Hartt's *Humorosities* (London: Australian Trading & Agencies Co., 1917), *The Anzac Book* (Campbell, AU: Australian War Museum, 1916/2010), *Shell Shocks* "by New Zealanders in France" (Peterborough, UK: Jarrolds Publishers, 1916/Europeana, 2016).

2. Canada's *The Brazier*, *In & Out*, *Listening Post*, and *Vie Canadienne* (all archived at Early Canadiana Online), England's *Blighty* (archived at the National Library of Scotland), Australia's *Kia Ora Coo-ee* written by troops in Egypt, Palestine, Salonica, and Mesopotamia (Sydney, AU: Cornstalk Publishing, 1918/1981) and *Dinkum Oil* (online at the Australian War Museum).

3. *Charley's War* (*Omnibus*, London: Titan Books, 2014), *White Death* (Portland: Image Comics, 2014), *To End All Wars* (Vancouver: Soaring Penguin Press, 2014).

4. *The Legendary Story of the 1914 Christmas Truce* (*Task and Purpose* online, December 2015), *Above the Dreamless Dead* (New York: First Second, 2014).

Works Cited

Ahmed, Maaheen. "The Great War in Comics: Workings and Imagery." *European Comic Art* 8, no. 2 (2015): 1–8.

Assmann, Jan. "Collective Memory and Cultural Identity." *New German Critique* 65 (1995): 125–33.

Australian War Memorial, editor. *The Anzac Book*. 3rd ed. Sydney, AU: UNSW Press, 2010.

Badsey, Stephen. "Blackadder Goes Forth and the 'Two Western Fronts' Debate." In *The Historian, Television and Television History*, edited by Graham Roberts and Paul Taylor, 113–25. Luton, UK: University of Luton Press, 2001.

Bailey, Penny. "Losing Face? The Symbolism of Facial Mutilation." Wellcome, Nov. 22, 2012. wellcometrust.wordpress.com/2012/11/22/losing-face-the-symbolism-of-facial-mutilation/. Accessed Nov. 7, 2019.

Bairnsfather, Bruce. *Carry On Sergeant!* Indianapolis: The Bobbs-Merrill Company, 1927.
Bairnsfather, Bruce. *Old Bill Looks at Europe.* New York: Dodge Publishing Company, 1935.
Campana, Aurélie. "Collective Memory and Violence: The Use of Myths in the Chechen Separatist Ideology, 1991–1994." *Journal of Muslim Minority Affairs* 29, no. 1 (2009): 43–56.
Casey, Jay. "'What's So Funny?' The Finding and Use of Soldier Cartoons from the World Wars as Historical Evidence." In *Drawing the Line: Using Cartoons as Historical Evidence*, edited by Richard Scully and Marian Quartly, 07.1–07.23. Clayton, Victoria, AU: Monash University ePress, 2009.
Chapman, Jane, and Dan Ellin. "Dominion Cartoon Satire as Trench Culture Narratives: Complaints, Endurance and Stoicism." *Round Table* 103, no. 2 (2014): 175–92.
Chapman, Jane, and Daniel Ellin. "Multi-Panel Comic Narratives in Australian First World War Trench Publications as Citizen Journalism." *Australian Journal of Communication* 39, no. 3 (2012): 1–22.
Chute, Hillary L. *Disaster Drawn: Visual Witness, Comics, and Documentary Form.* Cambridge, MA: Belknap Press, 2016.
Chute, Hillary L. *Graphic Women: Life Narrative & Contemporary Comics.* Kindle ed. New York: Columbia University Press, 2010.
Corrigan, Gordan. *Mud, Blood and Poppycock.* Kindle ed. London: Cassell, 2003.
Daughton, James P. "Sketches of the Poilu's World: Trench Cartoons from the Great War." In *World War I and the Cultures of Modernity*, edited by Douglas Mackaman and Michael Mays, loc. 766–1152. Kindle ed. Jackson: University Press of Mississippi, 2000.
Duncan, Randy. "Image Functions: Shape and Color as Hermeneutic Images in *Asterios Polyp*." In *Critical Approaches to Comics: Theories and Methods*, edited by Matthew J. Smith and Randy Duncan, 43–54. New York: Routledge, 2012.
Dunne, Frank. *Digger Days: Laughing through the Great War.* Sydney, AU: Snelling Printing Works, 1919.
Edwards, Brian. "The Popularisation if War in Comic Strips 1958–1988." *History Workshop Journal* 42 (1996): 180–89.
Fitzsimmons, Phil, and Daniel Reynaud. "Comics/Graphic Novels/Bandes Dessinées and the Representation of the Great War." In *The Great War in Post-Memory Literature and Film*, edited by Martin Löschnigg and Marzena Sokołowska-Paryż, 187–200. Kindle ed. Berlin: Walter de Gruyter, 2014.
Flothow, Dorothea. "Popular Children's Literature and the Memory of the First World War, 1919–1939." *The Lion and the Unicorn* 31, no. 2 (2007): 147–61.
Fussell, Paul. *The Great War and Modern Memory: The Illustrated Edition.* New York: Sterling, 2009.
Gage, John. *Color and Meaning: Art, Science, and Symbolism.* Berkeley: University of California Press, 1999.
Godley, Alex. "Introduction by Lieut.-General Sir Alexander Godley, K.C.B., K.C.M.G., General-Officer-Commanding New Zealand Expeditionary Forces." In *Shell Shocks* by New Zealanders in France, 4. Peterborough, UK: Jarrolds Publishers, 1916.
Hagener, Malte, and Thomas Elsaesser. *Film Theory: An Introduction Through the Senses.* Kindle ed. New York: Routledge, 2010.

King, Anthony. "Violent Pasts: Collective Memory and Football Hooliganism." *Sociological Review* 49, no. 4 (2001): 568–85.

Lehoczky, Etelka. "Songs of Innocence and Bitter Experience in 'Dreamless Dead.'" NPR.org, Aug. 22, 2014. www.npr.org/2014/08/22/341879645/songs-of-innocence-and-bitter-experience-in-dreamless-dead. Accessed June 20, 2015.

MacCallum-Stewart, Esther. "The First World War and British Comics." *University of Sussex Journal of Contemporary History* 6 (2003): 1–18.

Marshall, Bridget M. "Comics as Primary Sources: The Case of *Journey into Mohawk Country*." In *Comic Books and American Cultural History: An Anthology*, edited by Matthew Pustz, 26–39. London: Continuum, 2012.

Nelson, Robert L. "Soldier Newspapers: A Useful Source in the Social and Cultural History of the First World War and Beyond." *War in History* 17, no. 2 (2010): 167–91.

Obrdlik, Antonin J. "'Gallows Humor'—A Sociological Phenomenon." *American Journal of Sociology* 47, no. 5 (1942): 709–16.

Olick, Jeffrey K., and Daniel Levy. "Collective Memory and Cultural Constraint: Holocaust Myth in German Politics." *American Sociological Review* 62: 921–36.

Patrick, Kevin. "Review: Commando—ANZACS at War." *Comics Down Under: An Ongoing History of Comic Books in Australia*, Aug. 2007. comicsdownunder.blogspot.com/2007/08/review-commando-anzacs-at-war.html. Accessed Nov. 7, 2019.

Roper, Michael. "Nostalgia as an Emotional Experience in the Great War." *Historical Journal* 54, no. 2 (2011): 421–51.

Scott, Cord. "The Return of the War Comic: A Revival of Military Themes and Characters in Comic Books." *International Journal of Comic Art* 10, no. 2 (2008): 649–59.

Sokołowska-Paryż, Marzena, and Martin Löschnigg. "Introduction: 'Have You Forgotten Yet? . . .'" In *The Great War in Post-Memory Literature and Film*, edited by Martin Löschnigg and Marzena Sokołowska-Paryż, 1–15. Kindle ed. Berlin: Walter de Gruyter, 2014.

Spinney, Laura. "Melting Glaciers in Northern Italy Reveal Corpses of WW1 Soldiers." *Telegraph*, Jan. 13, 2014. www.telegraph.co.uk/history/world-war-one/10562017/Melting-glaciers-in-northern-Italy-reveal-corpses-of-WW1-soldiers.html. Accessed March 3, 2016.

Stone, D. "The Domestication of Violence: Forging a Collective Memory of the Holocaust in Britain, 1945–6." *Patterns of Prejudice* 33, no. 2 (1999): 13–29.

Sychterz, Jeffrey. "Scarred Narratives and Speaking Wounds: War Poetry and the Body." *Pacific Coast Philology* 44, no. 2 (2009): 137–47.

Waldmeir, Joseph J. "What's Funny About That? Humor in the Literature of Second World War." *Journal of American Culture* 12, no. 3 (1989): 11–18.

Wurtz, James F. "Representing the Great War: Violence, Memory, and Comic Form." *Pacific Coast Philology* 44, no. 2 (2009): 205–15.

Youde, Kate. "The Captain Who Gave Britain its Ultimate Weapon During World War One—Laughter." *Independent*, Nov. 1, 2014. www.independent.co.uk/news/uk/home-news/the-captain-who-gave-britain-its-ultimate-weapon-during-world-war-one-laughter-9833596.html. Accessed March 6, 2016.

3

A TALE OF TWO CUBAN CARTOONISTS

DIANA ÁLVAREZ AMELL

The violently shifting winds of Cuba's mid-twentieth-century political landscape in their turmoil altered the lives and artistic paths of two original Cuban cartoonists.[1] Antonio Prohías had been an established editorial cartoonist since the forties. Santiago Armada, who published under the pen name Chago, emerged at the end of the fifties as a cartoonist committed to a political cause as a combatant, having joined the militia rebels at the *Sierra Maestra*. While Prohías left the country for the United States early in the sixties, and Chago stayed, their works bear the imprint of the island's conflictive politics. While both explored elements of violence, political, physical, and psychological, in their cartoons, the violence of their time and place also crisscrossed their personal trajectories. Curiously, their cartoons, censored and suppressed at one time, have become influential cultural referents. Politics intervened violently, creating a cultural fissure in Cuba, and at first glance, it might appear that Prohías and Chago have little in common, given that these cartoonists followed diametrically opposing political paths. Yet in the work of both there is a search for a communicative, formal expressiveness in a popular cultural medium. Strikingly, the two very different cartoonists shared basic artistic tenets, arriving at very different results in their search to innovate the cartoons' themes and visual composition. Their cartoons pose philosophical inquiries in sequential frames with minimal if any use of words. The two cartoonists explored the expressive possibilities of the visual narrative based on schematic lines, privileging the geometric or almost abstract forms over text.

ANTONIO PROHÍAS

Prohías had been a highly successful Cuban cartoonist. In 1946, at just twenty-five, he received the most prestigious recognition in his field in Cuban journalism, the Juan Gualberto Gomez Award; and went on to receive six more awards and become president of the Cuban National Association of Cartoonists in the fifties. His black and white cartoons with few or no words were published in major dailies and magazines, such as *El Mundo*, *Diario de la Marina*, *La Prensa*, and *Zig Zag*, the latter being the most important Cuban cartoon magazine. Most notably, he created the comic strip character the Sinister Man and its offshoot the Sinister Woman, which were published in *Bohemia*, the weekly political magazine with the largest circulation in the Spanish language. Sergio Aragonés, the Spanish Mexican cartoonist who would later join *MAD* magazine, and became his good friend, drew himself as a giggling teenager in Mexico buying *Bohemia* to read the Sinister Man: "the cruelest character I have ever seen" (Ficarra 10). With insouciant black humor, the well-known character indulged gleefully with social impunity in slapstick cruelty. The violence in the Sinister Man's devilish malice had no direct historical or social referents (Quiroga 57), but Prohías's characters came to embody the violence in Cuba under Batista.

After the fall of Batista, Castro handed him the 1959 best cartoon of the year award. Undeterred, Prohías proceeded to take aim at the controversial measures the new government imposed, creating a new cartoon series titled *Tovarich* published in the newspaper *Prensa Libre*. Sinister Man, the unrepentant trickster, had been transformed into a comrade whose self-serving hypocritical offerings to workers would open a Pandora's box. In one cartoon, the helpful Tovarich hands tools to a worker who builds a cage to lock up a smug bourgeois whom, instigated by Tovarich, the worker drags to jail. In the last frame, both the capitalist and the now red-faced worker are crammed into the same cage under lock and key. Satisfied with the result, Tovarich stands smiling in the background (Prohías 255). The caricature emphasized the shared psychology of the capitalist and worker, both puffed up in their own delusions, in contrast with the thin, wily, and seemingly very *simpatico* Tovarich.

The first two years of the revolutionary government were a crucial political period of uncertain transition. The new government, not ostensibly under any ideological banner, was meant to restore democratic governance under the constitutional order. Associating the new government with communism, at a time when the revolutionary government was denying it, turned out to be risky. Castro countered in a speech denouncing Prohías as a counter-revolutionary CIA spy (Santiago 15). In 1960, Castro ordered the closing of the daily *Prensa Libre*, that published Prohías's work (Prohías 254). After Castro's verbal attack, Prohías's coworkers at *El Mundo* also held a meeting where they echoed Castro's accusations (Santiago 16). Political threats against him mounting, Prohías resigned fleeing to the United States. A few months after arriving, he presented his black and white cartoons to the editors of *MAD* magazine. He had revamped his triangular pointy Sinister Man into interchangeable Cold War spies, putting to artistic use the political accusation that had forced him to leave his country. Prohías's *Spy vs. Spy* cartoons first appeared in 1961 in *MAD*'s sixtieth issue, becoming that magazine's longest running series, an indelible part of American pop culture. When Prohías retired in 1987 due to his failing health, the editors commissioned other cartoonists to continue his series. His spies were franchised, appearing in books, board games, animated film shorts, video games, and in advertisements.

His cartoons tap into a particularly childish sense of glee at the wildly improbable destructive antics that his characters deploy against each other— a fanciful total annihilation of the other, only to be resurrected, undaunted, in the next installment, ready to scheme new tricks. This antiheroic slapstick approach stands in contrast to the comic book world of heroes whose identities, while concealed, are clearly individualized by their costume. Visually, his iconic spies are composed of mostly triangles, as was the Sinister Man before them. Prohías's spies are distinguishable only by the black and white triangles they wear, bereft of their Manichean meaning. Their extreme actions are devoid of any manifest ideology. Their unceasing comeuppance mixes the everyday with the conventional tricks of the spy trade. His reversible spies use recognizable objects that transform into the preposterous: a pole holding a basketball net becomes a rocket, a hair dryer, a gun. His inventive plots incorporate contemporary life, outlandishly: his spies perform brain transplants or cross-dress simultaneously to fool and entrap the other (Ficarra 21).

While the spy genre depends on the element of suspense, Prohías's spies are predictable. The unforeseen lies in the inventiveness of the spy's bag of tricks; the thrill is in the sheer exuberance of the expected slapstick silliness of the farcical means of destruction. The plot is often constructed as a situational irony: the initial aggressor usually ends up caught in his own trap; the comedic catastrophe is as devoid of pathos as of ideology. The nonsense deprived of justification contains the violence, while subverting the tenets of the spy genre. Prohías's comics turns the sinister into a child's game: the destruction one spy schemes against the other reduces the horrific to a receptive giggle, transforming what was menacing into manageable fun. Lewis Black argued that these short cartoons introduced satire to children and young people who were living through the Cold War, enabling them to laugh at the paranoia at a time when people were building bomb shelters in their backyard, all the while showing that "collective stupidity" could be deadly (Ficarra 7).

Prohías's spies have been interpreted as a statement on the pointlessness of the ideological confrontation between the two Cold War superpowers by making both antagonists equal losers and winners (Carabas). For Peter Kuper, a cartoonist who continued the series for *MAD*, Prohías's *Spy vs. Spy* was a commentary on the "futility of war" (Grundhauser). The improbable wrecking-ball no-holds-barred destruction is devoid of identifiers, national or ideological, yet the cartoons have become a sort of historical testimony about the violence of a polarized ideological world. The absurdity of scorched earth antics forms a two-pronged signifier since the violence is absurd on multiple levels. While his cartoons strip political violence of the terrifying nature of destruction, they void it as well of any rationale. The reader is left with a simple claim: political violence is madness, recalling the military acronym for "mutually assured destruction." The spies seek out with unbounded enthusiasm the destruction of the other for no apparent reason, save that he is the other. His spies are an invalidation of destruction masquerading as ideology. The moral that may be found in his cartoons—once one acknowledges the joy of the destructive inner child—is an indictment of justifying violence for political reasons: ideologically driven violence is senseless. It is a plausible conclusion for understanding the work of a cartoonist who witnessed and experienced violence imposed by dictators on the opposite sides of the political spectrum and who used the black humor of his cartoons to mock it.

ON THE OTHER SIDE: CHAGO

Chago's *Julito 26* cartoons have been interpreted as instrumental in communicating the revolutionary government's expectation for citizens: "Chago's strip served as a medium of visual indoctrination into the new rules for a new Cuba and its new citizen" (Regalado Someillan 168). Blanco de la Cruz (2000) argues that he was a "chronicler of a process he approached without prejudices, which allowed him to record the epic of a historic period in a very peculiar war" (178). Chago rose to prominence as a member of the Cuban Revolution celebrating a *miliciano* in his character Julito 26, a direct reference to the Castro-led July 26 militia. Chago's politically committed didactic cartoons appeared in *El Cubano Libre*, a mimeographed publication of the guerrilla forces. In the final December 1958 clandestine publication, his cartoon showed Julito 26 sweeping Batista away with a broom. The caption read, "A clean sweep for the New Year and a happy, free and democratic Cuba" (Catalá-Carrasco, *Vanguardia y humorismo* 176, my translation). The *Julito 26* cartoons continued appearing in *Revolución*, encouraging acts of revolutionary selflessness, and celebrating the new political measures, some as controversial as the Agrarian Reform, which gave the state control over arable land.

Chago's *Julito 26* series is conventional in its design using representational figures and text. In some of his political caricatures, he used heavy dark lines not far from expressionism, when, for example, he attacked the oil companies, in support of the revolutionary government's nationalization of the American-owned oil refineries in Cuba. The cartoonists who considered themselves revolutionaries understood their work not as propaganda but as a defense of the revolution, according to René de la Nuez, who worked with Chago in *Palante* and *El Pitirre*, revolutionary graphic magazines that appeared after *Zig Zag* was forced to close. Chago was named in August 1961 a member of the comic art section of the official Union of Artist and Writers of Cuba (UNEAC) and worked up until the end of his life in the design department of the official communist state newspaper *Granma* (Regalado Someillan 117–19).

His graphic work evolved with *Salomón*, which appeared in two publications, *Revolución* and *El Pitirre*, in the early sixties (Catalá-Carrasco 186). It was a remarkable departure in design and narrative from his previous political cartoons. *Salomón* is drawn almost as an abstract form; philosophical and metaphysical allusions are mixed with scatological and overtly sexual drawings. *Salomón* was last published in a September 1963 edition of *Revolución*, where it had first appeared. Chago's *Salomón* cartoons, with their abstract visual design and cryptic philosophical musings encapsulated inside oddly shaped balloons, were collected in a 1963 book titled *El humor otro*. Chago's revolutionary curriculum did not spare his cartoons from censorship. His Salomón strips were withdrawn from circulation. Despite this, some prominent cultural figures affiliated with the government made sly references to Chago's controversial cartoons. Lisandro Otero, a state functionary at the time, wrote its prologue. In a scene of the well-known 1968 film *Memories of Underdevelopment* by Tomás Gutiérrez Alea, the most celebrated film director of the time, the protagonist is reading a newspaper showing Chago's cartoons (Leyva Martínez). Even in the seventies, a sympathetic note differentiated Chago's work from "Yankee comics," with a picture of him dressed in military fatigues (Feijóo 536). His work reappeared in Havana's independent art scene in 1995 with the artist Sandra Ceballos's performance titled *Salomón with Me*.

CULTURAL POLITICS

As in other countries, the debate in Cuba about comics addressed cultural issues about their social influence, and the relative value of "high" and "low" cultures. In his 1964 landmark analysis of *Superman*, Umberto Eco pointed out that the redundancies of the repetitive scheme were an important element of popular narratives; he considered this type of cultural production as entertainment, escapism, and "substantially immobilistic" (144). Jorge Mañach had written in 1954 a short piece for *Bohemia* about the "regrettable" influence cartoons "exerted both in a child's psychology as well as its elementary use of language" (Hernández 2012). Mañach, a Cuban intellectual, had written two influential essays in which he deplored "*choteo*," a type of Cuban humor. In *The Crisis of High Culture in Cuba* and *An Inquiry into the Choteo*, Mañach called *choteo* "pernicious." This idiosyncratic type of humor disdains distinctions, especially authority; nothing is sacred or off-limits. The proclivity to disdain authority, seen as a negative national trait, had been criticized by Cuban intellectuals since the nineteenth century (Catalá-Carrasco 41).

Choteo's irreverent black humor that mocks the sacred and makes light of authority is found in Prohías's *Sinister Man*. In a 1960 cartoon, Sinister Man is strolling about and encounters several different officials with puffed up chests dressed in uniforms. In the last frame, he finally salutes the one wearing the most elaborate uniform, who turns out to be a hotel doorman. In another cartoon, Sinister Man exchanges a policeman's gun for a child's toy gun. Both the policeman and the little boy take off, guns in hand, in opposite directions, the policeman in hot pursuit of a criminal, while the boy goes to play with another child with the real, loaded gun (Prohías 22–24). For one American commentator, Prohías's shift from the very popular Cuban *Sinister Man* to his equally popular spies was a cultural adaptation, since *Sinister Man* proved too "desolate" for American readers (Grimes). Carlos Eire, who read the Sinister Man cartoons as a child in Havana, alludes as well to the national character of humor: "The cartoons of Prohías are hilarious. And his subtlety has a distinctly Cuban accent, unmistakably sardonic and paradoxical."

Since the nineteenth century there has been a strong tradition of Cuban comics (Regalado Somillan 58–59). American comics too enjoyed a wide circulation in prerevolutionary Cuba, since they were less expensive due to their syndication, a point made by Paquita de Armas and others who attribute their lower price as the reason for their acceptance. However, in the sixties the discussion centered around the political and ideological function of art and popular culture. Several critics branded American comic strips instruments of "imperialism." In a 1961 article in *Revolución*, American cartoons were called "opium," a clear product of American interference in Latin America, responsible also for contributing to the illiteracy of their own citizens. More articles appeared in that same state publication branding American comics neocolonialist and imperialist propaganda (Catalá-Carrasco, *Vanguardia y humorismo*, 269–70). Edmundo Desnoes in a 1964 article titled "*Humorismos*" criticized their negative influence, viewing the American syndicated cartoons that had flooded the market with their inexpensive cartoons a form of imperialism (Catalá-Carrasco, *Vanguardia y humorismo*, 211–12). In a 1970 issue of *Signos*, a publication dedicated to the visual arts, an article signed by Herminio Almendros blasted cartoons for being as addictive as "marihuana," offering a "degraded" image of reality in which "only the strong have the right to live and triumph." The filmmaker Pastor Vega weighed in writing for *Cine Cubano* about the lack of subtlety in the "neocolonialist" and "imperialist" intentions in American cartoons. He considered Tarzan racist, and Clark Kent a perfect example of the *petit bourgeois*. In another article, Fernando Pérez called Walt Disney "reactionary" (Hernández).

These interpretations by prominent cultural figures stand in contrast with a much earlier newspaper article written in the fifties by Alejo Carpentier. Then living in exile in Venezuela, the Cuban novelist had praised the innovations in American graphic humor, mentioning *MAD* and Saul Steinberg as examples. Although Chago, as well as the other cartoonists who published in *El Pitirre*, acknowledged Steinberg's and James Thurber's influence, in the sixties, the debate was political. The articles in Cuban publications followed a Marxist reading, that was popularized outside Cuba by the Chilean writer Ariel Dorfman in his 1971 book *How to Read Donald Duck*. In her survey of the political and social attitudes about comics, De Armas notes that for some critics, artists, and cultural functionaries, comics were considered "manipulative," a tool for "ideological *diversionism*," a term used by Raúl Castro in a 1972 speech (xii).

European Marxist theorists had already argued that ideology was embedded in all cultural production. The influential Italian Marxist theorist Antonio Gramsci, although conceding it could not be "the only one," still had argued in his "Prison Notes" that the "unitary national elaboration of a homogeneous collective consciousness" demanded "a wide range of conditions and initiatives. Diffusion from a homogeneous center of a homogeneous way of thinking and acting is the principal condition" (388). Louis Althusser's concept of "ideological state apparatuses" could include the media. These Marxist views of popular media's ideological function became since its beginnings a priority for the Cuban revolutionary government. Several official publications made extensive use of cartoons to spread their message. As a sign that the revolution considered cartoons a "valuable medium of communication with the public," Regalado Someillan points to the creation of the revolutionary cartoon magazine *Palante y Palante* in 1961, and the lifting of the restriction on professionalism:

> An explosion of cartooning took place with the Revolution. Cartoonists' unwavering focus on the revolutionary program and promoting new forms of belonging reflected an active engagement on their part toward building a new revolutionary society." (9)

Prohías, who created iconic cartoon characters in the fifties in Cuba and in the sixties in the United States, is largely ignored in the studies of Cuban cartoons or becomes at best a passing reference on a list. The exception is Hernández and Piñero (2007), who point out Prohías's place in Cuban cartooning. In the preface of *Más de Cien Años de humor político*, Prohías and the other caricaturists who left the country are labeled "traitors at the service of American imperialism" (Regalado Someillan, 110). The political repression from which he escaped, a state of "terror" he called it, and his remarkable American success make him an uncomfortable presence for those who argued theoretically about the imperative of the collective over the individual, and who viewed the influence of American comics as hegemonic in prerevolutionary Cuba. The communicative interaction between Cuban and American cultures which Prohías's cartoons so well exemplified became problematic. His iconic *Sinister Man* is mostly missing from the national cultural narrative. His erasure hides the consequences of the ideological imposition of what has been called "revolutionary humor" or "red humor." For Negrín (2003), the difference was not only ideological, but stylistic. These interpretations conflate the ideological content—the "revolutionary vanguard"—with the visual "vanguard." Both Prohías and Chago were interested in the minimalist lines and wordless narrative of the Romanian American Steinberg's cartoons published in the *New Yorker*. Both admitted having followed the innovations of *MAD*. Prohías was able to develop and master a popular medium in another culture, making a successful transition in humor, a perishable commodity that rarely travels well. Declaring his political admiration for Castro's measures, Art Spiegelman was circumspect in his assessment of Prohías's cartoons, which for him were a "variation on a narrow-theme-school of comics." While calling him a "minor god," he admitted to having been "affected" by Prohías's cartoons (Spiegelman 197).

Chago's graphic explorations of visual narrative with inchoate forms were cut short by censorship. His *Salomón* series was considered "controversial" and "misunderstood." As Blanco de la Cruz points out, *Salomón*'s strange ethereal, erotic, or scatological elements were not at the service of the Revolution. Gramsci's concept of the social use of art had argued for social "rationality" in the arts: it was a mistake to view rationality as coercion because cultural productions have a social function. Simply stated, art should fulfill its social function for, according to Gramsci, "ultimately it is always a question of 'rationalism' versus the individual will" (401). The commonplace assumption in Cuban cultural studies is that during the sixties there was greater latitude in the arts. The awareness, the attentiveness, and sensitivity concerning popular culture, the urgency in making it promote the new state line, tend to show that the ideological boundaries were marked earlier than is usually acknowledged. Juan Marinello, the *eminence grise* of the Cuban communist party, had argued in the fifties that in the arts it was a mistake to favor the geometric over the figurative. For Marinello, abstract art was bourgeois and imperialistic, and he recommended that artists adopt social realism, since true art is involved with reality. While Marinello addressed "high" culture, his argument emphasized the imperative of representing what is perceived to be in the social interest, instead of following individual pursuits. This mandate was imposed early in the sixties in popular media.

Although Chago had earned his revolutionary stripes, his *Salomón* cartoons were not apparently revolutionary enough. The 1965 exhibit of Chago's work in Havana was cancelled, though several critics in Cuba or sympathizers with the revolution tend to downplay the censorship as "misunderstandings" about his work.[2] Dalía García Barbarán, Chago's widow, said in an interview that for *Granma*'s editors *Salomón* was too existential and not political enough: "She felt Chago's attention to certain themes like death, sex, eroticism, *machismo*, existence, and love challenged the role of cartoons in revolutionary society and insisted that one needed a certain amount of culture, or intellectualism to fully enjoy his pieces"; Chago "was not well comprehended and his ability to exhibit his work in the late 1960s suffered, something which left him very bitter" (Regalado Someillan 122). Yet for some in the Cuban artistic community, his early participation in the militia, his close friendship with Ernesto Che Guevara, and his continued employment in *Granma* made him suspect. When asked in a 2018 interview about the rumors as to whether Chago had worked for state security, his close friend, Umberto Peña, a graphic artist who now lives in Spain and whose own work was censored, discounted the rumors, adding that Chago, who worked tenaciously, was a very sensitive artist who had become very "disillusioned with the process" (Aguilera 188; my translation).

Whether Chago kept his criticism "inside the Revolution" as Luis Camnitzer has claimed, or became disillusioned, as Peña states, *Salomón*'s ambiguity was unwelcome at a time when state-controlled cultural institutions expected optimistic affirmations of revolutionary fervor. Chago's artistic reputation and influence since has been mostly garnered because of his banned *Salomón*. With the opening of Sandra Ceballos's independent Havana art space *Espacio Aglutinador*, the creator of *Salomón* reappeared in Havana's visual culture. Gerardo Mosquera wrote the note for the 1995 exhibit. Ceballos held a 1996 performance titled *Salomón with Me*, tattooing the words on her left arm, a tribute to Chago, who with his creation *Salomón* had been, in her words, a "victim of censorship." For Ceballos, Chago's two characters Julito 26 and Salomón were "emblematic" of the sixties and served as an inspiration for artists who came after him. She points out that Chago kept receiving many letters from fans, who waited for the next installment of *Salomón* in *Revolución* (Ceballos, personal email, September 28, 2018). Chago's work was included in the 2017–2018 art exhibit *Adiós Utopia: Dreams and Deceptions in Cuban Art Since 1950*, which traveled to several American museums.

To compare the lives and art of both men makes an exemplary tale of the country's violent cultural divide. The two artists experienced a painful entanglement in their country's politics. Both addressed the ideological maelstrom of their time in their cartoons by developing visual innovations that offered significant interpretations of political narratives, while expanding the boundaries of the expressive range of the popular genre. Their confrontations with politics made their artistic choices more starkly interesting because both were involved with a popular medium that sought to directly address the issues of the times to a vast readership. Prohías was able to cross the cultural divide by successfully transforming his Cuban Sinister Man into the American phenomenon of the transnational wacky spies. Chago's cheerful and politically engaged *Julito 26* was abandoned for an enigmatic and morose *Salomón* that was banned. Their clearly divergent political trajectories and artistic choices were fundamentally embedded in the social debates of their time and addressed, although obliquely in some instances, the ideological schism of the period. The continued appeal of their artistic accomplishments is expressed in the acknowledged influence of their work. With time, their work has become fertile artistic and historical documents that have continued to exert their influence in the cultural world, seemingly fulfilling Peter Burke's claims that images constitute historical documents. Their graphic work in a popular medium has acquired testimonial value as symbolic representations of their historical time.

Notes

1. For a history of Cuban cartoons, see Piñero, Regalado Someillan, and Hernández.
2. See Camnitzer and Ceballos's catalog for a record of Chago's exhibits.

Works Cited

Aguilera, Carlos A. "Archivo y Terror. Operaciones entre literatura, política, teatro y arte." In *Umberto Peña: Bocas, Cepillos, Dientes, Restos*: 167–210. Virginia: Editorial Casa Vacía, 2019.

Althusser, Louis. "Ideology and Ideological State Apparatuses (Notes Towards an Investigation)." In *Lenin and Philosophy and Other Essays* by Louis Althusser, 85–126. Translated by Ben Brewster. New York: Monthly Review Press, 2001.

Armada, Santiago. "Prólogo, Otero, Lisandro." *El humor otro*. Havana: Ediciones R, 1963.

Armas, Paquita de. *La vida en cuadritos*. Havana: Pablo de la Torriente Editorial, 1993.

Blanco de la Cruz, Caridad. "Salomón, el perturbador." *Revista latinoamericana de estudios sobre la historieta* 1 (2001): 101–18.

Blanco de la Cruz, Caridad. *Always the Other One Salomón*." In *Cartooning in Latin America*, edited by John Lent, 241–51. Translated by Gisela Gul-Egui. New York: Hampton Press, 2005.

Blanco de la Cruz, Caridad. *Salomón. Siempre el otro*. Translated by Gisela Gil-Egui, Marizet Agrelo, and Daniel Díaz Mantilla. Asterisco Press, 2017.

Burke, Peter. *Eyewitnessing: The Uses of Images as Historical Evidence*. Ithaca, NY: Cornell University Press, 2008.

Camnitzer, Luis, and Sandra Ceballos, curators. "From Sierra Maestra to La Habana: The Drawings of Chago." *Drawing Room*. New York, 2001.

Carabas, Theodora. "'Tales Calculated to Drive You MAD': The Debunking of Spies, Superheroes, and Cold War Rhetoric in Mad Magazine's 'Spy vs. Spy.'" *Journal of Popular Culture* 40, no. 1 (2007): 4–23.

Castro Ruz, Fidel. "Discurso pronunciado por el comandante Fidel Castro Ruz, en la empresa petrolera Shell el 6 de febrero de 1959." www.cuba.cu/gobierno/discursos/1959/esp/f060259e.html.

Catalá-Carrasco, Jorge L. *Vanguardia y humorismo gráfico en Crisis: La Guerra Civil española (1936-1939) y La Revolución cubana (1959-1961)*. NED edition. Woodbridge, Suffolk; Rochester, NY: Boydell and Brewer, 2015.

Catalá-Carrasco, Jorge L. "Raising the Cuban Flag." In *Comics and Memory in Latin America*, edited by Jorge Catalá Carasco and Paulo Drinot, 33–58. Pittsburgh: University of Pittsburgh Press, 2017.

Ceballos, Sandra. "Re: De Sandra." Message to Diana Álvarez Amell. Sep. 28, 2018. Email.

Dorfman, Ariel, and Armand Mattelart. *How to Read Donald Duck: Imperialist Ideology in a Disney Comic*. Translated by David Kunzle. New York: OR Books, 2018.

Eco, Umberto. "The Myth of Superman." In *Arguing Comics: Literary Masters on a Popular Medium*, edited by Jeet Heer and Kent Worcester, 134–73. Jackson: University Press of Mississippi, 2005.

Eire, Carlos. "Antonio Prohías: A Brilliant Cuban Cartoonist in Exile." *BabaluBlog* (blog). Aug. 15, 2016. babalublog.com/2016/08/15/antonio-prohias-a-brilliant-and-extraordinary-cuban-cartoonist/.

Eschner, Kat. "This Cuban Cartoonist Drew the Cold War for MAD Magazine." *Smithsonian Magazine*, Jan. 17, 2017. www.smithsonianmag.com/smart-news/how-cuban-cartoonist-drew-cold-war-mad-magazine-180961787/#eqL6Eib3Oddjv1Wv.99.

Feijóo, Samuel. "Chago, el gráfico." *Signos* 21 (1978): 536–37.

Ficarra, John, ed. *MAD Presents Spy vs. Spy: An Explosive Celebration*. Forward by Lewis Black. New York: TI Inc. Books, 2015.

Gramsci, Antonio. *The Gramsci Reader. Selected Writings 1916–1935*. Edited by David Forgacs. New York: NYU Press, 2000.

Grimes, William. "Antonio Prohias, 77; Drew 'Spy vs. Spy' Cartoon." *New York Times*, March 2, 1998. www.nytimes.com/1998/03/02/arts/antonio-prohias-77-drew-spy-vs-spy-cartoon.html.

Grundhauser, Eric, "How Cuba's Greatest Cartoonist Fled from Castro and Created 'Spy vs. Spy'" *Atlas Obscura*, Aug. 11, 2016. www.atlasobscura.com/articles/meet-the-cuban-expatriate-who-created-spy-vs-spy.

Hernández, Arístides, Jorge Piñero. *Historia del humor gráfico en Cuba*. Lleida, ES: Milenio, 2007.

Hernández, Roberto. "La historieta en Cuba: desde la crítica destructiva a la defensa a ultranza." *Tebeoesfera* 13 (2014). www.tebeosfera.com/documentos/la_historieta_en_cuba_desde_la_critica_destructiva_a_la_defensa_a_ultranza.html.

Lent, John. "Cuban Political, Social Commentary Cartoons." In *Cartooning in Latin America*, edited by John Lent, 193–215. New York: Hampton Press, 2005.

Leyva Martínez, Yaima. "Un libro para descubrir a Salomón." *Inter Press Service en Cuba*, Oct. 20, 2017. www.ipscuba.net/espacios/altercine/convergencias/un-libro-para-descubrir-a-salomon/.

Marinello, Juan. *Conversación con nuestros pintores abstractos*. Havana: Imprenta Nacional, 1961.

Mañach, Jorge. *An Inquiry into Choteo*. Translated by Jacqueline Loss. Barcelona: Linkgua Ediciones, 2018.

Mañach, Jorge. *La crisis de la alta cultura en Cuba*. Barcelona: Linkgua Ediciones, 2009.

Mogno, Darío. "A propósito de la historieta en Cuba después de 1959. Charla con Roberto Alonso." *Revista Latinoamericana de Estudios sobre la Historieta* 19 (2005): 61–70.

Mosquera, Gerardo. "Existir en el cosmos." *Catálogo. Nace el topo*. Galería Espacio Aglutinador. Havana, April 1995.

Negrín, Javier. "El Pitirre. Humor Revolucionario." *Revista latinoamericana de estudios sobre la historieta* 3, no. 12 (2003): 193–228. http://rlesh.mogno.com/13/13_negrin.html.

Olson, Ray. Review of "Spy vs. Spy 2: The Joke and Dagger Files." *Booklist*, Nov. 1, 2007, 34. Academic OneFile.

Pizarro, Marta Rosa. "Snapshots of My Father." In *Spy vs. Spy: The Complete Casebook*, by Antonio Prohías, 17–18. New York: Watson-Guptill, 2001.

Prohías, Antonio. *Spy vs. Spy: The Complete Casebook*. New York: Watson-Guptill, 2001.

4

ARCHIVING THE PAST, DRAWING THE PRESENT, AND PRESERVING DISPLACED HISTORIES OF VIOLENCE IN NONFICTIONAL GRAPHIC NOVELS

NATALJA CHESTOPALOVA

The symbiotic, interactive kernel between the reader and the visual narrative on the page remains one of the reasons why comics continue to be such a popular narrative form for both readers and writer-artist collaborators trying to offer a voice for nonfictional and marginalized voices. The same concerns about representations of gender, race, identity, space, memory, and witnessing that exist in relation to television, film, literature, and performative arts surface in relation to comics, and have raised a lot of critical questions about comics as a medium that has taken on the work of *memorializing* and *archiving* histories.[1] Portrayals of violence and trauma in comics has evolved beyond the genres of superhero and autobiography into storytelling modes that can resist immediate identification because they embody the flow of changing cultural activist capital. This intersection between portrayals of violence, history, and ethics can become the basis for a much more rhizomatic understanding of *memorialization* through multimodal narration.

The pivotal focus of this chapter is part of an ongoing conversation about comics as a decolonizing medium and the creation of counter-hegemonic *narrative-archives* outside of institutionalized spaces and practices. I look at some of the specific ways contemporary comics and nonfiction graphic novels are capable of provoking new dialogues with regard to how readers *recognize, engage,* and *interpret* the narrative frameworks shaping the representations of *global-local* boundaries, *trauma-framed* spaces of violence, *displaced* communities, and their *disappearing* histories. Joe Sacco's *Palestine* (2001) and *Footnotes in Gaza*

(2009), along with more recent works such as Jeff Lemire and Gord Downie's *Secret Path* (2016) and Kate Evans's *Threads: From the Refugee Crisis* (2017), are becoming part of the unofficial multimodal archive that exists on the periphery of institutionalized memory. These graphic novels challenge conceptions of local and global spaces and shift the perception of the physical and emotional distance that occurs between the reader and sites of individual suffering, generational violence, and community trauma. As instances of collective memory, the works discussed here are indicative of the license to engage in nonfictional storytelling that builds on journalism as a method of witnessing. Whether addressing the violent past of the Canadian residential schools or the violence perforating refugees' lives, the narrative effects force the reader to view the sites of trauma from a variety of angles and experience multiple spatial and emotional relationships, from global to local to intersubjective.

There is a continuing need to examine Sacco, Lemire/Downie, and Evans's works as both culture-specific comics narratives and mediated tools instrumental for the preservation of individual and community histories. The immersive nature of multimodal storytelling not only breaks the boundaries between the reader as a passive spectator and a conscious subject but also incites questions about the methods of witnessing and archiving *global-local* histories. These graphic novels challenge conceptions of local and global spaces because they use the medium itself to take on the ethical responsibility of not only retelling and preserving a nonfictional story about violence and trauma, but a story that implies that a degree of responsibility is being transferred onto the reader as an active part of the narrative medium.

Any discourse about comics as a medium that can successfully embody the drive to *decolonize* narratives of suffering and violence must likewise become attuned to some of its internal idiosyncrasies. Writing about the capacity of comics to spur activism and foster human rights, Sidonie Smith points to the potentially exploitative quality at the core of *witnessing*, specifically offering the genre of *crisis comics* as one of the problematic modes of witnessing radical violence, since the narratives are often exploited due to their presupposed simplicity and accessibility. The comics form is then forced to abandon its decolonizing potentiality and instead create a narrative economy based on problematic agendas grounded in dangerous binaries or categorizations (Smith 62). Within the framework of human rights discourse, comics audiences can witness the same uncannily familiar subject categorizations in the form of perpetrator, victim, and rescuer. Smith takes a subtle but poignant stance when she writes that *crisis comics* "make public an archive of marginalization and suffering by visualizing representative subjects of particular forms of victimization" (Smith 62). Autographic comics[2] and nonfictional graphic novels as methods of witnessing are thus intrinsically responsible for ensuring that they remain conscious of the ethical and ideological biases they help to either confront or reinforce.

Similar questions arise about the medium in relation to affect-based topologies of multimodal narration and what connections comics can afford when it comes to portrayals of violence in displaced and marginalized contexts, both fictional and nonfictional. Even in serialized crime comics, Jared Gardner observes, there are complex dynamics governing the transformative ethical connotations. For Gardner, serialized crime comics are saturated with agency linked to the participatory modalities of comics as a popular culture form, where, on the one hand, popular culture is a medium for "mind-control—whether the minds being controlled belong to others or one's self"—or, on the other, popular culture is a "tool for breaking through the pasteboard mask to the deeper truths that lie behind" (Gardner 69–70). The philosophy of comics as a narrative form is thus a system of methodological interactive interplay between reader and page. Gardner establishes the reader as *complicit* in the comics narrative, maintaining that the reader is always "required to fill in the space between the frames with the missing action," in effect making all comics and graphic novels "necessarily collaborative texts between the imagination of the author/artist and the imagination of the reader who must complete the narrative" (Gardner 800). The gutter, panels, speech bubbles, and other functional and temporal elements of the comics narrative form necessitate "work on the part of the reader of a different nature than other narrative forms" (Gardner 800). This ongoing symbiotic work has become an essential constituent in a *decolonizing* comics medium toolkit, and in some cases facilitated the creation of a multimodal *narrative-archive*.

What makes Sacco, Lemire/Downie, and Evans distinct is that these authors contribute to the representations of *racialized* and *displaced* communities by questioning the conceptions of local and global spaces of violence and initiating a perceptual shift in the reader's construction of individual, communitarian, generational, and/or global suffering. Though Sacco, Lemire, and Evans may not share stylistic or genre preferences, all their works have a self-reflexive quality with respect to what *form* they want to implement in order to tell stories about *personal* journeys within *global* contexts. In part, the ethics of their respective visual narrative forms is connected to what is included and what is excluded from the storytelling. Barbara Postema observes that "comics, as an art form and as a narrative form, is a system in which a number of disparate elements or fragments work together to create a complex whole" (Postema xii). She notes that "to create meaning all the various elements contain and produce gaps, creating a syntax and semiotics (what Roland Barthes would call a language), in which fragmentation and absence become operative throughout as signifying functions, while at the same time the gaps invite readers to fill in the blanks" (Postema xiv). Postema's analysis of how signification is formed through syntactical and semiotic choices is an effective way to think about how Sacco, Lemire, and Evans have taken explicit care to both write and illustrate these works as spaces of individual and communitarian violence in a manner that would allow them to control the syntax and semiotics, and thus retain greater creative and ethical control over the depicted stories of trauma. I hold the view that the impact of this type of creative authorship is part of the impulse to decolonize the graphic novel medium, and multimodal media in general, by constructing immersive nonfictional graphic novels with sophisticated emotional economies.

Sacco's *Palestine* and *Footnotes in Gaza* are some of the earlier texts to include the impulse to decolonize, and they accomplish this in part by playing with genre expectations and how far narrative form can be used to critically respond to sites of violence and crisis. Sacco's autographic novels embody the genre shift from traditional journalism, and instead borrow from New Journalism and its key principles and epistemologies. James Murphy observes that New Journalism can be defined through narrative practices that range from "subjective to participatory to activist" (Murphy 28). Scholars of literary journalism propose that New Journalism was more than a "wider revolt into style" and that its in-depth reporting was a timely response to the publishing market opportunity created by social and political unrest (Pauly 590). Murphy's demarcation of New Journalism as a counterhegemonic method that applies "techniques of fiction to nonfiction" (Murphy 28) aligns well with Sacco's style of visual narration. Instead of privileging the preoccupation with the binary of fiction versus nonfiction, Sacco, as well as Evans, take advantage of New Journalism's reliance on reader response, acknowledged subjectivity, preference for intensive instead of extensive coverage, intuitive or instinctual writing, and literary-artistic techniques. The epistemological difference between traditional journalism or historical nonfiction and New Journalism is not grounded in objective or subjective writing, but rather the perception of individual and global histories through an ethical storytelling paradigm.

Building on this framework of New Journalism, Sacco's, and to an extent Evans's, nonfictional graphic narratives can function as spaces for the renegotiation of the relationship between global sites of racially charged conflict and trauma. *Palestine, Footnotes in Gaza,* and Evans's *Threads: from the Refugee*

Crisis are all examples of narratives that have this *regenerative potential* as they engage in two types of processes. First, these multimodal graphic novels play with the local and global space so as to manipulate the perception of the physical and affective distance between the reader and the sites of trauma. Second, they critically question the abstract nature of racialized boundaries by destabilizing the threshold between the reader as a passive spectator and as a conscious subject. The latter concern with abstraction of violence, conflict, and suffering has been a consistent part of the conversation about the value of comics and site-specific/immersive experiences in educational settings. For instance, research shows that nonfictional comics narratives have been successfully used in classrooms as accidental historical archives because their multimodal form can counteract the experience of desensitization and abstraction. Graphic novels can offer a storytelling space where the reader begins to question the idea that the violence of war is an "abstraction of sorts—something that exists, but that is tangential to their daily lives" (Decker and Castro 178).

Sacco's New Journalism–inspired visual storytelling contributes to this project of decolonizing complex representations of violence, race, boundaries, and history by using interviews and first-person accounts to create a series of multimodal location-specific narrative-archives. *Palestine* describes a two-month period in the early 1990s and combines textual panels with a series of images that mimic photographic journalism practices. The autographic novel's framing as a series of themed interviews with Palestinian refugees and visits to sites of conflict actively relies on the participation of the reader as a critical observer. The introduction to the collected edition of *Palestine* written by Edward Said picks up on a dimension of this dynamic when it proceeds to endorse comics as a legitimate medium that offers an alternative reading process. This alternative process, Said notes, intentionally distances the reader from "media saturated" and "controlled" filtered portrayals of local and global spaces that have over time become defined by a rigid "aura" of specific social, economic, or cultural conflict (Said iii). Part of the decolonizing potential in comics is the ability to question the problematic or institutional "aura" and offer counterhegemonic narratives, especially in terms of depicting sites of violence, trauma, racialized bodies, and racialized boundaries.

Consider an instance of such storytelling in *Palestine*'s chapter 5 as it narrates Sacco's visit to Ramallah in the Central West Bank. The chapter begins with a series of bleeding horizontal panels inviting the reader to follow Sacco from the hidden and protected space of the taxi, to the action-packed street, and then back to the hotel where he eagerly tells the clerk about his first "explosion" experiences, which instead turn out to be "percussion" or "sound grenades" used for crowd control and curfews (Sacco 117–18). The signification formed through syntactical and semiotic choices call on the reader to continually synthesize textual, visual, and temporal components in order to develop a multifaceted affective connection to events, interactions, and places. Sacco's storytelling captures complex affect-based relationships that depend on the audience's ability to conceptualize and engage with sites of conflict and generational, colonial, and racially framed contexts. Furthermore, the transition from passive spectator to conscious subject and the developing concern with ethical responsibility are contingent on the changing relationship to space and distance—a relationship that transcends the practices of desensitization and othering perspectives. Instead the graphic narrative form turns to a critical discussion of the localized perspective, compassion, and cultural value of everyday lives.

Another example of autographic storytelling in *Palestine* that tries to reconfigure the various aspects of distance and space can be experienced in the visual narration of Sacco's arrival at the Palestinian refugee camp in chapter 6 (Sacco 146–47). This two-page bleeding style panel is dependent on the reader's experience of *closure*, classically defined by Scott McCloud as the "phenomenon of observing the parts but perceiving the whole" (McCloud 63). Featuring no speech bubbles or captions, the effects of the two-page panel push the audience to view sites of trauma from a variety of angles and through multiple points of closure. As the reader's gaze follows each point of content, the contact with the page ensures that there is new affect being constantly produced and reevaluated. In an interview, Sacco attributed this intensity to the comics medium itself:

> The thing about comics, it has this very visceral impact. You open up the book, and if the drawings have a truth to them the reader is immediately in that picture. They see the architecture, they see the clothing, they see all that stuff, the background, and it sort of situates them immediately. And that's just by function of opening the book. (Holland and Dahlman 210)

The wealth of angles, points of closure, and moments of visceral impact ensure that the reader experiences multiplicitous spatial relationships, from global to local and communitarian to intersubjective.

In *Footnotes in Gaza*, Sacco continues to apply a similar immersive narrative style and syntax, but the added temporal juxtapositions suggest a more self-critical perspective, conscious of the medium's decolonizing potential.

Footnotes in Gaza is framed by two parallel storylines that contrast current spaces of crisis and ongoing conflicts with personal recollections collected by Sacco in relation to the 1956 incident when 111 Palestinians were killed in Rafah. A closer examination of a two-page bleeding style panel showing Sacco's fictionalized version of the 1956 "screening process" (Sacco 298–99) offers a moving take on accidental historical archive as it is rooted in the memories, fears, and hopes of real people. This nonfictional graphic novel is steeped in stories of loss, violence, and suffering as a historical record of personal and communitarian trauma, as well as a memorial that exists outside of the mainstream and institutional.

The second major distinction between *Footnotes in Gaza* and *Palestine* is that Sacco is dedicated to carefully narrating how he acquired the data necessary for writing this history-based depiction of the 1956 events. Sacco makes the reader part of the research process, insofar as the audience is continuously immersed in local community interviews with victims, relatives, and neighbors. This immersive process builds dual cognitive connections, where, on the one hand, Sacco wants to convey that everyone has a story worth listening to, and on the other, one has to continually work on not becoming desensitized to these stories. Comics scholars, including James F. Wurtz, view this duality as a point of discussion because an argument can be made that graphic depictions of violence, war, and trauma can "become so detail-oriented that the reader may become detached and unemotional" (Wurtz 205). In fact, Sacco confesses in an interview that as an author, "You're constantly thinking how much of the violence should I show" (Holland and Dahlman 211). Wurtz suggests that in addition to detachment, "artistic works of individual and national commemoration have tended to reduce the violence of the war to pure abstraction" (Wurtz 205). Through a conscious use of an ethically framed lens, Sacco, Lemire, and Evans are able to record the affective economies within disappearing and marginalized histories. The audience is invited to empathize with suffering on the page and, as this process is repeated over and over, the immersive modality of comics affects the emotional distance between the reader and the narrative, making them part of the process of historical memorialization.

An alternative way to decolonize the discourse, Sacco's visual narration embodies a retrospective quality Sandra Cox differentiates as an immersive "slow journalism" (Cox 199). According to Cox's interpretation of slow journalism, it takes advantage of the "temporal adjustment to reporting that may complicate how his audience receives the coverage" (Cox 199). Furthermore, "the delay between witnessing, reporting and proliferating the documented atrocities also implicitly demands a re-attending to the events" in a manner that parallels the experience of a "traumatized survivor" (Cox 199). Although Cox is unpacking the relevance of slow journalism specifically in relation to the coverage of rape as a war crime in comics, I want to extrapolate by suggesting that any act of traumatizing violence can temporally "bisect a life" (Cox 199) into before and after. The process of recording and archiving narratives of violent conflict, communitarian trauma, and individual suffering would be strengthened through a greater awareness of the psychology behind new experiences of time and temporality. The language of comics can provide a narrative form that resists attempts to "lock trauma into a single historical moment" and instead generates an immersive engagement reinforcing the "continued relevancy" (Cox 199) of stories about histories of violence as timeless.

Moving beyond Sacco's use of slow journalism, the applicability of the graphic narrative medium for archiving marginalized or disappearing voices takes on other forms in Jeff Lemire and Gord Downie's *Secret Path* and Kate Evans's *Threads: From the Refugee Crisis*. For the *Secret Path* project, Lemire collaborated on a historically situated graphic novel that was accompanied by a series of music tracks composed and performed by Gord Downie from the Tragically Hip. The narrative exemplifies one of the many cases of generational trauma caused by the aggressive assimilation practices implemented at the Canadian federally funded and primarily church-run residential schools. The forced enrollment of Indigenous children, rigid boarding school structure, and systemic physical and sexual abuse destroyed Indigenous communities, separated families, and created a legacy of generational trauma. *Secret Path* is therefore both a graphic narrative preserving the real memories of violence and injustice towards Indigenous peoples in Canadian history and a moving personal story of Chanie Wenjack. An Anishinaabe child from Marten Falls First Nation, Chanie was forcefully removed from his family, abused, and alienated at the Cecilia Jeffrey Indian Residential School located near Kenora, Ontario. The collaboration between Lemire and Downie commemorates Chanie's life and tragic death in 1966, when he tried to walk back home along the railroad tracks in order to return to his family and escape abuse at the residential school. *Secret Path* plays with the distance between the reader and the sites of affective and physical violence through its particular take on multimodal storytelling.

Lemire's reimagining of Chanie's suffering and journey home through the use of sequential panels without any text bubbles is instead accompanied by pages with printed song lyrics by Downie. This creates a narrative dynamic that relies on the audience as active readers as well as listeners. In one of these instances, three panels depicting a predatory sexual abuse shower scene appear on the left page, while Downie's lyrics for the song "Swing Set" appear on the right:

> Turning round and round in my seat
> Chains twisting over my head
> When the tension is complete
> And there is no way out of it (Lemire and Downie 2016)

The multimodal demands of the symbiotic relationship between comics and music create multiple ways in which the Lemire/Downie collaboration tries to resurrect, preserve, and archive individual and communitarian traumas. *Secret Path* was Lemire's first autographic work with the distinct aim of having a "specific conversation" (*Goethe Institute Interview*) about the Canadian residential school system and its impact on Indigenous histories. Not only are the proceeds from the sales of *Secret Path* being donated to the National Centre for Truth and Reconciliation at the University of Manitoba, this work is also becoming part of the Canadian school curriculum. In one of the interviews, Lemire recollects that even before he started working on the project with Downie, they wanted to create something "teachers could use to introduce this part of Canadian history to younger readers," as a kind of "access point" to the histories of Indigenous peoples and Canada's role in the individual and communitarian damage caused by the residential schools (Lemire).

Despite the narrative potential in *Secret Path* as an accidental archive and educational tool, it is important to note that any conversation about Indigenous past, present, and future must acknowledge Indigenous perspectives and ways of seeing. Writing about Indigenous cultural and intellectual resurgence, political mobilization, ways of being, and traditional governance, Leanne Betasamosake Simpson points out that any genuine attempt at decolonization or reconciliation would have to involve much more than an acknowledgment of the history of abuse, violence, and dispossession (Simpson 21). Simpson writes that most Canadians do not understand the "historic and contemporary injustice of dispossession and occupation, particularly when the state has expressed its unwillingness to make any adjustments to the unjust relationship" (Simpson 21). Her emphasis on Indigenous methodologies and cultural paradigms is likewise a commentary on the fact that nonfictional graphic narratives cannot exist in isolation from their past and current contexts as they continue to portray real histories of global, local, and generational violence and trauma. For comics to function as a decolonizing and regenerative medium, the narrative must therefore create a space where the reader can begin to take on the work of thinking through "the impetus, the ethical responsibility, the strategies and the plan of action for resurgence" (Simpson 20). Sacco, Lemire/Downie, and Evans's nonfictional graphic novels succeed as instances of narrative activism because they are able to provoke critical and ethical considerations about displaced or disappearing histories and individual voices.

The final, and chronologically most recent, example that embodies *activist* and counterhegemonic practices by preserving histories of marginalized people whose voices often only exist outside of institutional and censured spaces and media formats. Evans's autographic novel offers a counterbalance to Lemire and Sacco, in so far as it was not created as an educational work of graphic nonfiction, or as an homage to new journalism, but rather it is a first-hand account of her own contribution as a volunteer at a refugee camp in the French port town of Calais between 2015 and 2016. During that period, Calais served as a temporary housing and processing area for refugees that were attempting to get to the United Kingdom. Evans's account of her time at the camp utilizes a range of visual and storytelling techniques, from interviews and diary entries to collage and sketches. While Sacco is in some respects safeguarded by his use of the New Journalism genre, Evans's depictions of people coexisting in shipping containers without proper access to safety and toilet facilities are starkly personal. In one of the episodes Evans is visiting the camp, walking among flooded and broken-down tents, in order to distribute some lemons and oranges to families with young children. However, at the sight of a little girl Evans "breaks" down (Evans 64). In a central panel we can see Evans's face, mouth open in a painful grimace, tears streaming down her face:

> What are we fucking doing!?
> We can't solve this with oranges!
> The kids are all here!
> They're all stuck here!
> When does this stop being somebody else's problem?!!! (Evans 64)

Evans's stylistic and semiotic choices are directed at creating a multimodal storytelling environment that invites the audience to enter into a dialogical relationship with the page and question the limitations of their own affective or emotional boundaries.

This dialogical relationship is further complicated by Evans's perspective as a mother and an activist. Her emphatic as well as intuitive understanding of the therapeutic effects of *art* and *play* turn her portrait painting sessions into affective contact points during which refugees, both adults and children, find ways to ground themselves in situations that are dehumanizing. For one such portrait painting session, Evans uses an overlay of newspaper-style speech bubbles to shift the attention to the lack of global ethical accountability and the extent to which the lives and voices of these refugees remain out of focus:

> As I draw, I have no idea that this child has walked from Afghanistan over mountain ranges without food or water. That he's been held in slavery in Turkey and nearly drowned in the Mediterranean. That his eyes have been damaged by French police tear gas. To me, he's just a cute kid. He has no idea that he'll make it to the UK seven weeks later, in the back of a lorry. That the doors will be sealed shut, the oxygen levels will fall, and he'll very nearly suffocate along with fourteen other people. That he'll save all their lives with a text that he sends to the volunteers back in Calais: "I need halp . . . No oksijan in the car." We find out later. I do discover one thing at the time. He's another motherless child. (Evans 111)

Considered from an educational perspective, the immersive storytelling aspects in *Threads: From the Refugee Crisis* call for a perceptual shift which plays with the notions of responsibility and empathy, the latter being further complicated by a crucial distinction between *emotional* empathy and *cognitive* empathy (Jorenby 160).

The distinction between cognitive and emotional empathy is a vital one because it arises from a changed relationship between the reader and the sites of suffering and violence. Whether they are preserving refugee voices, capturing racially and historically charged conflicts, or calling attention to the generational trauma of Canadian residential schools—Evans, Sacco, and Lemire/Downie cultivate critical narrative relationships between the audience and the multiplicitous sites of suffering and violence. Their narratives take on the project of *decolonizing* portrayals of nonfictional conflict-based relationships in so far as they incite the reader to ask difficult questions about the ethics of power, global/local boundaries, and the problem of complicity and desensitization within modern spectatorship of suffering. Their immersive storytelling environments can function as *accidental* archives for the preservation of communitarian and individual histories beyond the agendas and practices imposed by institutions and mass media formats. *Accidental* archiving through the comics medium acts as a multimodal repository for stories that require a symbiotic creative process and engage the reader as an active collaborator. Sacco, Lemire/Downie, and Evans's nonfictional graphic narratives change the kinds of affective or emotional bonds the audience can build with the narrative by disrupting the sense that these histories are abstractions, removed spatially as well as temporally. The immersive potential of the comics medium as a multimodal *archive* can sustain methods of ethical witnessing, that is witnessing through an ethical lens based on cognitive and emotional empathy. These autographic novels prioritize the emphasis on defining access, memory, boundaries, accountability, transparency, and responsibility, in essence signaling the beginning of an activist type of *archiving* that looks outside of institutional practices for *immersive spaces* which would restore and protect stories that are *always* under the threat of being erased.

Notes

1. All use of italics in this paper is intended to draw the attention to terminology and invite the reader to track shifts in language and meaning associated with interdisciplinary discussions at the intersection of comics, archive, and media research studies.

2. Autobiographic comics are here denoting narratives that are both grounded in the author's autobiographical accounts and are created by, or under the direction of, the same author.

Works Cited

Cox, Sandra. "The New Slow Journalism of the Moral Draughtsman: Joe Sacco's Coverage of State Sanctioned Sexual Violence." *Journal of Graphic Novels and Comics* 9, no. 3 (2018): 195–213.

Decker, Alicia C., and Maurice Castro. "Teaching History with Comic Books: A Case Study of Violence, War, and the Graphic Novel." *History Teacher* 45, no. 2 (2012): 169–87.

Evans, Kate. *Threads: From the Refugee Crisis*. London: Verso, 2017.

Gardner, Jared. "Archives, Collectors, and the New Media Work of Comics." *Modern Fiction Studies* 52, no. 4 (2006): 787–806.

Gardner, Jared. "Serial Killers: The Crime Comics of Ed Brubaker and Sean Phillips" *Zeitschrift für Anglistik und Amerikanistik* 59, no. 1 (2014): 55–70.

Gilmore, Leigh. "Witnessing *Persepolis*: Comics, Trauma, and Childhood Testimony." In *Graphic Subjects: Critical Essays on Autobiography and Graphic Novels*, edited by Michael A. Chaney, 157–63. Madison: University of Wisconsin Press, 2011.

Holland, Edward C., and Carl T. Dahlman. "Graphic Geopolitics: An Interview with Comics Artist Joe Sacco." *Geopolitics* 22, no. 1 (2017): 204–14.

Jorenby, Marnie K. "Comics and War: Transforming Perceptions of the Other through a Constructive Learning Experience." *Journal of Peace Education* 4, no. 2 (2007): 149–62.

Lemire, Jeff. "Interview with Canadian Cartoonist Jeff Lemire." Interview by *Goethe-Institut Toronto*, April 27, 2018. https://www.youtube.com/watch?v=YvNqXJsb1Ec.

Lemire, Jeff, and Gord Downie. *Secret Path*. Toronto: Simon and Schuster, 2016.

McCloud, Scott. *Understanding Comics: The Invisible Art*. New York: Harper Perennial, 1993.

Murphy, James E. "Press Responsibility and New Journalism." *Journal of Communication Inquiry* 3, no. 2 (1978): 27–36.

Pauly, John J. "The New Journalism and the struggle for interpretation." *Journalism* 15, no. 5 (2014): 589–604.

Postema, Barbara. *Narrative Structure in Comics: Making Sense of Fragments*. New York: RIT Press, 2013.

Sacco, Joe. *Footnotes in Gaza*. New York: Metropolitan Books, 2009.

Sacco, Joe. *Palestine*. Seattle: Fantagraphics, 2011.

Said, Edward. "Introduction: Homage to Joe Sacco." In *Palestine* by Joe Sacco, i–v. Seattle: Fantagraphics, 2011.

Simpson, Leanne Betasamosake. *Dancing on Our Turtle's Back: Stories of Nishnaabeg Re-Creation, Resurgence, and a New Emergence*. Winnipeg: ARP Books, 2011.

Smith, Sidonie. "Human Rights and Comics: Autobiographical Avatars, Crisis Witnessing, and Transnational Rescue Networks." In *Graphic Subjects: Critical Essays on Autobiography and Graphic Novels*, edited by Michael A. Chaney, 61–72. Madison: University of Wisconsin Press, 2011.

Wurtz, James F. "Representing the Great War: Violence, Memory, and Comic Form." *Pacific Coast Philology* 44, no. 2 (2009): 205–15.

5

CALVIN AND HOBBES
A Case Study of the Cartoon Fight Cloud

JACOB MUREL

The Cartoon Fight Cloud (CFC) is an oft-utilized and traditional device for depicting violence in both animated cartoons and still comics. Despite its widespread use, however, the CFC has not yet undergone any extended examination in comics scholarship. Neil Cohn, one of the few comics scholars to analyze the CFC, refers to it as a "smoke-veiled fight," explaining how the CFC differs from other "morphemes" of comics iconography, e.g., actions stars, that replace representational depictions of violence in comics in that the CFC replaces only durated events, specifically fight sequences.[1] The CFC never stands in for a single action, but always the duration of an entire or large portion of a fight. In light of the CFC's highly specified signification, the question remains: what might the CFC signify about the *nature* of the violence it represents? When and for what reasons do cartoonists choose to signify a fight with a CFC rather than drawing the struggle itself? Does the CFC represent a specific kind of violence? And how might the CFC affect surrounding panels or the story arc in which it is placed? By better understanding the role of the CFC and the specific nature of the violence it signifies, comics readers and scholars can better understand the role and nature of cartoon violence in comics more generally. With this end in mind, the present essay examines Bill Watterson's newspaper strip *Calvin and Hobbes* as a case study of the CFC. Motivated by the above questions, I survey Watterson's use of the CFC throughout *Calvin and Hobbes*. In doing so, I argue that Watterson's use of the CFC both signifies and elides physical confrontation, requiring readers to imaginatively participate in the signified violence while drawing readers' attention to the violence's context rather than the acts of violence in themselves.

My reason for focusing on *Calvin and Hobbes* is due to both practical constraints of space and the nature of CFC and its appearance in Watterson's strip. The CFC appears almost exclusively within comedic comics. It is entirely absent from the work of largely noncomedic cartoonists such as Joe Sacco or Phoebe Gloeckner, and from the melodrama of conventional superhero comics, yet it appears time and again throughout Mort Walker's *Beetle Bailey* strip and Goscinny and Uderzo's numerous *Astérix* albums. The CFC's limited appearance to comics often labeled "funnies" reinforces its role as a comedic device for depicting violence in comics. In other words, cartoonists do not utilize the CFC when depicting noncomedic violence; the CFC is a visual device limited to light-hearted and humorous situations. As such, due to pragmatic restraints—there is simply not enough space or time in one essay to survey every use of the CFC across even one genre of comics, such as American newspaper strips—I have limited my present discussion to one comedic comic. I have chosen *Calvin and Hobbes* given it is known for both its visual creativity (particularly in its Sunday strips) and humor. Moreover, compared to other comedic comics like *Beetle Bailey*, the CFC makes relatively few appearances throughout *Calvin and Hobbes*. Watterson employs the sign only twelve times throughout the strip's ten-year run, and not at all during the strip's last three years, instead often opting to illustrate physical confrontations between Calvin and Hobbes as the two caught in resentful embrace. I believe that, given Watterson's selective use of this well-known sign, an analysis of the few individual instances in which he does employ it can reveal key aspects of the CFC's specialized signification. My intent in this essay is not to write an exhaustive treatise on the CFC or symbolic devices for representing violence in comics. Rather, I hope to initiate discussion about the CFC in comics, as well as other potential means for symbolically depicting violence in comics. To this end, the present essay focuses exclusively on the CFC as it appears in Bill Watterson's American newspaper strip *Calvin and Hobbes*.

Past scholarship has established the CFC as a motivated sign used to replace extended, physically violent interactions between two or more characters. Neil Cohn and Hannah Miodrag have remarked how, for comics signs like the CFC, there exists "a certain rationale behind the relation between signifier and signified," meaning that "these shapes encoded a representative *aspect* of a signified, if not a visual characteristic."[2] In being a "partially motivated, partially conventional" sign whose general form draws from elements traditionally associated with physical brawls, the CFC as conventionally used signifies physical violence, as opposed to emotional or mental violence.[3] The CFC's typical cloud-like appearance is motivated by the flaying limbs and dust kicked up during a brawl, while its vortex iteration draws from the whirling bodies and disorientation involved in such encounters. This representational element of the CFC is involved in its primary signification for external, interpersonal, physical conflict. Of course, other symbols and signs are often used to represent physical violence in comics, most notably action stars. As Neil Cohn aptly remarks, however, CFCs are distinct from action stars due to the former's implied duration. Cohn writes, "Action stars are a punctive event, implying a single momentary action. You cannot infer multiple punches or an exchange of punches in an action star."[4] By contrast, Cohn writes, CFCs "imply durative events, occurring across a span of time. Here, there must be multiple actions (hits, kicks, bites, etc.) and cannot be only a single action."[5] In this way, both action stars and CFCs signify physically violent actions "but evoke subtly different inferences about those events."[6] I do not argue against Miodrag and Cohn in this essay. Rather, using their work as a starting point, and drawing from other comics scholars, I hope to demonstrate the CFC's additional nuances as the CFC appears throughout *Calvin and Hobbes*.

More than just signifying sequences of physical violence, Watterson's use of the CFC throughout *Calvin and Hobbes* often serves to signify specific stages of physical confrontation. Though the two eponymous main characters often argue with one another, the CFC never appears until their confrontation becomes physical. An example of such physicality is the Sunday strip dated September 20, 1987,[7] in which Calvin and Hobbes argue over who should lead their trip to the Yukon wilderness. While several panels show the two in verbal confrontation, the CFC does not appear until their argument turns physical. The two argue until Calvin remarks, "You can't be the leader! See, I've got the commander hat." In response, Hobbes mimes the action of rolling up his sleeves and retorts, "That can be easily remedied." The following panel contains a CFC accompanied by dust clouds and stars, followed by another panel of dirt-covered Hobbes donning the commander hat to Calvin's protestations. While Calvin and Hobbes's verbal argument is depicted in detail in this strip, their physical confrontation is represented in a single panel through the CFC. Moreover, Watterson appears to use the CFC to signify specific degrees or forms of physical violence. For instance, one Sunday strip dated October 11, 1987, features a common motif of the series: Hobbes pouncing onto a surprised Calvin upon the latter's return home from school. Although this scenario transpires many times throughout the strip's ten-year syndication, Hobbes's savage impact is never accompanied by a fight cloud until his pounce develops into an extended conflict with Calvin, as in the above-mentioned strip. Here, Hobbes's initial impact with Calvin is accompanied by action stars and an onomatopoeic POW!, but in the following panel, the vortex ring serves the same purpose as the traditional CFC, suggesting an ensuing brawl between the eponymous main characters. But in this panel, the vortex serves as a transition between Hobbes's impact with Calvin and the depictions of their wrestling in subsequent panels, thereby signifying the characters' transition from a one-off impact into a wrestling match. In this instance, then, the CFC indicates a specific stage in the two characters' fight.

Other Sunday strips—specifically, those dated June 7, 1987, and September 24, 1989—similarly feature the CFC as a means of representing a change in fight intensity between two characters. In both strips, Calvin and Hobbes's physical altercation begins in one panel with the CFC occupying the subsequent panel. The first panel depicts Calvin and Hobbes wrestling, as if caught in a static struggle. The CFC's individual components—that is, the flailing limbs, kicked up dust, and impact stars—in the subsequent panel suggests this struggle evolves into an extended brawl, as if the two characters move from their brotherly wrestling match into a battle complete with punches and kicks. In these strips, then, the CFC depicts an increase in the intensity of physical violence as the two characters move from wrestling to brawling. Moreover, as quoted by Cohn above, the CFC carries with it a temporal connotation. But this time is never specified. Not only does the CFC suggest the conflict's intensity increases, but that Calvin and Hobbes's confrontation transpires over an indeterminate amount of time. The CFC's accompaniment alongside more overtly indexical depictions of fighting demonstrates how it can signify not only a fight but a specific form—or rather intensity—of fighting that lasts for a nonspecified length of time. In such instances, rather than standing in for the whole fight, the CFC signifies the indeterminate amount of time spent in one stage of fighting.

Watterson's use of the CFC to signify heightened intensity in physical violence further appears to represent the climax of the strip's or sequence's physical confrontation. In other words, Watterson appears to use the CFC to signify the instant of greatest intensity within a single, physical battle. The few strips following the CFC panel contains an illustration of Calvin and Hobbes fighting; these panels indicate a steady decline in vigor and energy, a narratological feature observed in the aforementioned October 11, 1987, strip as well. In that strip, although the CFC does provide a transition from Hobbes's impact to the wrestling between him and Calvin depicted in subsequent panels, the CFC nevertheless signifies a peak of physical intensity. The CFC's vortex in the October 11, 1987, strip connotes the rapid spinning and tumbling of Calvin and Hobbes as they hit the ground, reeling from Hobbes's high-powered pounce onto Calvin. As with action lines for depicting speed in comics, the blurring of characters suggests rapid movement and high energy. The shift from CFC to an actual image of Calvin and Hobbes wrestling in the following panels suggests a loss of speed and lowering of physical intensity in their confrontation as they are distanced temporally from Hobbes's initial impact with Calvin. In this way, the CFC represents the moment of peak physical intensity in their confrontation. In this way, the CFC's use within this strip makes Cohn's claim that "both action stars and fight clouds play specific roles as 'Peaks' in the narrative structure of sequences—the culmination of actions and events in a visual sequence."[8] Even when serving a transitory function within a panel sequence, the CFC signifies the peak of physical intensity for a given violent encounter.

As a means for signifying the combative peak in a strip or sequence, the CFC may also represent the sequence or strip's narrative climax, though it does not necessarily need to do the latter. Two such examples of this are the *Calvin and Hobbes* daily strips circulated on December 12 and December 13, 1989. In each of these strips, Calvin and Hobbes debate the earnestness behind Calvin's performative kindness in an attempt to get onto Santa's Nice List. In the final panel of both strips, Calvin and Hobbes's verbal argument turns into a physical fight that is represented by the CFC. Accompanied by joke dialogue, the CFC—being the climax of physical violence—coincides with each strip's comedic and narrative climaxes. Here, by signifying the combative peak between two or more characters, the CFC also signifies the narrative climax in the strip. But if the physical action and violence is not central to the sequence's narrative arc, the CFC may very well not signify the narrative climax. Take, for example, the September 21, 1990, and July 19, 1992, Sunday strips, in which the CFC panel appears during the first half of the strip, serving as part of the narrative build-up to the strip's punchline or climax. As these strips demonstrate, the CFC merely signifies the climax of physical violence within a comic, not necessarily the narrative climax, although these two peaks may be coextensive within a panel.

As I have argued thus far, CFCs signify durated, physically violent events with comedic undertones that function as the peak moment of violence within a given panel sequence. But despite this limited signification, the CFC provides few, if any, specifics of the signified fight. In this way, as Neil Cohn writes of comics signs and symbols, the CFC "hereby forc[es] a reader to infer a 'hidden' event."[9] Though the CFC signifies the peak of a physical and comedic battle, it is not specific about the details of the event's content and duration, instead leaving the fight's specifics to the reader's imagination. In this way, the CFC functions as an imaginative space, a site of ambiguity and mystery, in which each reader visualizes the actual fight between Calvin and

Hobbes. By abjuring a representational illustration of Calvin and Hobbes's conflict in drawing a CFC, Watterson leaves readers to imagine what happens during the course of the two characters' fight, their respective combat styles, even how long the fight lasts, etc. Throughout the series, panels containing CFCs almost always appear between two other panels—the previous panel depicting Calvin and Hobbes in heated argument and the subsequent panel illustrating their near-exhaustion. The interstitial CFC panel connects these two instants of the comic narrative via an imaginative link. It signifies that Calvin and Hobbes move from a verbal argument (or even physical impact) to exhaustion through a physical fight signified by the CFC. What specifically happens during the fight and how longer, however, is never explicitly stated, instead left to each individual reader. In its role as a connective and imaginative space, the CFC—comprising a whole panel as it nearly always does—operates in a way similar to the gutter, as conceived by Scott McCloud in *Understanding Comics* (1993).

Though there have been numerous developments and alternative theories on the significance and function of the gutter in comics, the McCloudian gutter resonates with the CFC here conceived through both element's involvement of the reader's imagination as supplying elided action and violence. McCloud speaks of the gutter as the empty space between panels in which readers mentally supply all the unrepresented instants of a panel sequence. McCloud terms this act of filling in the gaps "closure," the process in which the reader mentally connects the ostensibly disparate panels of a comics sequence into a unified stream of action consistent with human experience.[10] Due to the reader's imaginative provision, "Every act committed to paper by the comics artist is aided and abetted by a silent accomplice. An equal partner in crime known as the reader."[11] By way of example, McCloud offers a two-panel sequence suggesting the given character's death, the first depicting a character being attacked by zombies, the second depicting that character's scream above a city skyline. Of this sequence, McCloud writes, "I may have drawn an axe being raised in this example, but I'm not the one who let it drop or decided how hard the blow, or who screamed, or why. That, dear reader, was your special crime, each of you committing it in your own style."[12] For McCloud, when a character's death or harm is left unillustrated, transpiring figuratively within the space between two panels, the reader imaginatively provides the details of that violence, making the reader a participant in the violent act. I argue that McCloud's conception of the gutter here equally applies to the CFC: readers must imaginatively supply the individual acts of the physical violence signified by the CFC, thereby making readers active participants in the represented violence.

As a symbol signifying an indeterminate series of combative acts, the CFC indicates a (violent) moment in the narrative sequence the reader must complete via closure, much as the McCloudian gutter. The reader knows a fight is transpiring, but the specific actions of its violence—who hits who, how, when, and with what degree of intensity—are supplied by the reader's imagination. A previously mentioned Sunday strip from September 20, 1987, serves as an apt example here. In the strip's third row of panels, Calvin and Hobbes argue over who can rightfully serve as leader of their expedition to Yukon. Upon Calvin's inference that he is the rightful leader because he wears the leader hat, Hobbes marches towards Calvin, fist at the ready. The next panel consists of a CFC, followed by a panel portraying a newly hatted Hobbes beside an angry Calvin, both smeared with crosshatching to signify the residue of their recent tussle. It is significant here that the CFC panel in this strip possesses no frame. In this way, the CFC may be understood as visually appearing within the gutter space that connects the two surrounding panels. Without the CFC between these two panels, readers are left to ask how the hat has come to rest on Hobbes's head or how both characters go from being clean to covered in dirt and scratches. While the CFC does not specify how Hobbes comes to bear the leader hat, the CFC nevertheless signifies the terms under which these transitions occur. The specifics, such as Hobbes's tactics in overpowering Calvin, are left to be supplied exclusively by the reader. Much like the McCloudian gutter, then, the CFC requires readers to actively participate in the comic strip's violence. Through the use of the CFC, violence shifts from something passively viewed by the reader into a narrative and visual element readers themselves imaginatively produce.

When the CFC appears between two panels, readers must imagine what particular acts of violence have transpired to produce the shift from one panel's state of being to another's, and it is precisely these surrounding panels which allow readers to effectively fill in the CFC's signified gap. The CFC's function as a McCloudian gap demands reader participation, as the violence that is undrawn yet represented by the CFC is left to be filled in by readers. This is to the advantage of a newspaper strip such as Calvin and Hobbes, as each reader can imagine a brand of comedic fighting that corresponds to their own comedic preferences. But the contextualizing panels, those drawn around the CFC, define the limits and boundaries within which the reader's imagination may work. As such, readers cannot imagine the represented violence completely however they wish. My use of the term *boundaries* here is not intended to be negative, as though the CFC or reader's imagination were tyrannically constrained by the surrounding panels and narrative. Rather, these boundaries are precisely what allow the CFC to operate by invoking reader participation. Readers cannot imaginatively supply the details of the signified fight within a vacuum. Returning to the Yukon Sunday strip of the previous paragraph: seeing the CFC with accompanying limbs emerging therefrom, readers may know the CFC signifies a fight. Nevertheless, they cannot imagine the individual actions of that fight without the surrounding panels. For example, without the surrounding panels, readers do not know that Calvin and Hobbes are fighting over ownership of a toy helmet, whether (and if so, which) one of them currently holds the helmet, whether there are other parties (for example, Susie Derkins) involved in the fight, and so forth. Without the imaginative limits provided by the CFC's surrounding panels and narrative, the CFC's signification becomes potentially limitless, and so, I daresay, meaningless as a narrative device. Readers cannot fill in the CFC's signified fight without the imaginative boundaries dictated by the surrounding panels. In fact, I suggest the CFC may highlight the surrounding panels over and above its own represented physical violence.

Turning to other scholarship of the gutter following McCloud, we can see how the CFC is not only a symbol-gap representing physical violence, but also a visual ellipsis eliding that violence to emphasize the surrounding events. In her own extended analysis of the gutter, Barbara Postema writes that gutters "are gaps that stand in for moments and events that go unrepresented in the comics sequence, moments that are not pictures but that are nevertheless evoked by the empty space . . . gutters do not 'stand for' or represent anything beyond elision."[13] This elision-function does not apply to the CFC unconditionally—as explained above, the CFC represents violence, not elision itself. But Postema's analysis of the gutter draws attention to the CFC's elision-function. By replacing a sequence of physical violence, the CFC elides violence, thereby drawing attention away from the physical combat the CFC signifies and directing attention to the combat's surrounding events, conditions, and panels. This redirecting of attention through elision may be observed in the *Calvin and Hobbes* September 20, 1987, Sunday strip. In the panel immediately before the CFC, Hobbes charges a taunting Calvin. In the panel that follows the CFC, Hobbes dons the designated leader helmet despite Calvin's complaints. Here, much like the gutter, the CFC serves to connect two moments in the narrative sequence. Of course, readers do not witness any single moment of the fight, as the CFC elides the whole confrontation. By replacing the fight with a partially abstract symbol, the CFC moves the fight to the background, turning Calvin and Hobbes's physical confrontation into a mere transition between two depicted states of affairs. The fight and its violence become secondary to whatever instigates or results from it.

By highlighting the before and after moments of violence, the CFC highlights the fight's context, emphasizing that no violence transpires in isolated space, but that all acts of violence have both a cause and consequence, a build-up and aftermath. In other words, the fight itself becomes less important than the events that narratively surround it. Take, for instance, another of Watterson's Sunday strips dated August 6, 1989. In this strip, as Calvin and Hobbes play baseball, they eventually end up in an argument over whether Hobbes had pitched a strike or ball. The argument quickly devolves into a physical confrontation. But here, Watterson abjures the CFC, opting instead to illustrate Calvin and Hobbes locked in an angry embrace, surrounded by action stars and tiny dust balls to indicate the action and effects of their fight, such as dizziness or pain. In illustrating the actual physical confrontation rather than infer it through the CFC, Watterson makes the fight an event in itself. Depicting the actions of Calvin and Hobbes's physical confrontation makes the confrontation a tangible event within the narrative, one stage in the sequence of action. By contrast, by representing a fight with the CFC as in other strips, Calvin and Hobbes's conflict shifts from an event to a transition. For example, returning again to the Yukon Sunday strip, the CFC serves as a connecting visual device explaining the transition in ownership of the commander hat between Calvin and Hobbes. While an illustration of the physical fight draws attention to the fight as an event in itself, the CFC visually elides the fight, moving attention away from the fight to its surrounding narrative parts, the fight's context. In this way, the CFC causes the fight and its incumbent violence to fade into the strip's narrative background as a mere transition between two other events (which are implied to be of greater narrative importance), whereas a depiction of the fight's individual actions foregrounds the fight as one event among many. But what of those strips in which the CFC comprises the final panel? How can the CFC retain its transitional elision-function when it has no following action or event into which it may transition?

When the CFC occupies the final panel in a sequence, the CFC obviously no longer functions as a transition, yet this loss of transition-function does not necessarily mean the CFC loses its function as a visual ellipsis. Transition is only one function of the ellipsis, and it is not a necessary trait. Here, I turn to two paired *Calvin and Hobbes* daily strips, dated December 12 and 13, 1989, in which the CFC comprises each strip's final panel. The December 12 strip comedically functions via the build-up of Calvin's anger resulting from Hobbes's repetitive jibes against the former's self-proclaimed good behavior. The strip's concluding CFC panel serves only to signify that these barbs have led to a fight between the eponymous main characters. The fight itself—how each character battles, their specific combative actions, the fight's duration—is largely, if not entirely, irrelevant to the strip's narrative and humor. All that is important in this regard is that the reader understands that Calvin and Hobbes are fighting, and that Hobbes's sarcastic protestations against Calvin's claims to amiability have led to a physical battle between them. The same is true of the final CFC panel in the following December 13 strip, although here, an additional layer of humor arises in the repetition of action, that Hobbes's sarcastic responses to Calvin have once again developed into combat. In both the December 12 and 13 strips, the CFC signifies a fight while simultaneously drawing the reader's attention away from the fight toward the events comprising its build-up: Calvin's rant, Hobbes's caustic gestures, and finally, both characters' taunting dialogue as they fight. The CFC's function as an ellipsis contributes to the strip's comedic narrative by preventing readers from dwelling on any sensationalism of the comedic violence and instead focusing on the strip's primary comedic components, such as Hobbes's gestures or the taunting dialogue that accompanies the CFC.

Although the CFC may conclude a strip, it is worth noting that it never begins a strip in all of *Calvin and Hobbes*' run. In fact, I propose the CFC's ellipsis-function is precisely what prevents it from initiating a strip. Given the quotidian and serialized nature of newspaper comic strips, the first panel of each daily installment must establish the scene and premise of the individual strip's narrative and joke. When the CFC begins a comic, readers are robbed of crucial contextual information necessary to comprehend the comic's narrative. The December 13 strip begins with a drawn depiction of Calvin and Hobbes's fight, however after two panels of the characters mocking one another, the strip concludes in a CFC panel. Should the given day's strip begin with a CFC, readers would enter the strip unaware of who was fighting and why (unless they read and remembered the previous day's strip). The CFC's inability to coherently initiate a comics narrative highlights the function of the beneficial, imaginative boundaries established by the CFC's surrounding narratological and visual material. Without any preceding narrative and visual material, the CFC's potential signification becomes limitless within the reader's imagination; as discussed above, the limits of signification provided by the CFC's surrounding, and especially preceding, material is crucial for the CFC's efficacy as a meaningful symbol. In fact, the CFC's reliance on this contextual matter points to its function as an elision of physical violence. This strip shows how the CFC not only represents but further elides its represented physical combat by shifting readers' attention to the context of that violence. In this way, the CFC's elision function highlights how, for both the strip's narrative and humor, the violent act is often less important than its conditions.

By drawing attention to the fight's context, the CFC manifests the comics principle of contextualization specifically in relation to physical acts of violence. Comics scholars have often spoken of the comics sequence as a network in which each panel is connected to every other. For example, Theirry Groensteen writes that "every panel exists, potentially if not actually, in relation with each of the others";[14] and Barbara Postema writes how "the panels of a comic constitute a network, and even a system."[15] Much like the comics panel, acts of physical violence can only be properly understood and interpreted in light of their context, the conditions within which they occur. This is perhaps the latent philosophy of violence that manifests in comics through the CFC—that no act of physical violence transpires in a vacuum. By highlighting the narratological conditions of a confrontation and eliding the physical fight, the CFC highlights the conditions (whether personal or systemic) that gave rise to the confrontation. In any of the above comics strips, it is not Calvin and Hobbes's fight that is important, but the surrounding conditions, the causes and aftermath, to which Watterson draws readers' attention. This is not to say that the written word or other art mediums are incapable of calling attention to the conditions or context in which a violent action occurs, only that this mode of contextualization is inherent to the structure and visual layout of comics. In a visual medium like comics, violence can easily devolve into sensationalism—and no doubt such comics do exist. In abjuring an overt depiction of violence, the CFC avoids such sensationalism while manifesting the important narratological principle on which the comics medium's visual structure rests. But there remains one aspect of the CFC not discussed henceforth, its comedic nature, the point at which this essay began.

Given the CFC seems to appear exclusively within comedic comics, one may naturally wonder whether this visual device makes light of violence. This is not unjustified, as the replacement of physical (potentially grotesque) violence with cartoon cliches may seem to deny the seriousness of violence, be it specific, physical acts or systemic processes. I argue that this is far from the case, however. By replacing a violent battle with a comedic device like the CFC, comics make the specific violent acts less important than the conditions under which they occurred. The implication here is that acts of violence are perhaps less important than the often-unseen narrative and systematic structure in which they are produced. Perhaps in this way the CFC does make light of physical violence itself, but in doing so, the CFC moves readers to consider instead the conditions that led to the physical battle. By emphasizing the context of a violent act or actions, the CFC trains readers to contextualize physical acts of violence within the narrative structures they encounter on a daily basis and among, even through, which they live.

Notes

1. Neil Cohn, *Visual Language*, 46, 53.
2. Hannah Miodrag, *Comics and Language*, 173, 183.
3. Miodrag, *Comics and Language*, 170.
4. Cohn, "Being Explicit," 79.
5. Cohn, "Being Explicit," 79.
6. Cohn, "Being Explicit," 79.
7. All references to the content and dates of *Calvin and Hobbes* strips refer to their appearance in Bill Watterson, *The Complete Calvin and Hobbes*. All *Calvin and Hobbes* strips here referenced are publicly accessible and may be searched by date at gocomics.com/calvinandhobbes.
8. Cohn, Visual Language, 52.
9. Cohn, *Visual Language*, 112.
10. Scott McCloud, *Understanding Comics*, 66–67.
11. McCloud, *Understanding Comics*, 68.
12. McCloud, *Understanding Comics*, 68.
13. Barbara Postema, *Narrative Structure*, 50.
14. Thierry Groensteen, *System of Comics*, 146.
15. Postema, *Narrative Structure*, 158.

Works Cited

Cohn, Neil. "Being Explicit about the Implicit: Inference Generating Techniques in Visual Narrative." *Language and Cognition* 11, no. 1 (2019): 66–97.

Cohn, Neil. *The Visual Language of Comics: Introduction to the Structure and Cognition of Sequential Images*. London: Bloomsbury, 2014.

Groensteen, Thierry. *The System of Comics*. Translated by Bart Beaty and Nick Nguyen. Jackson: University Press of Mississippi, 2007.

McCloud, Scott. *Understanding Comics: The Invisible Art*. New York: William Morrow Paperbacks, 1994.

Miodrag, Hannah. *Comics and Language: Reimagining Critical Discourse on the Form*. Jackson: University Press of Mississippi, 2013.

Postema, Barbara. *Narrative Structure in Comics: Making Sense of Fragments*. Rochester, NY: RIT Press, 2013.

Watterson, Bill. *The Complete Calvin & Hobbes*. 3 vols. Kansas City: Andrews McMeel Publishing, 2005.

6

WHITE BLACK MEN AND BLACK WHITE MEN

Reading Race as Violence in Mat Johnson and Warren Pleece's *Incognegro: A Graphic Mystery*

JOANNA DAVIS-McELLIGATT

Mat Johnson and Warren Pleece's critically acclaimed graphic novel *Incognegro: A Graphic Mystery* was first published by Vertigo, an imprint of DC Comics, in 2008. The comic tells the story of Zane Pinchback, a light-skinned Black journalist who, like Walter White of the NAACP, leverages his ability to pass as white in order to surveil and infiltrate Ku Klux Klan lynching parties in locations throughout the Deep South. Writing under the pseudonym Incognegro, Pinchback publishes the names of those in attendance at lynchings in the *New Holland Herald*, a northern Black newspaper. In the novel's initial printing, Pleece renders all subjects, Black and white, in spare black ink outlines with only minimal shading—as Johnson notes in an interview with Alex Dueben in the *Los Angeles Review of Books*, "The style matches comic strips of that era—not a lot of shading, mostly just inks. It fits stylistically for the period, that was the artistic justification."[1] Given the lack of black and gray hues, both Black and white skin tones are represented by default as the same flat white of the page, which assumes no variation. Racial difference is instead apprehended through racial phenotype, in which physical characteristics—including Pinchback's racially ambiguous features—become the exclusive signs of racial identity, depicted through remarkably subtle markers, such as lip size, nose width, and hair texture and style, as well as dress and speech acts. This makes it difficult, if not at times impossible, for both readers and characters to discern what precisely makes a white man look white, what makes a Black man look Black—or what makes a Black man look white. Pleece's minimalist black-and-white style in the 2008 edition, as I will explore in greater depth later in this essay, underscores the central role that perception plays in racial categorization; after all, Pinchback is able to pass because others fail to perceive in his features Black phenotype or, as the case may be, choose to read his features as representative of a white phenotype. To that end, readers of the comic are encouraged to rethink their inclination to categorize a subject's race based solely on their perceptions of that subject's phenotype.

Yet in the novel's second printing in 2018, published by Berger Books, an imprint of Dark Horse comics, Johnson and Pleece drastically alter the comic's visual style by shading subjects and their environments in heavy gray and black hues. In the 2018 printing, the flat white page no longer functions as a universal baseline for each character's skin tone, an effect that in the 2008 printing served to frustrate readers' attempts to make firm determinations about a character's race simply by looking at them; rather, the enhanced shading serves to fix subjects along scales of lightness and darkness that more precisely and immediately concretize characters into specific racial categories. As Johnson explains, the visual revisions were intentional:

> Honestly the discussion we had was: Why the hell didn't we do this in the first place? . . . The artistic justification this time—and I think we should have done this before—is that book owes a lot more to noir film than it does to comic strips. The shading to me connects it with film noir, and I like that it looks more cinematic in this version. It's an opportunity to create this film noir version of a story that could never have been made at that time, but that both speaks to this time and that time.[2]

On one hand, Pleece's attention to the aesthetics of film noir, with its trade in chiaroscuro lighting, stark contrasts between black and white, and heavy use of dark shadows, draws the reader's attention more closely to the possible slippage between embodied Blackness and whiteness, largely by rendering all subjects, regardless of their race, in shades of black and gray. On the other hand, however, the 2018 edition's insistence on skin tone as a marker of racial difference—or, as the case may be, the appearance of racial sameness—frustrates the 2008 edition's efforts to trouble the perceptual foundations of racial categorization. For example, characters whose racial phenotype in the 2008 edition might be read as racially ambiguous emerge as much more clearly raced in the 2018 edition—Pinchback's skin tone in the 2018 edition aligns him with white subjects, but functions as an expression of an intangible racial ambiguity that resists easy categorization in the 2008 edition.

In this chapter I argue that the discrepancies between the 2008 and 2018 editions of *Incognegro* help to elucidate the process of reading race and inscribing its meaning on Black bodies, complicating readers' attempts to arrive at comfortable conclusions about a subject's race or ethnicity based on either phenotype or skin tone alone. I argue that though both editions interrogate the slippage between modes of racial recognition and categorization in everyday life and the process of perceiving the race of characters on the comics page, they do so in different, and ultimately contradictory, ways that trouble how readers perceive and categorize racialized subjects in each text. Given that racial perception and categorization are necessary precursors to targeted racial violence, I make the case that reading race both on the comic's page and in the real world is always a potentially violent encounter, given that white supremacist social structures code light-skinned white-presenting subjects as more inherently valuable and thus worthy of greater protection than dark-skinned Black subjects, whose phenotype and skin tone often consigns them to death. I first consider how methods and modes of recognizing race in everyday life serve as a necessary precondition for reading race in comics first. I then examine the entanglement of physiognomic logic and racial representation in the comics language, as a way to explore precisely how race is represented in the medium. Finally, I explore how racial perception and categorization in both editions of *Incognegro* function as a mechanism for capitulating to or resisting racial control for both characters and readers; more specifically, I examine how both editions of *Incognegro*, at the visual and narrative level, convolute processes of racial categorization by highlighting the highly disjunctive, imprecise, and inherently violent process of reading race.

OPTIC POLITICS: PHYSIOGNOMIC SYNTAX AND THE VIOLENT GRAMMAR OF CARTOONING

In white supremacist systems, such as the United States, the optic politics of cartooning are a critical reflection of the broader sociocultural machinations of race thinking and representation; as a consequence, the stakes of representing and recognizing embodied subjects are as high on the comics page as they are in the world beyond it. How artists render race in the comics language, and how readers make sense of racialized syntax and vocabulary in the medium, hinges on a mutuality of apprehension fundamental to the creation and reception of signs. Will Eisner contends that any effective communication of comics grammar between creators and readers requires the artist to "evok[e] images stored in the minds of both parties. The success or failure of this method of communicating depends upon the ease with which the reader recognizes the meaning and emotional impact of the image. Therefore, the skill of rendering and the universality of the form chosen are critical."[3] These mental images are shaped and structured by a number of factors, including time, place, race, nationality, gender identity, and class, among others. To that end, comics is a dynamic language, in which the internal logics of its representation of embodied subjects—and their reception—are intimately related to the external social, historical, and political conditions that inform its creation. As an inherently visual language system, comics is structurally concerned with and imbricated in the politics of looking at and being seen—a fraught process in any racially inequitable society. Aldo Regalado has argued that the development of the comics language cannot therefore be understood as distinct from the language of race: "Comic book creators and audiences engaged the language and imagery of race, either consciously or unconsciously, because it existed (and continues to exist) as part of their lived experience. Appropriating this racial language, comic books creators manipulated its contours, and employed it in giving voice to their desires, fantasies and longings."[4] The appropriation of the grammar of race by the language of comics requires that we think critically about not only how race is represented in the medium, but likewise how we read race both on and off on the page.

Karen E. Fields and Barbara J. Fields argue that the logics of race in action—or what they call "racecraft"—in part "depend[s] on what another person looks like, at a glance, to a viewer observing quickly and superficially."[5] In their formulation, race thinking and doing, such as monitoring segregated spaces or instances of police brutality, "all stand in reference to a person as a seen 'object.' That reference entails, besides, a seeing object and of course a seeing subject."[6] These forms of looking enforce racecraft precisely because they are essentially "superficial" and fantastical processes in which human difference is "quickly" reduced to an essence that reinforces and reinscribes racist white supremacist norms. Central to Fields and Fields's understanding of the function of race in society is the interaction between seeing subjects, whose sightline through a process of objectification reinforces violent social codes, and seeing objects, whose looking back troubles and complicates their objectification. These modes of looking, which "occur together or in rapid sequence, and in constantly shifting perspective," are

> intimate yet public practices that organize individual perception of physical appearance, including one's own, as subject.... In fact, Americans observe themselves and each other through their own eyes and those of others, all the while classifying and evaluating. Thus

racecraft has an inner horizon that turns out to be densely populated with sometimes peculiarly selected physical traits. A living person, to be met presently, ascribes meaning to the shape of his jawbone.[7]

As seeing subjects and seeing objects look at and read one another and themselves, they ascribe very real meaning to physical characteristics—the "jawbone," eye shape, skin color—thereby linking their appearance to particular racialized character and personality characteristics, affectual processes, and ethical and moral propensities. In the formation of a "lexicon of bio-racism,"[8] physicality is overdetermined and made meaningful through spectacular optics that reinforce violent constructions of human being and doing.

Given that the optic politics of racecraft are appropriated by the comics language, they in turn structure cartoon grammar. Art Spiegelman notes that the comics language "makes use of the discredited pseudo-scientific principles of physiognomy to portray character through a few physical attributes and facial expressions. It takes skill to use such clichés in ways that expand or subvert this impoverished vocabulary."[9] Indeed, Rodolphe Töpffer, the inventor of the cartoon language, explicitly structured what he called "literature-in-pictures"[10] around the logics of physiognomy, or the art of deciphering or divining the moral and intellectual makeup of an individual based on a study of their facial features. E. Wiese argues that Töpfferian cartooning requires artists to "perfect an intelligible grammar of physiognomic expression,"[11] which enables readers to immediately correspond visual representations of personality and character types to their ostensible real-world counterparts. This process is both explicitly and implicitly raced. In "Essay on Physiognomy," Töpffer argues that the representation of human forms in a cartoon language necessitates a distinction between the use of permanent signs, or dispositional traits representing "what we mean by the general term *character*; also the habitual quality of reflection, alertness, and ability that goes by the general term *intelligence*,"[12] and nonpermanent signs, which "depict . . . all that we include in the general term *feelings*."[13] As Wiese makes clear, both permanent and nonpermanent signs do the work of portraying human affect, personality, and type by appropriating "the fundamental rules according to which we instinctively 'read' the character, capabilities, and immediate emotional set of the individual confronting us."[14] This physiognomic syntax—or the grammar of cartooning—was for Töpffer merely an extension of the processes that operate in the world beyond the comic. To that end, cartoon syntax might be seen as an aesthetic expression of racecraft in which seeing subjects and seeing objects confront themselves and one another on the page. In point of fact, Töpffer contended that the grammatical rules for cartooning representations of people only function because in ordinary interpersonal interchange there exists already "a hierarchical ordering of expressive shapes.... Involuntarily, we scan a set of features to classify correctly, friend or foe, the stranger bearing them."[15] Cartoon grammar, then, is an aesthetic extension of the interactive processing of racecraft; the mechanics of reading human affect and personality in cartoons are therefore essentially the same as those used to read the bodies and behaviors of real people.

As Töpffer explains, physiognomic syntax and vocabulary in cartoon grammar functions as a system comprising particular features such as eyes, ears, or jawlines; expressions of emotion and feeling; and character type that overdetermine the meaning of the image within the context of the comic and simultaneously correlate it to a referent in the world outside it. If, in other words, a reader can ascertain that Richard Felton Outcault's Mickey Dugan, or the Yellow Kid, with his big ears, gap teeth, bald head, and tattered nightshirt, is a representation and condensation of the white immigrant poor, then the physiognomic syntax and lexicon has operated effectively. Because cartoon grammar is intimately related to cultural and social modes of individual and interpersonal perception, the logics of cartoon grammar shift and change over time as artists and readers abandon outmoded terms, adapt to emerging sociocultural visual politics, and expand visual syntax to represent new perspectives. Even so, cartoon art has always derived its meaning from the practice of looking, a process that cannot be divorced from the politics of what it means to see and be seen in everyday life. To that end, cartoon images are always and very particularly loaded with cultural meanings that are reflective of the optic politics that inform their production.

The notion that cartoonists necessarily peddle in crass stereotypes and caricature is therefore to some extent true; as Spiegelman admits, comics do have "a predisposition toward insult."[16] This is particularly the case given that physiognomy attempted to prove longstanding white supremacist propositions about the value of human beings according to their facial structure and features. In his discussion of the meaning of facial features, for example, Töpffer suggests that "among the signs that show moral qualities, or character, the lips are especially significant, and it is commonly said . . . that extremely thin, tight lips are a sign of spitefulness or even insensibility. Contrariwise, very thick lips pass for a sign of an easy-going nature, or even of weakness."[17] The drawings which accompany the above statement consist of a nontemporal sequence of several images of the same face in profile, each rendered with a different mouth shape. The progression of the faces and their mouths is intended to depict a collection of differing stock characters: one dull-witted, another regal, yet another uptight. For contemporary readers, Töpffer's description of the difference between "thin" and "thick" lips might call to mind racist caricature and hyperracialized images of the minstrel Jim Crow, which is no coincidence—indeed, as Spiegelman suggests, the comics language is really a "compression of ideas into memorable icons."[18]

The technique of rendering and reading race in comics predisposes both artists and readers toward enacting the violence of racial recognition. Given that creators and readers of comics always-already come to the comics page familiar with the visual-phenotypical lexicon of embodied Black inferiority, the processes of image-making and the meaning made of them are thus sustained by those racist logics. Even so, comics creators—writers and artists—can resist and seek to transform the inherent violences of physiognomy and racial recognition by working simultaneously within and against white supremacist logic, interrupting the flow of seeing subjects and seeing objects, and inventing new grammars of racial difference.

WATCH ME GO INVISIBLE: THE VIOLENT LOGICS OF PHENOTYPICALITY IN THE 2008 EDITION OF *INCOGNEGRO*

The 2008 edition of *Incognegro* eschews skin color as a marker of racial difference, which, I argue, precipitates a crisis of racial classification and recognition for readers who must see Zane Pinchback as both Black and white. Given that comic books require intense looking in order to make sense of the action, in the absence of any variance in skin tone readers must rely exclusively on other less concrete phenotypical markers, such as the shape of one's nose, eyes, or lips, to determine the race of characters. *Incognegro* immediately brings this into sharp relief. The novel begins with a single page spread of a lynching in Tupelo, Mississippi, in the early twentieth century. White men, women, and children mill around a tree, each subject rendered in black-and-white ink outlines with minimal or no shading. Though there are visual signposts that signify their whiteness, such as straight blonde hair, represented by empty space and straight lines, we rather understand these characters as white because of the situational politics of the narrative. The central subject of the page is a shirtless man in rags standing on a box, strung up by the neck to the tree—though drawn from a distance, there are some physiognomic suggestions of Black racial phenotype in the boxy shape of his black hair and slightly wider nose. Yet his race is more overtly indicated by his positionality, insofar as the lynched body calls to mind images that have been circulated most prominently in picture postcards that were routinely sold at lynchings to white patrons as remembrancers of the event. The second panel features a close-up of the man at the center of the single page spread, moments before he is castrated and murdered. In this instance, his Black phenotypicality is represented more clearly; though his bruised face is twisted in panic and covered in tears and mucus, his black hair is textured, his nose broad, and lips full. Yet these physiognomic markers are given meaning in part because of his position as lynched subject, which, I argue, overdetermines the way readers interpret phenotype on the comics page. In other words, Johnson and Pleece draw our attention to the ways Blackness is interpellated through violence, and explicitly given meaning both phenotypically and narratively because only Black bodies can be so thoroughly destroyed.

Megha Anwer argues that Johnson and Pleece provide a "behind-the-scenes documentation of lynching—an 'inside view' that lynching photographs . . . often failed to do."[19] As lynchings were socially transformed from acts of disorganized mob violence into public community events, Anwer suggests that "the act, and . . . visual representation of lynching, becomes readable . . . as a somewhat desperate attempt at salvaging a sense safety from the detritus of the old order, a paranoid effort, paradoxically, to hold at bay and restore 'order' by unboundedly violent means."[20] Johnson and Pleece make direct reference to this attempt to preserve white supremacist social structures through appeals to the spectacular in subsequent panels, as we see a photographer capturing images of the corpse, now dressed in a clown costume, his face smeared in makeup. Pinchback, who serves as the scene's voiceover narrator, notes that white attendees "take pieces of the body as keepsakes. Pictures are taken to remember the special day."[21] The opening pages of the comic encourage readers to confront the historic compulsion to enact and capture acts of violence against Black peoples as a form of entertainment, given that readers are positioned to bear witness to the unjust violence of lynching, while simultaneously observing the event as a community voyeur.

Reinforced by the comic's integration of photographic technology in its opening pages, *Incognegro* suggests that, like photography, racial recognition and categorization is a relatively immediate process. Eve C. Willadsen-Jensen and Tiffany A. Ito argue that "faces are incredibly rich stimuli from which a wide range of social information can be extracted, including emotional state, health status, personal identity, social category membership, and traits, interests, and intentions."[22] The work of analyzing faces, however, also functions as a type of racecraft; indeed, Willadsen-Jensen and Ito note that "studies of face perception show that race information is processed very quickly and often automatically even when perceivers are asked to attend to nonracial attributes."[23] To that end, just as readers make immediate perceptive sense of the race of the lynched subject in the comic's opening pages both physiognomically and because he experiences forms of white supremacist violence historically reserved primarily for Black people, readers are likewise encouraged to read Zane Pinchback as phenotypically, and therefore physiognomically, indistinguishable from the white subjects around him. In Pinchback's first full-body appearance in a close-up single-page spread that structurally echoes the lynching scene, in which he poses as the photographer's assistant, he has straight hair, a large but straight nose, and a thin top and full bottom lip, all indicative of European phenotype. When Pinchback is eventually identified as passing, it is not because he is physiognomically other, but because he is wearing a suit, writing in a notebook, and lying about his affiliation with the photographer; in other words, Pinchback is revealed to be passing because his behaviors, not his looks, are out of step.

Even so, Pinchback is *not* white, and must undergo a physical transition before crossing the color line. In the single five-panel sequence readers see of Pinchback's transformation, as he stands before a mirror and drags a hot comb through his wavy hair, straightening it, Pinchback describes his transformation into Incognegro as a form of "camouflage" in which he becomes "invisible."[24] The performance of whiteness for Pinchback is both a political mask and a form of ontological nonexistence, an act of extreme self-erasure. Yet Pinchback also regards his white "disguise" as an act of "revolution" in which his "assimilation" into whiteness simultaneously destabilizes it.[25] This disguise, Pinchback argues, is possible because white people "think they're just normal, that they are the universal, and that everyone else is an odd deviation from form. That's what makes them so easy to infiltrate."[26] Even so, as Keshia L. Harris notes, as a consequence of the logics of hypodescent, in which individuals with any amount of African ancestry are classified as Black, "the normative image of Black people became a broad range of skin tones, body shapes, and hair textures while the image of White people became quite narrow (i.e., fair skin, straight hair, narrow noses and lips, blue eyes, etc.)."[27] Pinchback's European physiognomic register enables him to pass, even as his racial ambiguity classifies him as Black; indeed, as he himself explains: "American Negroes are a mulatto people; I'm just an extreme example. A walking reminder."[28]

Phenotypicality and its physiognomic counterpart in the comics language are not the sole markers of whiteness or Blackness, however, and, because Pinchback can look white and yet be Black, the comic makes it plain that racial recognition is not exclusively predicated on phenotype and physiognomy, either. Pinchback's ability to infiltrate white communities suggests that whiteness is not a stable and impenetrable category of being; indeed, if it can be impossible to tell that someone is Black by looking at them, then it is equally impossible, as Pinchback proves, to definitively identify an individual's whiteness using phenotype. Pinchback's narrative archnemesis, a white Grand Wizard Ku Klux Klansmen from the national headquarters in Birmingham, Alabama, named Huey, has a similarly shaped nose and mouth, but blonde straight hair; Huey serves, alongside the lynched Black man at the comic's beginning, as Pinchback's double, positioning Pinchback both within and outside the Black/white binary. Because Pinchback understands himself to be Black and, when not passing, is positioned socially as a Black man by others, his representation troubles attempts to classify and categorize the race of another simply by looking at them.

At the comic's end, Pinchback determines that, despite its perils, he will continue to work as Incognegro, but will also pursue an arts of the Harlem Renaissance column under his own name; living this dual existence, Pinchback argues, will enable him to embrace his identity as "open-ended."[29] As a point of revenge, Pinchback determines that before moving on he will unveil the identity of Incognegro in a multiply syndicated newspaper article to be published in papers across the US, including in the Deep South. However, rather than publish a picture of himself, Pinchback uses a photograph of Huey in the unveiling. It is possible for Huey, a white Klansman, to be classified as Black for precisely the reasons it is possible for Pinchback, a Black man, to be read as white—phenotype as an unreliable indicator of racial identity (again, Huey's physiognomic markers are not particularly distinct from Pinchback's), and racial classification is a spectacular phenomenon overdetermined by the inherently contradictory logics of white supremacy that make it impossible for a white-looking man with African ancestry to actually *be* white. Because the 2008 edition does not rely on skin tone as a marker of racial difference, readers are confronted by the fundamental illogics and inherent violence of white-supremacist racial classificatory systems that are predicated on any form of phenotypicality. As soon as the newspaper article is published, Huey is recognized and immediately confronted by a growing white mob. The novel's final image mirrors its first; readers are asked to consider how lynching functions once again in a white supremacist society as a form of revenge, and as a way for white people to violently maintain their own boundaries. Indeed, that no one stops to verify whether Huey actually *is* Black signifies the fundamental instability of whiteness as an identity category, and the destructive optic processes that police it.

LIGHT AND DARK: PERIPHERAL BLACKNESS AND SKIN TONE BIAS IN THE 2018 EDITION OF *INCOGNEGRO*

In light of Pinchback's ability to pass and the mob's (mis)classification of Huey as Black, the reader's guide located at the end of the 2018 edition of *Incognegro* suggests that "it's impossible to distinguish race by sight."[30] Indeed, as I argued in the previous section, the structure of physiognomic markers in the 2008 edition make it very difficult to categorize Pinchback's race simply by looking at him, given that the lack of skin tone variance in the 2008 edition requires readers to read race through more ambiguous physiognomic markers, such as nose and lip shape, which are not as clearly indicative of racial identity. Yet in the 2018 edition Johnson and Pleece revise the visual narrative to include skin tone variance in the form of black and gray shading—and so it *becomes* possible to determine the race of characters simply by looking at them. When readers first encounter the lynched subject in the novel's opening page in the 2018 edition, for example, the central figure hanging from the tree is visibly darker-skinned than the people who crowd around him. When we see a close-up of his face and body in the second and third panels, his skin tone appears in striking contrast to the white skin and Klan robes of his torturers. To that same end, when we first encounter Pinchback in his first full-body appearance in a single-page spread, it is immediately apparent that he is as light-skinned as both the white people who surround him *and* as Huey. To that end, though in the 2008 edition Pinchback is immediately positioned as a mirror image of both the lynched Black man and Huey, in the 2018 edition he is aligned visually with white characters and rendered as more profoundly phenotypically distinct from Black people. Because, as Hitomi Shimakura and Katsuaki Sakata argue, "humans use the natural appearance of facial skin tone to judge perceptibility and acceptability,"[31] Pinchback's skin tone paradoxically reinforces his Blackness and, at the same time, invisibilizes it. While passing as a white man, Pinchback becomes imperceptible and acceptable; however, the moment he is identified as passing, his Blackness becomes both perceptible and unacceptable.

The visual distinctions between light- and dark-skinned Black people in the 2018 edition matter precisely because skin tone is materially consequential. As Ellis P. Monk Jr. contends, skin tone continues to be "a significant predictor of personal and family income.... Darker-skinned blacks have less income and are more likely to be unemployed or in poverty, have lower occupational prestige and wealth, and have worse health outcomes, such as high blood pressure."[32] To that end, Monk argues, for Black folks "there are at least two dimensions of inequality: (1) between blacks and non-blacks;

and (2) within the black population according to gradations of skin tone."[33] Differences in skin tone are made meaningful not only between white and Black people, but among Black people; to that end, dark-skinned Black people are more subject to systemic interracial and intraracial violence because, in a white supremacist system, variations in light and dark skin tone are given vastly differential meaning by onlookers. As Keith B. Maddox and Stephanie A. Gray argue, skin tone bias "is a tendency to perceive or behave toward members of a racial category based on the lightness or darkness of their skin tone."[34] By drawing visual distinctions between light- and dark-skinned characters in the 2018 edition, readers are asked to confront the logics of skin tone bias that, in the 2008 edition, were merely tacit. Given that comics are not created in cultural vacuums, and because skin tone bias operates as a social mechanism both on and off the page, the comic's colorization of characters both underscores and performs the violent marginalization of dark-skinned Black people.

One of the more striking examples of this visual-racial shift is made apparent in the figure of Mildred, the fiancée of Carl, Pinchback's closest friend—like Pinchback, Carl is light-skinned and able to visually pass as a white man, despite the fact, the text makes clear, he is unable to convincingly act the part. Mildred is physiognomically and phenotypically ambiguous in the 2008 edition; because her nose is wide and lips full, her almond-shaped eyes and straight hair make it impossible to determine her racial identity, though, given her closeness to Pinchback and Carl, readers are perhaps inclined to read Mildred's phenotypical ambiguity as a sign that she, too, is able to pass. In the 2018 edition, however, Mildred is unquestionably phenotypically Black, her skin shaded as dark as the lynched man at the novel's beginning. When Pinchback learns he must return south again to rescue his younger brother, Alonzo "Pinchy" Pinchback, who has been falsely arrested for the crime of murdering a white woman, Carl volunteers to go with him because he is also able to pass; in the 2018 edition, however, readers understand that his visibly Black fiancée would be unable to travel with them without blowing their cover. Among the consequences of the 2018 edition's stark racialization of characters at the axis of physiognomics and skin tone is the visual alignment of passing Black characters with white people, and the consequent relegation of Black characters to the narrative and visual margins. Given that light-skinned Black characters predominate the novel's action, the 2018 edition's literalization of skin tone serves to eclipse dark-skinned Black characters, who have historically been overwhelmingly the proper objects of antiblack violence. As a consequence, dark-skinned Black people serve as visual intensifiers for white and light-skinned Black characters at the visual-narrative level, and come to occupy a visually and narratively peripheral position in the narrative.

The peripherality of dark-skinned Blackness begins in the novel's opening pages. Though readers bear witness to the lynched subject's pain—he is repeatedly beaten, castrated, hanged, and his corpse is defiled—we never learn his name, or any other concrete details about his life. There is never any suggestion that Pinchback will intervene to prevent the lynching from taking place. The lynched Black subject's peril, rather than serving as an end in itself, instead both visually and narratively foreshadows and intensifies Pinchback's peril as a light-skinned Black man in passing. As Michael A. Chaney argues, "Pinchback is not there to save the lynch victim, who remains confined to a domain of pictorality, which further demarcates the space of historical death that he occupies."[35] The "domain of pictorality," in this sense, is a static location, a space that cannot be articulated or actualized. The full-color cover image of the 2018 edition underscores the peripheralization of dark-skinned Blackness, in a visual structure that resembles a photograph taken with a fish-bowl lens in the moments before the Black subject is hanged from the noose. At the top of the image is a large leafy tree from which dangles an empty noose in the upper-right corner. Pinchback stands front and center at the back of a large crowd of white people who are dressed in various pink, orange, yellow, and mauve hues; Pinchback is pensively looking over his right shoulder at the camera's eye, his eyebrows contorted in distress, his lips curled in an expression of disgust and fear. Only the brown-skinned head of the lynched Black subject is visible, slightly above and to the left of Pinchback's head; surrounding his body are men in bright-white Klan robes, who viciously beat him. A large shadow in the shape of a Black man's profile appears on the back of Pinchback's beige suit, a visual symbol representing the Blackness he both possesses and hides from the mob around him. The cover image literally peripheralizes the degree of antiblack violence meted out against dark-skinned Black bodies; indeed, the image suggests that Pinchback's danger as a white-passing Black man is both equal to and greater than that of the dark-skinned lynching victim. In other words, the cover image reinforces the idea that the literalization of antiblack violence against dark-skinned Black people is inevitable and also peripheral to the mere threat of antiblack violence against light-skinned Black people.

Dark-skinned Black people are in other ways visually and narratively marginalized, often serving as supports for Pinchback, such as Josiah Ryder, a local Black man whom Pinchback coerces into helping him rescue his brother. In one scene, after narrowly escaping from a white supremacist cult, Ryder confronts Pinchback about his callous misuse of his labor: "You almost got me killed. That offends me very much. It might not bother you, but I have to take exception to things like that."³⁶ The stakes of Ryder's participation in Pinchback's schemes are exponentially greater than they are for Pinchback, not merely because Ryder is more likely to be subject to antiblack violence than Pinchback. Though Ryder attempts to resist Pinchback's coercion, he is subsumed by his plot until he is, at text's end, peripheralized into narrative oblivion. Though Ryder occupies a significant portion of the narrative, he remains a marginal figure.

In the 2018 edition, dark-skinned Black people appear as warnings, as signposts, and as narrative transitions. As is the case with Pinchy, Pinchback's dark-skinned and kinky-haired brother, dark-skinned characters provide visual contrast for light-skinned white and white-passing characters; Pinchy highlights the extent to which Pinchback can pass, but Pinchy's legitimate peril is narratively peripheralized in favor of Pinchback's. Indeed, at novel's end, when Huey is read as Black and confronted by a mob, the optic logics of phenotypicality in the 2018 edition reinforce the notion that antiblack violence is not motivated by skin tone bias, but by situational and local politics—and to that end is open to anyone, light- and dark-skinned both.

CONCLUSION

In their treatment of phenotypicality and their expression in the physiognomic structure of the comics' language, the 2008 and 2018 editions of *Incognegro* do radically different work. In the 2008 edition, the clear line work and lack of skin tone variance frustrate attempts to read race simply by looking. In doing so, Johnson and Pleece highlight not only the dangerous absurdity of reading race onto Black bodies, but the inherent violence of doing so. The 2018 edition, however, in its deployment of skin tone variance as a phenotypical marker and a physiognomic visual fact, peripheralizes the experiences of dark-skinned peoples, while simultaneously undermining the 2008 edition's attempts to challenge the convention of seeing and reading race on bodies. By qualifying Blackness as a matter of skin tone, in the 2018 edition Johnson and Pleece make it easier, not more difficult, for readers to align their conceptions of characters with their preconceived notions of race and racial identity rooted in the inevitability of skin tone bias.

Yet as we see over and over again in both editions of the comic, the act of reading, classifying, and recognizing a person as Black subjects them to violence in the form of brutality and death. Representations of race in the comics language—the optic logics of racial representation, the function of forms of looking and seeing, the structures of white supremacy that inform readers, narratives, and their contexts—substantively structures how readers make sense of images on the page, and how they read or resist dominant modes of racialized meaning-making. I am not contending here that representations of racial difference that emphasize skin tone variance cannot resist white supremacist optic logics, and neither am I claiming that the absence of skin tone variance is a more perfect representation of the physiognomy of racial difference. Rather, I hope to draw our attention to the difficulty that cartoonists and readers have in rendering and reading race, and to consider how these renderings and readings can enforce, compound, or undermine the very real violence of recognizing and reading raced bodies, both on the page and in the world beyond it.

Notes

1. Alex Dueben, "Comics and Storytelling: A Conversation with Mat Johnson." *Los Angeles Review of Books*, April 21, 2018. https://lareviewofbooks.org/article/comics-and-storytelling-a-conversation-with-mat-johnson/.
2. Dueben, 2018.
3. Will Eisner, *Comics and Sequential Art: Principles and Practices from the Legendary Cartoonist* (New York: W. W. Norton & Company, 2008), 7–8.
4. Ibid., 86.
5. Karen E. Fields and Barbara J. Fields, *Racecraft: The Soul of Inequality in American Life*. (London: Verso, 2012), 70.
6. Ibid., 70.
7. Ibid., 70.
8. Ibid., 43.
9. Art Spiegelman, "Drawing Blood: Outrageous Cartoons and the Art of Outrage," *Harper's Magazine* (June 2006), 45.
10. Rodolphe Töpffer, *Enter: The Comics*, 3.
11. Ibid., xviii.
12. Ibid., 17., his emphasis.
13. Ibid., 17, his emphasis.
14. Ibid., xviii.
15. Ibid., xviii.
16. Spiegelman, 45.
17. Töpffer, 16.
18. Ibid., 45.
19. Megha Anwer, "Beyond the Photograph: A Graphic History of Lynching." *Journal of Graphic Novels and Comics* 5, no. 1 (2014): 15.
20. Ibid., 16.
21. Mat Johnson and Warren Pleece. *Incognegro: A Graphic Mystery*, 9.

22. Eve C. Willadsen-Jensen and Tiffany A. Ito, "Ambiguity and the Timecourse of Racial Perception," *Social Cognition* 24, no. 5 (2006): 580.

23. Ibid., 581.

24. *Incognegro*, 2008, 18.

25. Ibid., 18.

26. Ibid., 19.

27. Keshia L. Harris, "Biracial American Colorism: Passing for White," *American Behavioral Scientist* 62, no. 14 (2018): 2075.

28. *Incognegro*, 2008, 18.

29. Ibid., 129.

30. Mat Johnson and Warren Pleece, *Incognegro: A Graphic Mystery* (New York: Berger Books, 2018), 142.

31. Hitomi Shimakura and Katsuaki Sakata, "Color Criteria of Facial Skin Tone Judgment." *Vision Research* 193 (2022): 2.

32. Ellis P. Monk Jr., "Skin Tone Stratification among Black Americans, 2001–2003." *Social Forces* 92, no. 4 (2014): 1313–14.

33. Ibid., 1314.

34. Keith B. Maddox and Stephanie A. Gray, "Cognitive Representations of Black Americans: Reexploring the Role of Skin Tone." *PSPB* 28, no. 2 (2002): 250.

35. Michael A. Chaney, *Reading Lessons in Seeing: Mirrors, Masks, and Mazes in the Autobiographical Graphic Novel* (Jackson: University Press of Mississippi, 2016): 152.

36. *Incognegro*, 2018, 92.

Works Cited

Anwer, Megha. "Beyond the Photograph: A Graphic History of Lynching." *Journal of Graphic Novels and Comics* 5, no. (2014): 15–28.

Chaney, Michael A. *Reading Lessons in Seeing: Mirrors, Masks, and Mazes in the Autobiographical Graphic Novel*. Jackson: University Press of Mississippi, 2016.

Dueben, Alex. "Comics and Storytelling: A Conversation with Mat Johnson." *Los Angeles Review of Books*, April 21, 2018. https://lareviewofbooks.org/article/comics-and-story telling-a-conversation-with-mat-joh.

Eisner, Will. *Comics and Sequential Art: Principles and Practices from the Legendary Cartoonist*. New York: W. W. Norton & Company, 2008.

Fields, Karen E., and Barbara J. Fields. *Racecraft: The Soul of Inequality in American Life*. London: Verso, 2012.

Harris, Keshia L. "Biracial American Colorism: Passing for White." *American Behavioral Scientist* 62, no. 14 (2018): 2072–86.

Johnson, Mat, and Warren Pleece. *Incognegro: A Graphic Mystery*. New York: Vertigo, 2008.

Johnson, Mat, and Warren Pleece. *Incognegro: A Graphic Mystery*. New York: Berger, 2018.

Maddox, Keith B., and Stephanie A. Gray. "Cognitive Representations of Black Americans: Reexploring the Role of Skin Tone." *PSPB* 28, no. 2 (2002): 250–59.

Shimakura, Hitomi, and Katsuaki Sakata. "Color Criteria of Facial Skin Tone Judgment." *Vision Research* 193 (2022): 2.

Spiegelman, Art. "Drawing Blood: Outrageous Cartoons and the Art of Outrage." *Harper's Magazine*, June 2006: 43–45.

Töpffer, Rodolphe. "Essay on Physiognomy." In *Enter: The Comics: Rodolphe Töpffer's Essay on Physiognomy and the True Story of Monsieur Crépin*. Edited and translated by E. Wiese. Lincoln, NE: University of Nebraska Press, 1965.

Willadsen-Jensen, Eve C., and Tiffany A. Ito. "Ambiguity and the Timecourse of Racial Perception." *Social Cognition* 24, no. 5 (2006): 580.

7

VIOLENCE TRYING *PATIENCE*

Daniel Clowes, Gender, Semiotics, and the Duo-Parallel-Critical Alternative to McCloud's World-Image Typology in Comics

STEVEN S. VROOMAN

INTRODUCTION: A CLOWES BOOK

To this day we inflict Wimsatt and Beardsley's "The Intentional Fallacy" on students of literature and popular culture. We explain that the answers to questions of meaning in a text are not to be gained by looking to the author's intent, or, in their words, "Critical inquiries are not settled by consulting the oracle."[1] This leaves us in choppy waters when looking at work that is not only self-referential, but, in the case of Daniel Clowes's *Patience*,[2] referential to the entire enterprise of comic art. Thus, although Foucault[3] and Barthes[4] go so far as to bump off the author entirely, we find that Clowes, our oracle, whose comic is strewn with violence, is willing and able to fight off this range of theorists from the New Critics to the poststructuralists.

What of such art that seeks critical commentary outside of itself? There are many comics about comics in Clowes's repertoire, and in his book *Ice Haven*, a character, Harry Naybors, who identifies himself as a comic book critic, unleashes a structuralist schema for understanding comics after we watch him pee, while eating dry cereal and wearing only underwear.[5] That is critique of theory in the vehicle of art. The rub here is that an author is not the boss of their text's meaning, or, for Foucault, a function that allows us to reduce the uncomfortable complexity of a text, "the great peril . . . with which fiction threatens our world."[6] But this should not stop us from upending the usual model, which is to use theory or critical tools to replace the author as the arbiter of what a thing means, and instead allow a creative work to suit up and enter the fray and perhaps tell us a thing or two about ideas.

Clowes's intent (feel the skeptical shivers!), as Ito reports, was to reimagine the relationship between text and images in *Patience*, as he looked back on the works of comics past, from Harvey Kurtzman to Jack Kirby.[7] What I found in the course of this project is that Clowes's book locates its pivot on questions of word and image around issues of gender and violence, and suggests a different semiotics for all those relationships. It is a deconstruction of comics structuralism, particularly the type embodied by the pop-academic work we teach in so many first-year student classes in college, Scott McCloud's *Understanding Comics*. Martin Jay's gloss of Derrida's thoughts on art plays like a plot summary: "For Derrida, the act of drawing itself necessitates a moment of nonseeing in which the artist depicts the ruins of a previous vision."[8] Derrida further suggests that attempts to build structuralist models (like McCloud's) are haunted by "incidence of menace, at the moment where imminent danger concentrates our vision."[9] It is as if Clowes's text is a riff on Derridean notions of dangerous visions.

A different plot summary would be that the protagonist in *Patience*, Jack, travels through time to save a murdered woman from danger caused by his own time-travelling rescue attempts. The loopy recursions only accelerate as the book continues. In the past he does what is, on first read, a shocking amount of waiting around. The reader is tempted to lose patience while Jack loses Patience, but gains her back, only to have *Patience* lose Jack in the end, his embers drifting into a void after he leaves Patience with a previous or perhaps alternate version of himself, a Jack who doesn't know Jack. These loops of narrative and irony structurally flow around acts of visceral violence that ground the plot, as we might expect in a murder whodunit. But they also unsettle, in their habit of spilling beyond the comic's visual language.

One more plot summary, in a different tenor, would be that *Patience* shares its title with its lead female character, who is named after time itself, or, more precisely, an attitude about time, a word whose origins are in suffering, as in being a patient. Patience, as a concept, then, is what Irigaray calls a "geometric prop" or "copulative link"[10] that gives meaning to a structural or semiotic system (with the *copula* and *copulation* joke in play in her original text), in this case an attitudinal link between an amount of time and a person who experiences it. Real women flow and blur the lines of such linkage systems, for Irigaray, while the opposing pressure, from both real men and men as discursive subjects, is to paralyze her voice, to freeze it.[11] Such movements happen in the plot, as Patience occupies multiple identities through the timestreams while acts of violence are wielded by characters to seemingly lock down her role as object. In the end, Patience says, "It's okay. I know everything," and the time-travelling Jack disappears into the void.[12] She ends up with not only power as a character, but as a kind of proxy author. The question remains as to whether or not violating comics apparatus is enough for Patience to become a subject.

This essay's intent is to use what Clowes develops in *Patience* in order to take an axe to Scott McCloud's prevailing theory of word and image relationships in comics. I deploy an analysis of Clowes's work, most specifically its depictions of gendered violence, to develop a different semiotic tool than McCloud's theory of word and image relationships in comics. This tool, which we will call the *duo-parallel-critical continuum*, is useful in and of itself, and should also demonstrate the further need for semiotic revisions to the structuralist moments in comics criticism overall.

A CLOUDED SYSTEM

Before we can try our *Patience* on comics theory, we need to deconstruct one. Scott McCloud's influential *Understanding Comics* develops a series of typologies by which we might analyze the structural languages of comics. The clearest of these lists are of panel transitions, abstraction levels, and word-image relationships, the latter of which will be my focus. In short, his typology of word-image relationships in panels is this:

> *Word Specific.* The text has almost "complete" meaning.
> *Picture Specific.* The image has almost "complete" meaning.
> *Duo Specific.* The text and image have the same meaning.
> *Additive.* Either the words or the images "amplify" the other meaning, which seems more primary.
> *Parallel.* The words and pictures tell seemingly different stories.
> *Montage.* The words are treated like pictures ("**BOOM!**").
> *Interdependent.* Words and pictures, "hand-in-hand to convey an idea that neither could convey alone."[13]

One is tempted to agree with Julia Round that the *interdependent* category may be everything, really, with the rest as matters of degree,[14] or of "blending," to use Mario Saraceni's phrasing.[15] For my part, the first three do require what we would understand, post-Derrida, as an impossibly certain grasp of the complete meaning of a discursive object. So does *parallel*, really. The difference between *additive* and *interdependent* is obscure, and McCloud's examples seem to suggest *additive* relationships have a more "knowable" meaning, where his six *interdependent* examples involve ambiguity, including questions asked by the text or image and not answered by the counterpart. Yet this ambiguity is constricted as the play possible between specific kinds of images and word relations which clearly signal ambiguity (a hilarious three-word phrase, that), as if such uncertainties are not typical or normal in the complex set of signs that make up a comics panel. And what of *montage* elements, which seem to signal both clarity on one hand and a barely contained excess on the other?

McCloud does suggest most comics panels are *interdependent*, but since his first five categories rely on impossible assumptions of certainty, we are left in the same position as Roman Jakobsen, rejecting arch structuralist Ferdinand de Saussure's "atomizing, neogrammarian" system that loses the "perpetual interplay" of signs.[16] Although Jakobsen's concerns are multiple, a key piece of his legacy for our purposes is his work on pushing Saussure's concepts of the syntagmatic and paradigmatic relationships between words into the field of social semiotics. A sign's "meaning," if you will, coheres around the syntagmatic (expanded by Jakobsen to be the relationships amongst signs within a text) and the paradigmatic, originally "associative" relationships in Saussure, where signs are "associated with memory" and drawn from a constellation of possibilities in a cultural sphere in what Jakobsen calls an "intuitive" choice.[17]

In other words, a sign is in a paradigmatic relationship with all the other signs that could substitute for it in a text. Jakobsen's "intuition" here is filled out in the field of media studies, where paradigmatic choices are constructed as more ideological: "The meaning of the unit chosen is defined by the relationship to the others in the paradigm that were not,"[18] or in their "substitutability."[19] Those relationships are sites of ideological struggle.[20]

To clarify, in a mystery text, as in the first part of *Patience* when Jack tries to find out who killed her, the image of the scene of the crime contains clues, as we have been trained to divine by TV shows. Her body lies there, head and arm at awkward angles. We might look at the broken lamp and the rumpled rug and the splay of her hair and develop a theory of the crime based on the syntagmatic relationships between those signs. Paradigmatically, we note the specific callout to the extreme closeup on Marion Crane's dead eye in *Psycho* in the small panel at the bottom and perhaps generate the idea of a serial killer. Two pages after finding her dead body, Jack imagines a perp with a melting face, too abstract to be identifiable. We've also been trained to try to figure out who that really is based on suspects we might have. In a Poirot novel's denouement, we'd have specific characters to replace the molten perp with. In this book, we have yet to meet any suspects but can sift through imagined options: Jack himself, a robber, a rapist, a serial killer, an old enemy only later to be revealed. My corrective to McCloud, then, would be to suggest that we look to syntagmatic relationships between everything in a panel, but specifically for our purposes, words and images. The paradigmatic adds the notion of what's not there or could be there and how that affects the meanings we read in the text.

THE *DUO-PARALLEL-CRITICAL CONTINUUM*

McCloud's *duo*, with image and word identical, is impossible. So is his *parallel*, given that they are totally separate. Hillary Chute has argued that readers perform a "disjunctive back-and-forth of reading and looking for meaning" along those "two narrative tracks."[21] Thus, it seems that readers will try to draw connections between the *parallel* modes of word and image, and indeed many comics utilize this perhaps inevitable process to develop additional layers of meaning. We move between those impossible poles of *duo* and *parallel*, as we semiotically work through the field of signs, but we are also pulled toward another pole, a *critical* one McCloud doesn't include, where one channel's apparent meaning challenges the others. This pole is also a bit impossible, so we find ourselves, as readers, moving along this pivot, finding ways the two modes cohere and then disjunct.

Indeed, many comics seem to live primarily in the space of play in that *duo-parallel-critical continuum*. A. David Lewis notes places in *Watchmen* (Alan Moore and Dave Gibbons, 1986) where the verbal and visual have two different narrators, creating "a schism between the two."[22] A similar effect is created when Superman's text-box critiques of Bruce Wayne appear in *The Dark Knight Returns* (Frank Miller and Klaus Janson, 1986) before he arrives in the art, germinating the seed of their final fight. A more complex effect is created in *Batman: The Killing Joke* (Alan Moore and Brian Bolland, 1988), where the visual cueing makes it seem like a certain set of memories are the Joker's while the text "actively denies this,"[23] but we cannot simply rest easy in the *critical* notion, as the text propels us to further question. Even in Karline McClain's analysis of *Amar Chitra Katha*, where texts about the life of the poet Tagore and Gandhi's call for nonviolence are set alongside images of a British massacre, the anticolonial criticism is not simple given that Gandhi brings a nonviolent critique, but also the memory of the Partition, and Tagore's views on anticolonialism were anything but simple.[24] Chris Ware's "I Guess" (1991) provides one more useful example of the way a comic can be constructed in such a way as to propel us through constant tension on that *duo-parallel-critical continuum*. The textual narration involves a child telling a mundane story about his grandfather while the images show a superhero tale. A. David Lewis argues this creates "narrative polyphony" (79), but we can explicate that a bit further. In the third panel, the man reading the newspaper with surprise can easily be either the not-yet-costumed hero or his grandfather worried about what he wears before he goes outside, inviting us to analyze while holding both options in critical tension. So do we believe the narrator at the end who says he's fine with his grandfather's death? Or is there secret love for his secret hero? Or, as with real life, is it probably all of it and more?

Patience is an extended exploration of the artistic and narrative possibilities of this kind of construction, from its opening panels. It doesn't seem like it at first. The first is just a block lettering of the year, 2012, over what looks to be semen in a vagina. The second shows sperm not quite entering an egg. Then we see a pregnancy test only in silhouette as two silhouetted people discuss whether two lines are good or not. And we don't know yet whether pregnancy or not constitutes "good." This kind of experience of reading such moments in comics is an experience of being continually unsettled in our temporary reading stances. The structure of comics' "manifest handling of its own artifice" encourages a more critical and searching semiotic read across the seams of the panel.[25]

McCloud suggests that these issues are more complex than his typology, but he turns to a scales model, whereby either text or images are the primary weight on the fulcrum. He grasps the fluidic work of audiences, but he isolates the wrong seam. The balance we seem to need to find is to locate the tension of the panel between the impossible poles of *duo specific* and what we will call a totally *critical* relationship, with *parallel* another impossible balance in between. Michael Riffaterre, writing about fiction, suggests that when confronted with metatextual complexity of this kind, for our purposes here the divergence between the text and image, we have a moment of "double-take" where we must experiment with potential meanings,[26] which resonates strongly with Hillary Chute's notion that comics require us to "look, and then look again."[27] In that moment we connect with the unsaid, the undepicted, the paradigmatic others that might be there instead, and we find ourselves selecting options based on Riffaterre's "subtext"[28] or the way the nonexplicit implications of the text connect with our larger cultural imaginary. I contend that the text-image relationship is perhaps the primary syntagm in our apprehension of a comic. Our paradigmatic search intensifies the further toward *critical* that seems to fall.

PATIENCE WITH VIOLENCE

To explore this contention, every panel in *Patience* that depicts or implies an out-of-panel or "offscreen" act of contemporaneous violence was analyzed. Any act of physical aggression, including punching or grabbing or any use of a weapon, was coded as an act of violence. There are no "playful" acts of violence in the book, thus simplifying the procedure. The remnants of past acts of violence were not included, for example, when Jack discovers Patience's dead body on pages 12 and 13.

Why violence? To start, on first read I was viscerally struck by the way the acts of violence violate our vision with such devices as stacking a floating frame over the scene to occlude our sight or having the acts spill out the hidden edges of the panels. It's as if those acts were pulling at the seams of the book itself even as those acts pull at the seams of the trippy reality of the plot. As a teacher of McCloud to my undergraduates, this was something that directly challenged those structuralist typologies.

Theoretically, Derrida expects violence when we disrupt a structuralist system, but it also seems to be the locus in which other critics have looked to disruptions between text and image. For example, Christopher Pizzino argues that for Gilbert Hernandez, violence "functions as a lynchpin in the dynamics of comics making and reading,"[29] and Jonathan Gaboury's work points to the connections between the hybridity of characters and comics techniques in *We3*.[30] Hillary Chute, in *Graphic Women*, points to the connections between women, violence, and trauma in comics. Although she is primarily focusing on autobiographic graphic novels by women, her notion that graphic narrative theorizes "trauma in connection to the visual"[31] applies to a much larger scope of comic art. Chute contends that unlike film, which manipulates the viewer into a particular duration of vision for acts of violence, comics release the reader "to be in control of when she looks at what and how long she spends on each frame."[32]

Table 1 demonstrates how I coded each of the sixty-three panels of violence in the book.

I have violated my arch antistructuralist commitments, obviously, by generating such a table, and even more problematically by coding panels as duo, parallel, and critical, conditions that I have argued panels don't really clearly sit within. These categories, in this table, represent, given how different those three options are, the closest option for each panel in my reading. The same follows for some additional analytic lenses, the degree to which the visual and the textual is either seen, partial/obscured, or absent. The way the text shifts its patterns across these matrices in rough thirds corresponds to the

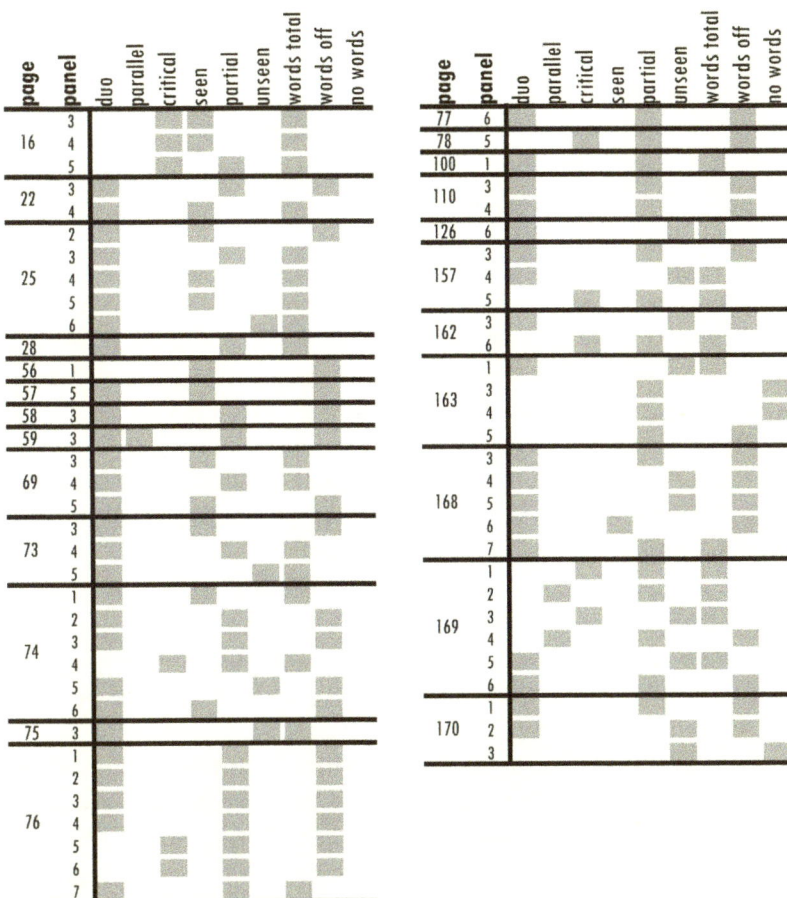

Table 1. This chart shows every panel of the graphic novel that includes an act of violence, coded on the duo-parallel continuum, the degree to which the act of violence is seen in the panel, and the use of words.

ways that Patience lurches free(ish) of her narrative constraints and toward an almost authorial subjecthood. The text doesn't quite get there, but the way it connects its use of violent comics deconstruction with issues of gender power demonstrates perhaps the limits of the progressive possibilities that can be achieved in a violent tale set in the masculinist world of noirish sci-fi.

PATIENCE WITH JACK'S VIOLENCE

Throughout the whole text, most panels are *duo* in structure. The majority of nonviolent panels are moments of dialogue between characters who seem to do little enough visually that we'd be tempted to call these *word-specific* or perhaps think of the images as merely *additive* to the words. But there are subtle resonances as we are trained by the panels to look to the pictures to draw emotional and relational meanings, which slowly reveal themselves to be more important than the often-expositional dialogue. Our first clues to this come from the panels depicting violence. The first violent panel is also the first *critical* panel in the comic. It is a pink monochrome with a liquidy perp who attacks Patience in Jack's imagination as he meets with his lawyers in jail. The boxed narration from Jack on page 16 says, "I stopped giving a shit about myself a long time ago" while his smallish alter ego in the image tries to stop the perp from strangling her. Although the rest of this first section, before the jump back in time to 2006, contains no other clearly *critical* panels of violence, we are induced here to read the violent panels in the comic as places where images tell simple truths that our protagonist's untrustworthy thoughts in the other panels refuse to reveal. The violence begins to serve as a critical counterpoint to the rest of the book.

This sets up a series of mundane depictions of "righteous" violence, like an older Jack naturally aged into 2029 pummeling a future Patience lookalike's attacker on page 25 or a young Patience and a time-traveling Jack fighting off boys in the woods in 2006, who attempt to trick her into a sex act they secretly film on pages 55–58. There is no critical word-based commentary on these acts of violence, but each sequence ends with Jack hitting someone extra hard with a weapon of some kind, lines of force demonstrating the ferocity of his attack, blood and perhaps chunks of something (teeth?) flying off. In each there is a large *montage* sound effect splayed across each panel, our vision often occluded in some way by having the head of the victim being hit shown off-panel or in silhouette. Are we being trained across this first section of the text to develop an unwritten critique that perhaps he is getting out of control and that once violence starts he can't quite help himself? He does, in other panels, suggest that life and now time travel have messed up his self-control, but not in these two moments. We have to see that for ourselves, to the extent we can given what is not shown in the panel.

As the images begin to push out of view in the more extreme moments of violence in the first "real" fight on page 25, the words likewise begin to slide away. Here a "THUK" and a "CRACK!" flow over the white gutters. When Jack attacks the young men in the woods in 2006, their faces are not only obscured in silhouette, but their heads are also obscured by the montage words, one of which is presumably a "CRACK!" of which we can only see the "CRA" because it is now crossed "under" the gutter into invisibility. In the aftermath of the attack, we also see the text bubbles follow under the gutter, something we saw for the first time on page 56 when one of the young men is unzipping his fly and Patience's dialogue disappears under the gutter.

Still, in this first segment of the book, much of this formal experimentation is subtle. It escalates when Patience is attacked by her ex-boyfriend Adam, just out of jail and now violently jealous on pages 73–76. When he first touches her, covering her face and mouth, his dialogue, "Shut your fucking mouth now," partially covers her speech bubble, which reads as, "Pleas I don." The majority of these panels have words or images or both occluded or in partial view. The apex of this is in the middle of page 74, where it seems as if Adam is punching the wall near her head, but we can't fully see because another panel floats on top of that scene, obscuring all but his back on the left and his fist and Patience's hair both against the wall on the right. That panel shows Jack in silhouetted darkness, watching from inside the closet through a cracked door, a monochrome yellow sliver of violence in view, similar to the monochrome pink panels on page 16. Jack sees Adam, his arms radiating some force, while we see only Patience's sagging legs. In neither panel can we see her face or what is happening to her. The speech bubbles and a "THUD!" in the original panel slide off the edges while Jack's interrupted narration box in the floating panel is the first text to broach the *critical* pole of the continuum for sixty pages: "Oh Lord, oh Jesus Christ, what have I done? What have I."

When Jack bursts out of the closet with his ray gun, the collapse of the visual continues as the violence escalates. The ray gun flies out of a panel over the gutter, the only time that happens in the graphic novel. More often than not words are slipping off the side of the panel or obscured by other speech bubbles. The layered bubbles give a quick, argued dialogue sort of effect, and the words sliding off the edge give a feeling of events spiraling out of control, perhaps even the narrator's control. Words are now no longer trustworthy, not, perhaps, because we have reason to disbelieve them, but because they keep flying off the page or hiding from our sight. Speech bubbles then become so occluded under the gutters that only the little curved spike of the bubble that comes from characters' mouths are visible. Montage words slip and slide, and in the last panel, while Jack has him on the floor, Adam's entire face is off-panel in the gutter as bloody chunks fly and lines of force radiate, the montage words are so occluded that we can see only a "CHU" three times. I am not entirely sure what sound effect that actually is supposed to be.

In the panel after that, Patience picks up the ray gun, levels it at Jack, and orders him to stop. In the panel before it, Jack's narration returns, claiming clarity as he says he's at last pummeling her murderer. In this sequence of panels the text pivots. We soon discover Jack is wrong about this, and although the panel is structured in *duo* form, both words and images critique each other in retrospect when we find out Jack has mistaken the murderer. It is good he stopped Adam's violence, but killing him on the floor is not justified. Thus, Patience finally lays claim to the story. Jack's narration is worried about Patience's murder because it "ruined my life," which, for all his pretensions of blundering heroism up until now, finally reveals that for him Patience is only the Irigarayan copula linking his life as a loser with a crappy job in the first pages of the book with an imagined future as a family man and father that ends with Patience's death.

Jack jumps to 1985 after that to kill Adam as a child. He's unable to pull the trigger. He jumps to 2012 where Patience, having taken some control of her life, finds out that Adam has taken control of his and is a changed man. Jack, unknowing, finds him and ties him up in a shack, which he's rigged with explosives, which are accidentally ignited when Bernie, the inventor of the time machine, arrives to seek vengeance on Jack, his own ray gun firing. Adam is gone and Jack drives to surveil the scene of the crime, hoping he's stopped it.

He hasn't. Patience arrives home to see one of the boys from the incident in the woods, now grown up and missing an eye from Jack's violence on that night, holding an iPad with a video call from the boy who'd tried to initiate the sexual encounter, now a famous politician, perhaps the president, who'd been on televisions throughout the comic up until this point. Patience takes aggressive control of the encounter, her speech bubbles covering the two real, in person and on the device. Patience hits her original-timeline killer with the lamp we saw broken next to her body at the beginning in the most double-take-worthy panel in the book. A giant "CRASH" covers her face entirely, as if by this act she erases herself from the copulative structure built to encase her. There is a kind of odd absence or white light on the killer's head as the lamp shatters on impact, the only use of that technique in the entire text. She is breaking the timeline here, breaking her identity as victim written into the stories of men, and now breaking the pattern of the visibility of violence. Here the place of impact is simply whited out, not teased out of the frame of the panel. She crushes the iPad, her speech bubbles as she yells "Motherfucker!" growing as large as the montage sound effects of "CRASH" and "KRA," all sliding out of frame as the violence escalates. Half of the following violent panels in that sequence, now from Patience's point of view, have the action totally hidden. And the panels where vision is partial are far more partial than the partial visibility panels were earlier in the book. We simply cannot fully see what is happening.

As she is overpowered by her intruder, she, for the first time, takes over the rectangular narration boxes, which are yellow, as opposed to Jack's white. The first panel on page 169 places the first box right in the middle of her forehead. The panels turn black as she momentarily blacks out while being choked. Her text here, about the nature of her experience as reality, moves across the entire *duo-parallel-critical* continuum. Any sense of patterning across all the elements noted in table 1 breaks down. The climax of Jack's narrative leads ultimately to his nonbeing, as result of the costs of time travel, but pages before that, the panels break apart the logic of his role, a self-interested avenger seeking to secure Patience's life as the vessel for his family. It feels much like Irigaray's revenge, a woman flowing past patterns to find her own will, her own voice, as she takes control of the narrative, her narrative, for good.

IRIGARAY'S REVENGE?

The first third of the book shows us most of the images and all the words as violence occurs, even as the images tell us truths Jack's words don't reveal. In the second third Patience begins to wrest control of the story, and specifically the violence, as the words, hers or reflected through her perspective, discipline images. Words and images in the violent scenes begin to slip out of view and out of frame, as the violence begins to expand beyond the ability of comics-panel grammar to maintain. In the final third, the relationships between images and words become increasingly fragmented. The visuals become coded as Jack's story, the story of men who write her as a copula and which are increasingly erased in frames where she takes power. And the words, her words, slowly overtake and overwhelm the story as she writes Jack out of existence, the visuals of Jack literally melting to nothing by the end, when he departs existence in full-page art that combines imagery of space and the microscopic.

Violence, which at the beginning of the comic feels like the typical crime-and/or science fiction-story tool for disciplining women into the dominant structure, ends up being the mechanism by which the character breaks out of those structures, structures created by a character who tries to rewrite her life, while also metonymically bursting the structures of Clowes's comic, or at least the rules he teaches us to read it by through his manipulation of the *duo-parallel-critical* continuum. It is deft work by Clowes.

We might claim it for Irigarayan feminism, even given its flaws in that regard, but Jack's response to a newly empowered Patience is for his identity to melt into a squishy nonworld where he appears as a fetus homunculus before his existence falls apart entirely into a spacy void of orifices. Although this notion that male subjecthood has no existence without a woman object as the geometric prop of the ideological and symbolic system has a bracing tang of salt to it, Clowes doesn't quite pull it off. The critique in the end works so hard across the semiotic planes just to give Patience subjecthood, but it is unable to imagine a way to give Jack an alternative subjecthood when he no longer needs to write her identity for her. Those answers might be a lot to ask for, but perhaps something more than a void, Jack's fetal return to the enormous Lacanian Lack Irigaray mocks, should be forthcoming.

In terms of McCloud, I believe this essay has demonstrated the effectiveness of replacing his word-image typology with a sense of semiotic continuum, and I have found the *duo-parallel-critical continuum* a helpful replacement. I hope, also, that this essay has skated along the lines of hypocrisy well enough, both citing deconstruction and using a structuralist table we might expect of *S-Z*–era Barthes. After Derrida, there sometimes seems little but hypocrisy left in work that attempts to rescue structuralism from itself and push forward. In my defense, Derrida does suggest that all criticism is secretly structuralist at that, and I'd rather put structuralism in play rather than generate fealty to it on the one hand or be haunted by it on the other.

Notes

1. W. K. Wimsatt Jr. and M. C. Beardsley, "The Intentional Fallacy," *Sewanee Review* 54, no. 3 (1946), 487.
2. Daniel Clowes, *Patience* (Seattle: Fantagraphics, 2016).
3. Michel Foucault, "What Is an Author?" in *The Critical Tradition: Classic Texts and Contemporary Trends*, ed. David H. Richter, trans. Josue Harari (Boston: Bedford, 1989), 978–88.
4. Roland Barthes, *Image Music Text*, trans. Stephen Heath (New York: Fontana Press, 1977).
5. Daniel Clowes. *Ice Haven* (New York: Pantheon, 2005).
6. Foucault, 987.
7. Robert Ito, "The Making of Daniel Clowes and a Golden Age for Comics," *California Sunday Magazine*, Feb. 2016, https://story.californiasunday.com/daniel-clowes-patience.
8. Martin Jay, *Downcast Eyes: The Denigration of Vision in Twentieth-Century French Thought* (Berkeley: University of California Press, 1993), 522.
9. Jacques Derrida, *Writing and Difference* (New York: Routledge, 1978), 4.
10. Luce Irigary, *This Sex Which Is Not One* (Ithaca, NY: Cornell University Press, 1985), 108–9.
11. Irigaray, 112.
12. Clowes, *Patience*, 177.

13. Scott McCloud, *Understanding Comics: The Invisible Art* (New York: Harper, 1993), 153–55.

14. Julia Round, "Visual Perspective and Narrative Voice in Comics: Redefining Literary Terminology," *International Journal of Comic Art* 9, no. 2 (2007): 320.

15. Mario Saraceni. *The Language of Comics* (New York: Routledge, 2003), 27.

16. Roman Jakobsen, *Selected Writings II: Word and Language* (Berlin: Mouton, 1971), 721, 722.

17. Jakobsen, 719.

18. Tim O'Sullivan, John Hartley, Danny Saunders, Martin Montgomery, and John Fiske, *Key Concepts in Communication and Cultural Studies* (New York: Routledge, 1994), 215.

19. Leah Vande Berg, Lawrence A. Wenner, and Bruce E. Gonbeck, *Critical Approaches to Television* (Boston: Houghton Mifflin, 1998), 101.

20. Valentin N. Volosinov, *Marxism and the Philosophy of Language* (Cambridge, MA: Harvard University Press, 1973), 10.

21. Hillary Chute, "Comics as Literature? Reading Graphic Narrative," *PMLA* 123, no. 2 (2008): 452.

22. A. David Lewis, "The Shape of Comic Book Reading," *Studies in Comics* 1, no. 1 (2010): 78.

23. Mervi Miettinen, "Past as Multiple Choice—Textual Anarchy and the Problems of Continuity in *Batman: The Killing Joke*," *Scandinavian Journal of Comic Art* 1, no. 1 (2011): 12.

24. Karline Marie McClain, "Whose Immortal Stories? *Amar Chitra Katha* and the Construction of Indian Identities," Austin: UT Austin, 2005. PhD dissertation, 15.

25. Chute, "Comics," 457.

26. Michael Riffaterre, *Fictional Truth* (Baltimore: Johns Hopkins University Press, 1990), 86.

27. Hillary Chute, *Graphic Women: Life Narrative and Contemporary Comics* (New York: Columbia University Press, 2010), 33.

28. Riffaterre, 37.

29. Christopher Pizzino, "Autoclastic Icons: Bloodletting and Burning in Gilbert Hernandez's Palomar," *ImageTexT: Interdisciplinary Comics Studies* 7, no. 1 (2013), http://imagetext.english.ufl.edu/archives/v7_1/pizzino/.

30. Jonathan Gaboury, "The Violence Museum: Aesthetic Wounds from *Popeye* to *We3*," *ImageTexT: Interdisciplinary Comics Studies* 6, no. 1 (2011), http://imagetext.english.ufl.edu/archives/v6_1/gaboury/.

31. Chute, *Graphic*, 24.

32. Chute, *Graphic*, 32.

Works Cited

Barthes, Roland. *Image Music Text*. Translated by Stephen Heath. New York: Fontana, 1977.

Chute, Hillary. "Comics as Literature?: Reading Graphic Narrative." *PMLA* 123, no. 2 (2008): 452–65.

Chute, Hillary. *Graphic Women: Life Narrative and Contemporary Comics*. New York: Columbia University Press, 2010.

Clowes, Daniel. *Ice Haven*. New York: Pantheon, 2005.

Clowes, Daniel. *Patience*. Seattle: Fantagraphics, 2016.

Derrida, Jacques. *Writing and Difference*. Translated by Alan Bass. New York: Routledge, 1978.

Foucault, Michel. "What Is an Author?" In *The Critical Tradition: Classic Texts and Contemporary Trends*, edited by David H. Richter, 978–88. Translated by Josue Harari. Boston: Bedford, 1989.

Gaboury, Jonathan. "The Violence Museum: Aesthetic Wounds from *Popeye* to *We3*." *ImageTexT: Interdisciplinary Comics Studies* 6, no. 1 (2011). http://imagetext.english.ufl.edu/archives/v6_1/gaboury/.

Irigary, Luce. *This Sex Which Is Not One*. Translated by Catherine Porter and Carolyn Burke. Ithaca, NY: Cornell University Press, 1985.

Ito, Robert. "The Making of Daniel Clowes and a Golden Age for Comics." *California Sunday Magazine*, Feb. 2016. https://story.californiasunday.com/daniel-clowes-patience.

Jakobsen, Roman. *Selected Writings II: Word and Language*. Berlin: Mouton, 1971.

Jay, Martin. *Downcast Eyes: The Denigration of Vision in Twentieth-Century French Thought*. Berkeley: University of California Press, 1994.

Johnston, Paddy. "Exploring Ghost Worlds: A Review of 'The Daniel Clowes Reader.'" *Comics Grid: Journal of Comics Scholarship* 3, no. 1 (2013). https://www.comicsgrid.com/articles/10.5334/cg.ag/.

Lewis, A. David. "The Shape of Comic Book Reading." *Studies in Comics* 1, no. 1 (2010): 71–81.

McClain, Karline Marie. *Whose Immortal Stories?: Amar Chitra Katha and the Construction of Indian Identities*. Austin: UT Austin, 2005. PhD dissertation.

McCloud, Scott. *Understanding Comics: The Invisible Art*. New York: Harper, 1993.

Miettinen, Mervi. "Past as Multiple Choice—Textual Anarchy and the Problems of Continuity in *Batman: The Killing Joke*." *Scandinavian Journal of Comic Art* 1, no. 1 (2011): 4–25.

O'Sullivan, Tim, John Hartley, Danny Saunders, Martin Montgomery, and John Fiske. *Key Concepts in Communication and Cultural Studies*. 2nd edition. New York: Routledge, 1994.

Pizzino, Christopher. "Autoclastic Icons: Bloodletting and Burning in Gilbert Hernandez's Palomar." *ImageTexT: Interdisciplinary Comics Studies* 7, no. 1 (2013). http://imagetext.english.ufl.edu/archives/v7_1/pizzino/.

Riffaterre, Michael. *Fictional Truth*. Baltimore: Johns Hopkins University Press, 1990.

Round, Julia. "Visual Perspective and Narrative Voice in Comics: Redefining Literary Terminology." *International Journal of Comic Art* 9, no. 2 (2007): 315–29.

Saraceni, Mario. *The Language of Comics*. New York: Routledge, 2003.

Saussure, Ferdinand de. *Course in General Linguistics*. Translated by Wade Baskin. New York: Philosophical Library, 1959.

Vande Berg, Leah, Lawrence A. Wenner, and Bruce E. Gonbeck. *Critical Approaches to Television*. Boston: Houghton Mifflin, 1998.

Volosinov, Valentin N. *Marxism and the Philosophy of Language*. Cambridge, MA: Harvard University Press, 1973.

Ware, Chris. "I Guess." *From Dusk Till Drawn* (blog). 2016. https://fromdusktilldrawnblog.wordpress.com/2016/09/18/i-guess-by-chris-ware-usa-1990/.

Wimsatt, W. K., Jr., and M. C. Beardsley. "The Intentional Fallacy." *Sewanee Review* 54, no. 3 (1946): 468–88.

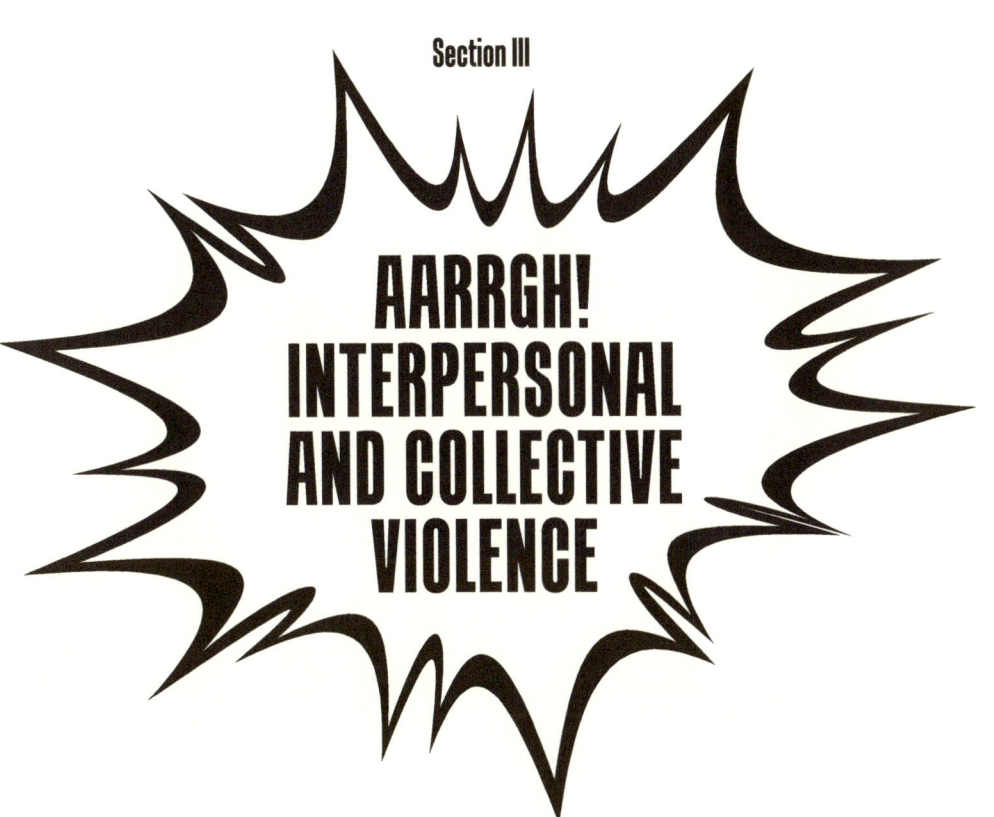

8

GENDER-BENDING AGGRESSION

A Comparative Study of Superheroine Aggression in *Hulk* (2016), *Captain Marvel* (2017), and *The New Wolverine* (2017)

KIERA M. GASWINT

We live in a moment where representations of physically aggressive females are finally breaking into contemporary popular culture. However, women continue to face stereotypes when expressing violence on screen, on the comic book page, or even in our daily lives. Representations of aggressive women have long been depicted exclusively through images such as raging mothers, women seeking revenge for themselves or a loved one, or through representations of women specifically coded as and/or actually Black, Asian, or Indigenous. With superhero films continuing to grow in popularity, the opportunity for new, more diverse characters has become far more likely than we have seen in the past. One specific and interesting batch of superheroes who have begun to enter the filmic arena are gender-bending characters like Captain Marvel, She-Hulk, and X-23. All characters whose personas were originally men, Carol, Jen, and Laura are all independent, female characters who have the same superpowers as their male counterparts. While these characters are fairly new to the big screen in the Marvel Cinematic Universe (MCU), their stories began long before the current moment. Most importantly, their stories have made waves by exploring how representations of aggression change when a personality, trope, or title is passed between gendered bodies.

Aggression can be understood as many things, such as physical violence, verbal assault, methods of intimidation, and acts of vandalism, to name a few. Dana Crowley Jack in *Behind the Mask: Destruction and Creativity in Women's Aggression* defines aggression as "an act that is 'done with the intention to harm another person, oneself, or an object.' It is the actor's intent that defines an act as aggressive" (7). Crowley Jack's approach engages gender by making a connection between a woman's destructiveness and her relationships.

Specifically, relationships are the most common justification for a woman's aggressive acts. In comparison to Crowley Jack's definition, Maud Lavin defines women's aggression "as the use of force to create change—fruitful, destructive, or a mix of the two," and "as a drive, expressed emotionally, and/ or as a key element of action" (1). Lavin's approach acknowledges the influence of a woman's relationships but emphasizes that female violence primarily functions to define boundaries and maintain cohesive social order. According to Lavin, women's aggression represents a drive for change. Together, Lavin and Crowley Jack's specific understanding of women's aggression is central to my understanding of violence and pugnacity in comic books.

Superhero personalities are inherently violent. But contrary to Fredric Wertham's arguments that violence in comic books has a negative impact on readers, creative representations of violence are largely used as a learning mechanism for the reader. As Jane Mitchell and Joseph George put it in their article about comic books and special education, "Most [superheroes] use their unique powers to fight an evil force, and they protect innocent people from imminent disaster" (92). Comic book violence has long been an educational tool used to teach readers about complex concepts like justice and politics, or a mechanism to help readers learn how to cope with horrible events like war. Gerard Jones explains his own revelation with the importance of violent representations in his book *Killing Monsters: Our Children's Need for Fantasy, Heroism, and Make-Believe Violence*:

> I'd seen fight scenes as a necessary evil to induce kids to read the more valuable contents of my stories—but I'd made the most meaningful contact with [a] reader *through* the fights. The characters, plots, and themes mattered, but the truly affecting, truly transformative element of the story was the violence itself. The violence had helped a timid adolescent tap into her own bottled-up emotionality and discover a feeling of personal power. (5)

Representations of aggression can be used to understand emotions associated with violence or empower individuals in the face of violence, contrary to popular beliefs about the negative influence of violent texts on individuals who read, play, or watch violent material. In this context, the representation of different bodies in violent and aggressive stories is crucial to the ever-continuing cultural conversation about the development of self-identity and inner strength.

The comic book realm offers a unique opportunity to explore the relationship between aggression, violent acts, and gender because characters and tropes have been recycled through differing ages and differing bodies over and over again: one heroic personality is passed from man to woman and is able to traverse race, sexuality, or other social descriptors based on a comic's story arc. Gender-bending characters—or female characters who have been derived from preexisting male characters by simply having the male's powers mapped onto a female body—have been around for some time and are scattered throughout comic book history. Characters like Supergirl, Batwoman, and Hawkeye are different from simply female superheroine characters. A classic gender-bending example can be seen between Superman and Supergirl. Created several years after Superman, Supergirl is a superheroine who directly reflects Superman's abilities of strength and flight, and in her overall costumed design (Marnell 2019). There are only two notable differences between Superman and Supergirl: their genders and Superman's life on Earth. The very idea and powers of Superman were simply mapped onto a female body and transcended gender, unlike characters like Wonder Woman, who was a female with superpowers that uniquely originated with her persona. Gender-bent comic book characters present a unique opportunity for analysis that other mediums of popular culture have yet to approach because they were so simply conceptualized and written, we can draw direct connections through the reflections in their gender-opposing characters.

In this chapter, I analyze three of the most famous gender-bending Marvel characters—She-Hulk, X-23, and Captain Marvel—in an attempt to understand how expressions of violence change as a unique set of superpowers is passed between specifically and differently gendered bodies. I argue that in comparison to the male incarnation of a super personality, the female gender-bending character mitigates their aggression by engaging methods of reactive, tactical, and mirrored violence in order to be taken seriously as a hero, and more importantly outperform their male counterpart. Lavin and Crowley Jack's gender-specific definitions outline the importance of drive, intent, and a woman's relationships to fully understanding female aggression. These elements largely define how characters such as She-Hulk, X-23, and Captain Marvel justify their violent actions, justifications to violence that their male counterparts—Hulk, Wolverine, and Captain Mar-Vell—never need.

"EVERYTHING IS NOT OKAY"[1]: CONTAINING AGGRESSION

Bruce Banner, otherwise known as the Hulk, is famous because of his fantastically violent anger-management issues. While Marvel revealed that there is an entire planet of Hulks in 2006, the Hulk had a female counterpart much earlier than the 2000s. Jennifer "Jen" Walters entered the Marvel universe in 1980, making her first appearance in *Savage She-Hulk* #1, "The She-Hulk Lives." Jennifer Walters, Bruce Banner's cousin and a successful lawyer in Los Angeles, is nearly killed by a mob boss; in order to save her life, Bruce gives her a life-saving blood transfusion, thereby transferring his Hulk powers to her. Given her early start in comics, Jennifer's powers have made an important and lasting statement about women's ability to handle ugly feelings like anger because her transformations into She-Hulk rely on her emotions.

She-Hulk became particularly central to the Marvel Comics universe in 2016, when Marvel fans—and Jen—came upon tragedy in the events of *Civil War II*. This storyline heavily involved Bruce and Jen as the series confronts politically charged questions about superheroes, including Jen's fight for superpowered people's rights in court, and whether or not it is acceptable to rely on an individual's ability to see into the future for political action. Ultimately, these questions result in events that lead to Bruce's murder for a crime he had not yet committed.[2] It was following these events that for the first time Jen was featured in a storyline titled *Hulk* (Tamaki et. al 2016), dropping "She" from the title and solidifying the finality of Bruce's death. For Jen this chain of events was catastrophic, given that she would have to find a way to grieve her cousin's death while avoiding any emotionally charged, She-Hulk-sized breakdowns. Throughout the storyline of *Hulk*, Jen struggles against symptoms of posttraumatic stress disorder and against her role as an acknowledged superhero in a society where she "feel[s] like an idiot." Jen says in *Hulk* #1, "Deconstructed: Part One"—"I'm a fricking super hero, but I'm eating pudding and watching Judge Judy. I should be out there doing something at least a little bit super" (6). Jen recognizes that she needs to get back to normal life and work through her grief, but she risks setting off the deep rage within her at her dear cousin's death and transforming into a Hulk. These "incidents," as Bruce often referred to them, are a bane.

Throughout the first few issues of *Hulk*, Jen struggles to retain her composure. In "Deconstructed: Part Three," Jen regularly breaks things in her office as a result of being unable to channel her emotions. She describes her increasing anger by using her transformation abilities as a metaphor: "It used to feel strong. Changing. Becoming something powerful. Now it feels like dying. Like a truck driving through my heart. Like every hurt is right there, pouring through me" (Tamaki 18). Jen has to manage her anger and aggression differently than Bruce because, unlike Bruce, society and gender norms regulate angry women and their emotions differently. To better understand Jen's struggle, Crowley Jack explains that "throughout history, women have been punished for obvious displays of aggression. They have been forced to camouflage their intent to hurt others, their oppositions, and even their positive forcefulness, to deliver their aggression in culturally sanctioned but more hidden ways" (4). Jen has the ability to be superempowered by her rage but must resist this power because embracing her rage physically changes her body outside of the cultural expectations of a women's size. In this moment, Jen is trying to avoid her superpowers as the ultimate obvious display of aggression that Crowley Jack describes above.

When all else fails and Jen is not able to maintain her cool, the *Hulk* storyline uses trauma as a plot device to justify Jen's public displays of rage, thereby fitting her into the mold of acceptable aggressive womanhood described in the introduction of this chapter. In the storyline featuring Jen following Bruce's death, a female client who rarely leaves her home comes to Jen desperate for protection from eviction. As Jen digs deeper into the case, she discovers her client was beaten and left for dead by a gang hired by the client's ex-boyfriend. The trauma Jen's client experiences from this incident causes her to fear the outside world, which becomes so intense it manifests as a physical being of dark energy. While a storyline that focuses on trauma does not necessarily have to be a feminized one, it is no coincidence that this narrative of intense trauma is coupled with Jen's struggle with grief and PTSD. Aggression is specifically understood in a gendered sense: men can be aggressive and women cannot. Plot lines such as this exploit trauma narratives in order to maintain a status quo between representations of gender; by extension, the client's overly traumatized story justifies extreme violence in return. Thus, in order for Jen to be able to activate the extent of her true abilities and access her rage, the story must compensate for Jen's overstepping her bounds as an actively aggressive woman. In this way, Jen and her client act like literary foils: Jen's client's trauma narrative is highly feminized, which allows Jen to finally confront and engage with her own rage in a way that maintains the gender status quo. This story arc teaches Jen how and when to contain her emotions, but also when she can no longer ignore her feelings. It is only when she is able to admit that everything is not okay that she is able to justify confronting her emotions and transforming into the Hulk to save the day.

In the sixth installment of *Hulk* we finally witness Jen's rage manifest physically against the embodiment of her client's fear. In classic Hulk fashion her body doubles in size, her speech becomes garbled, and her clothes are shredded to pieces as she unleashes her fury at the monster who is manipulating her client and destroying the neighborhood. Jen favors hand-to-hand combat similarly to Bruce and receives blow after blow in order to overcome her opponent. Notably though, Jen's Hulk appearance changes following

Bruce's passing. Prior to the events of *Civil War II*, Jen in Hulk form was green and muscular, but also noticeably sexualized to accentuate her femininity compared to Bruce's Hulk. However, in the 2016 *Hulk* series, Jen's Hulk form is grey and more rugged looking, with bright green scratches all over her body. These green marks reveal the extent of her physical and emotional trauma made manifest on her body. Over the course of the first six comics in the 2016 *Hulk* series, we see Jen struggle to contain her grief by avoiding her Hulk form. Even in a society that is working on accepting superpowers and super-people, Jen cannot risk the repercussions of her abilities because she is trying to return to her everyday, seminormal life. She works hard to hide her grief by only expressing and processing these emotions when she is by herself—much to the detriment of the destroyed furniture in her apartment and office space. Jen discovers that hiding her emotions does not help process her grief. It is only when she reconciles with herself that she needs to openly express her rage and grief that she is able to begin healing.

In many ways, Jen's containment of her rage is characteristic of women's aggression at large because she feels forced to hide it, and by extension her Hulk form. Jen's control of her Hulk form makes Jen's Hulk stand out in comparison to Bruce's irrational Hulk, and ultimately justifies her need to display her rage openly. While becoming the main character in the *Hulk* storyline is progressive for representations of women's aggression because she is no longer relegated to the gendered "She"-Hulk name in Bruce's absence, the fact that the storyline has to leverage trauma narratives and more to justify her rage, grief, and emotions renders this story arc regressive.

"IT'S NOT THAT I'M A VIOLENT PERSON—SOME THINGS JUST REALLY NEED PUNCHING AND I'M REALLY GOOD AT PUNCHING THINGS"[3]: INTENT, DRIVE, AND AGGRESSION

A superhero's intent is a no-brainer—a superhero acts for the greater good. Crowley Jack describes aggressive intent as moments when "women stand up to inner or outer authorities, when they hurt something purposely, [or] when they positively fight for justice—these are critical points of change" (1999, 21). Considering intent and aggression, Captain Marvel makes a particularly interesting case. Known as Ms. Marvel at the time, Carol did not officially take over the title of Captain Marvel until 2012 (Bundel 2019). Captain Marvel is one of the most well-known gender-bending characters, given that Walter Lawson, the original Captain Marvel, died in 1968 and at that time passed his powers to his love interest, Carol Danvers. Eric Diaz writes about Captain Marvel's journey by paying attention to the characters that preceded her, and articulating what makes her different: "By the time Carol [Captain Marvel] debuted as a hero, the idea of the female analogue to a popular male superhero had been around for decades. Superman had Supergirl, Batman had Batgirl, DC's Captain Marvel (no relation) had Mary Marvel, etc." Diaz notes that "Carol Danvers would be the first female 'spin-off' character to not only supersede her male counterpart in popularity and overall importance, but also take his name and rank from him on a permanent basis.[4]" Carol's permanent place within the Marvel Comic Universe marks her importance within Marvel's canonical group of popular superheroes; however, the fact that she was able to supersede a male counterpart and maintain his powers into the popular culture of the 2000s is important to understanding how aggression in superheroic bodies functions.

In a 2017 comic entitled *Generations: Captain Mar-vell and Captain Marvel*, Carol is unexpectedly transported to the past and is reunited on a distant planet with Walter Lawson, the original Captain Marvel whom she knew as a scientist on Earth. Despite their previous acquaintance, Walter has no memory of Carol nor his time on Earth. This scenario confounds Carol, as the two were close on Earth. As she spends time with him, she concludes that she was sent back in time and has in fact met Walter before their acquaintance or his time on Earth ever happened. Though confused about her spontaneous transcendence of time and space, Carol and Walter go on an adventure to save the peaceful planet Mydon from invaders by burrowing into the planet and finding Mydon's attacker, Annihilus. However, while Captain Marvel might be the name they both share, their reunion in this comic is quite revealing about the differences between Carol and Walter because of how Walter treats and underestimates Carol throughout their adventure simply because she is a woman.

Carol's aggression is highlighted throughout the comic because they are on a planet inhabited by passive creatures. In juxtaposition to the creatures who call the planet home, Carol is exceedingly aggressive because the aliens live a completely passive life. When Carol protects the aliens from invaders, she does not understand why they do not fight back, just as the inhabitants do not understand why she would fight. Carol's belligerency can be directly compared with Walter because she is the future inheritor of his superpowers. As Carol and Walter fight, their fighting styles are extremely similar; in fact, their fighting skills are so similar that in every panel they are fighting together, they are using exactly the same superpower to fight different bad guys. However, though Carol is able to fly at will, Walter must use boosters to fly. This small difference in power foreshadows Carol's discovery of further hidden powers by the end of their adventure.

It is clear that Carol can compete with Walter on a physically aggressive front. Throughout the beginning of their adventure together Walter suggests that he thinks men are superior to women and more often then not, makes an effort correct or belittle Carol for her femininity by mansplaining.[5] When Walter makes these comments, he clearly does not understand or pick up on Carol's distress. For instance, when Carol and Walter are traveling deeper into the planet to find the antagonist, Walter reassures Carol, "Don't worry about the Scavengers, as long as I'm here, I won't let anything happen to you." In this way, he attempts to stake a kind of ownership over her wellbeing. Carol, lighting the room with her superpowers while he stands and looks heroically at nothing, states "Funny, I was thinking the same thing." Carol's comment goes over Walter's head, and he laughs interpreting the comment as a joke. She responds, "Do these Lady-Biceps look like I'm Lady-Joking?" (Stohl 12). In addition to Carol's physical skills, her aggression is highlighted here by her quick wit to retort disagreeable comments and to stake her own claim over her wellbeing. Though they need each other to accomplish the mission, Carol and Walter argue because of Walter's overt verbal sexism. Unfortunately, Carol must contend with these comments over and over again throughout the narrative. Later as Carol addresses the inhabitants, Walter insists on explaining their objective once again after Carol finishes—a moment that perfectly demonstrates mansplaining alluding to Solnit's anecdote describing her creation of the term in *Men Explain Things to Me*. Carol is clearly perturbed by this and recognizes the case of mansplaining herself: "Still interrupting when he thinks he knows best!" While she respects Walter for the man she knew back on earth in her own experience, she refuses to put up with being belittled and makes sure to push back against his comments, which is clearly perceived by Walter as aggressive.

The *Generations* comics offer a direct comparison of Walter and Carol's personalities and abilities because they are forced to work as a team. Walter and Carol's personalities clash because of Walter's painful shortsightedness when it comes to a woman's strengths—something that comics have struggled with themselves for years now. In this way, this particular *Generations* comic actively works to make a comment about the language of past comics in an attempt to correct it. This comic creates a space for Carol to comment on and correct Walter's outmoded and offensive way of thinking about gender equality. Walter's commitment to stereotypical gender norms is ultimately what leads to his failure at the end of the comic, but also what allows Carol to teach him a lesson about women's aggression and their ability to be more successfully violent than men. In addition to rewriting the language of older comics culture, this also rewrites the past understanding of women's aggression—that "while men are naturally aggressive, women are naturally unaggressive" (Crowley Jack 18). In addition to Carol's willingness to protect the inhabitants of Mydon, fighting alongside Walter shows that Carol is willing to make her own choices and is capable of acting forcefully in response to Walter's negative comments, which continue throughout the narrative until the main antagonist is defeated. When they find Annihilus, Mar-vell attempts to be heroic when he announces: "Allow me to show this villain the proper way to treat a lady!" (Stohl 26). He is overtaken by the villain, and Carol flies in to protect him from what would surely be a deadly blast. In sacrificing herself for Walter, one way that this comic justifies her aggression, Carol finds newfound strength, and she overtakes the villain with her adept fighting abilities and the energy beams that come out of her fists. The villain stands no chance against her kickboxing fighting style combined with the lasers she can shoot from her hands, a much different story from the humiliating defeat that Walter suffers from panels before. The comic ends with Carol flying out of the ship and off into the galaxy, holding Walter in her arms since he can't fly. While Carol's physical victory justifies her superhero status, her moral victory against Walter's sexist conception of women defines where Walter's character comes up short in comparison.

It is Carol's dedication to doing good and her moral ideals that define her in contrast to Walter. Carol's aggression does not stem from being a naturally violent person; instead, she understands who she is (Captain Marvel, Superhero), what she wants (peace), and what she is good at (fighting bad guys). At the beginning of *Captain Marvel: Rise of Alpha Flight*, she says, "What I've realized about myself is pretty simple. . . . It's not that I'm a violent person, it's just that some things really, really need punching. And I am really good at punching things" (Butters 3). Unlike Jen, Carol revels in her abilities so much that she risks being hurt by a nuclear bomb so that she can toss it into space. In the name of traditional representations of aggressive women, Carol addresses and seeks to rewrite gender issues in past comics by confronting Walter about his comments and by demonstrating that her abilities are superior to Walter's. While Walter physically fought villains as a superhero, Carol offers a multifaceted form of aggression that seeks justice beyond the page and into the social sphere of the reader by acknowledging how comics have addressed women in the past through Walter's intent and speech, and by allowing Carol to defeat villains in physical battle on the same panel. Though it took almost four decades for her to take the title of Captain

Marvel, Carol's appropriation of the name signified that comics were ready to take a step forward from a gender exclusive past.

"SHE'S COMPLETELY BROKEN, AND SHE'S STILL COMING"[6]: SURPASSING THE LIMITS OF PHYSICAL AGGRESSION

While Jen and Carol are both violent and physically aggressive, they rarely are shown experiencing it in their own bodies and don't appear to take pleasure in it. In other words, we do not see Jen or Carol kill anyone, and we do not see Jen or Carol's bodies suffer from fighting. And while Jen's body is covered with scars when she is transformed in *Hulk* (2016), these markings only appeared in the comics following Bruce's murder, indicating that these scars are emotional in nature. Representations of Jen and Carol's aggression differs from representations of violence by Laura Kinney. Otherwise known as X-23, Laura has sharp adamantium claws that she can extend from her hands and feet. First appearing in *NYX* #3 in 2004, Laura is a clone made from the Wolverine's—Logan's—DNA in a program attempting to recreate Weapon X. The experiment was a success and Laura was born a clone in a lab that trained her to be a weapon. Laura's upbringing—her training—makes her very different from Jen and Carol, because she did not have access to a genuine childhood and family to inspire her sense of intent, morality, and drive as a superhero.

At the core of her character, Laura simply struggles to retain any sense of humanity, which is apparent through the violent nature of her aggression. Similar to Logan, Laura possesses claws on her hands that rip her opponents to shreds. However, Laura also has access to claws on her feet, which allow her the ability to be more aggressive than even Logan is. In the 2017 series *Generations: Wolverine and All-New Wolverine*, Logan is forced to acknowledge the tactical advantage of Laura's additional claws and her ability to use them. At the beginning of the *Generations* comic, Logan is working on a solo mission when he is ambushed; his attackers are close to defeating him when Laura comes from nowhere and fends them off, allowing Logan to recover and the duo to obtain the upper hand. While observing her fight his attackers, he thinks: "She's not as strong as me. But she's faster. Sharper. She's composed. Doesn't waste a single cut. She's surgical" (Taylor 7). This moment is specifically important because women's aggression has traditionally been understood only in relation to male aggression. Crowley Jack writes that "almost all of what psychologists have thought and have felt about aggression has been shaped by a male perspective. This means that we understand aggression from the point of view of those who have been dominant" (3). In this moment, the reader gets a glimpse into Logan's appreciation for Laura's execution of physical violence. We see this again as the two fight undead ninjas together, when he comes to realize that he's not the true threat when fighting alongside her. In one panel, Logan stabs one person with both claws. In the next panel, Laura stabs and takes out four people using both hands and both feet. The juxtaposition of these two panels is stunning as a demonstration of each of the characters' powers, but the display of Laura's raw power in comparison to Logan's shows exactly how savage and capable of violence she is. When the fight concludes, even Logan is forced to admit that "I was the best there is at what I do . . . At least, I thought I was" (6). Logan and Laura offer a unique comparison because Laura is clearly the better fighter on many levels; not only is she younger, faster, and more tactical, she isn't held back by her humanity as Logan is when she's fighting. Laura's separation from her emotions while fighting is atypical for a female superhero. While characters like Jen depend on the control and restraint of emotions, Laura has been trained to disconnect from her emotions in such an extreme way that she worries she will lose touch with humanity. Laura is not compatible with the stereotype that women are more emotional because she was created to be a humanoid weapon devoid of emotions at all.

In the realm of the comics universe, Laura's ability to look past her emotions when it comes to fighting is a unique representation of femininity. However, like Jen and Carol, Laura also struggles to overcome the weight of gender stereotypes because of the way she dresses. In the *Generations* comic, Logan—who doesn't know that he's Laura's father yet—remarks that he's surprised she didn't choose to wear a dress when Laura decides to wear a pantsuit. She refutes him by speaking about the tactical element of her clothing choice, and proceeds to recommend that he wear the dress because "the matching heels would have accentuated [his] calves" (17). Laura's reasoning contends with a longstanding issue that women have been subjected to in comic books: How is a woman supposed to be able to fight bad guys in a dress and heels? Unlike Carol, who reacts negatively to Walter's suggestions, Logan's comment did not make Laura angry because she is out of touch with gender expectations forced on Jen and Carol.

Laura's displays of violence can be jarring, even inside of the realm of comic books. Laura's surgical execution of violence in the *Generations* comic is staggering because of how much violence Laura is involved in, because of how tactical she is about that violence, and because of how detached she is from that violence. Crowley Jack acknowledges this relationship between violence and gender, noting that "women do resort to physical force, but usually only when hitting back self-defensively against male aggression. They often demand changes and then 'lose it,' with an explosion that simply lets off pressure and then continues that status quo of power in the relationship" (50). In other words, women are only physically violent when retaliating to an attack. This is not the case for Laura, who uses aggression tactically for her own purposes. For instance, after saving Logan from scores of undead ninjas, Laura misses beheading a ninja. While Logan chastises her, she explains that she actually meant to miss and pulls a piece of cloth from the sword that they can use to follow the ninja back to where he came from. This distinct difference between Logan and Laura points directly to a difference in gender—while Logan acts impulsively and ragefully towards his enemies, Laura carefully strategizes each move and uses her physical fighting skills to her own benefit in the long scheme of things.

While Logan is excessively violent in comparison to heroes like Bruce Banner or Walter Lawson, the *Generations* comic departs from even this kind of violence through Laura. When Laura pursues Sabretooth, Logan thinks about how much their perseverance is similar. To his surprise, Laura stabs Sabretooth through the throat with one of her claws, to which Logan thinks "Okay. That's different" (Taylor 28). Logan's surprise demonstrates that Laura departs even from his level of aggression because of her delivery of violence in this moment. All in all, whether it is purposely leaving a survivor in order to track them to their source or stabbing four people at once, Laura does not use violence as a response to overwhelming emotion or a crossing of boundaries; rather, she owns violence and tactics as a method to achieve an end and does it better than the very person she was cloned from.

CONCLUSION

Jen Walters, Carol Danvers, and Laura Kinney pose as interesting subjects through the lens of women's aggression because their superpowers were adapted from preexisting male characters. Traditionally, the superpowers of Bruce Banner, Walter Lawson, and Logan have been the locus of masculinity for these male characters because these powers focus on violence; between Bruce's incidents, Walter's use of his powers to establish patriarchal idealism and peace, and Logan's violence that can only be characterized as animalistic, these men are characterized by violence that is not uncommon of superheroes. Their female counterparts, on the other hand, do not have the freedom to use their powers without repercussion, and must use these superpowers through the lens of what is acceptable by society—Jen must contain her rage to avoid transformation and to continue on with her life, and Carol and Laura have to be subjected to gender stereotypes in order to justify their aggression on the page. However, these women overcome barriers of society and stereotypes through a steadfast intent and drive to do good or to achieve a means to an end.

In a very basic understanding of aggression, these women have used varying forms of force to create change. But in many ways, they've operated to make bigger changes socially than their super-male counterparts by commenting on past and present social conversations started by comic books. What's special about these female characters is that they do the same things—and more—than their male counterparts in the body they were written in. In addition, because these characters are replicas—or in Laura's case, a clone—of their male counter parts, they are able to make social commentary about larger issues that comic books have sustained in the past, such as in the Captain Marvel *Generations* issue. While the core marketing strategy of these gender-benders was to offer a more inclusive market for readers and to therefore deepen Marvel's pockets, these characters stand out because they are able to be a direct comparison to their male counterparts, which opens space for gender discussion. On a broader spectrum, these comics that feature female characters add to the overall conversation about representations of aggression, but also allow readers of all ages and genders to better understand such complex concepts as violence, aggression, and inner strength. By overcoming the barriers of femininity and exacting aggression in their own ways, Jen, Carol, and Laura create new boundaries, examples, and representations of women's aggression.

Notes

1. Mariko Tamaki, (w.) and Nico Leon (p.), "Deconstructed: Part Five" *Hulk* #5 (New York: Marvel Comics, 2016), 22.

2. One of the most successful Marvel comic book story lines to date, *Civil War II* is an event that gathered many of Marvel's superheroes and allegorized the debate between determinism and free will in the realm of superheroes. One of the main points of division during this event was how to address destructive events that Ulysses—an Inhuman who could see the future—had seen but had not happened yet. One day Ulysses has a vision that Bruce will become the Hulk and destroy all superheroes. When confronting Bruce about his secret experiments to rid himself of the Hulk, Hawkeye shoots Bruce and kills him to prevent Ulysses's vision from coming to fruition.

3. Tara Butters (w.) and Michele Fazekas (pi.), "Rise of Alpha Flight," *Captain Marvel* (New York: Marvel Comics), 2016.

4. Eric Diaz, "How Carol Danvers Became CAPTAIN MARVEL After 45 Years."

5. Coined by Rebecca Solnit in her book *Men Explain Things to Me*, "mansplaining" is when a man explains something to a woman unnecessarily in an "overconfident" and "clueless" manner.

6. Tom Taylor (w.) and Jorge Molina (a.), *Generations: Wolverine & All-New Wolverine*, 2017, 28.

Works Cited

Bundel, Ani. "Marvel's New 'Captain Marvel' Isn't Trailblazing like 'Wonder Woman'—But It's Still a Lot of Fun." *NBC News*, March 9, 2019. https://www.nbcnews.com/think/opinion/marvel-s-new-captain-marvel-isn-t-trailblazing-wonder-woman-ncna981276.

Butters, Tara (w.), and Michele Fazekas (p.). "Rise of Alpha Flight," *Captain Marvel* (2016). Yew York: Marvel Comics, 2016.

Claremont, Chris (w.), and John Byrne (a.). *Civil War II*. New York: Marvel Comics, 2015.

Claremont, Chris (w.), and John Byrne (a.). "Snowfire." In *Iron Fist* #14. New York: Marvel Comics, 1977.

Crowley Jack, Dana. *Behind the Mask: Destruction and Creativity in Women's Aggression*. Cambridge, MA: Harvard University Press, 1999.

Diaz, Eric. "How Carol Danvers Became CAPTAIN MARVEL After 45 Years." *Nerdist*, Feb. 13, 2019. https://nerdist.com/article/how-carol-danvers-became-captain-marvel-after-45-years/.

Jones, Gerard. *Killing Monsters: Our Children's Need for Fantasy, Heroism, and Make Believe Violence*. New York: Basic Books, 2002.

Lavin, Maud. *Push Comes to Shove: New Images of Aggressive Women*. Cambridge, MA: MIT Press, 2010.

Lee, Stan (w.), and John Buscema (p.). "The She-Hulk Lives." In *The Savage She-Hulk* #1. New York: Marvel Comics, 1980.

Marnell, Blair. "Supergirl Origins and Evolutions." SuperHeroHype.com, Oct. 26, 2015. https://www.superherohype.com/features/356735-supergirl-origins-and-evolutions-2.

Michael Bendis, Brian (w.), and Olivier Coipel (a.). "Civil War II." In *Civil War II*. New York: Marvel Comics, 2016.

Mitchell, J. P., and J. D. George. "What do Superman, Captain America, and Spiderman have in Common? The Case for Comics Books." *Gifted Education International* 11, no. 2 (1996): 91–94.

Quesada, Joe (w.), and Joshua Middleton (a.). "Wannabe: Part Three." In *NYX*. New York: Marvel Comics, 2004.

Solnit, Rebecca. *Men Explain Things to Me*. Chicago: Haymarket Books, 2014.

Stohl, Margaret (w.), and David Nakayama (p.). *Generations: Captain Marvel & Captain Mar-vell*. New York: Marvel Comics, 2017.

Tamaki, Mariko (w.), and Nico Leon (p.). "Deconstructed: Part One," *Hulk* #1. New York: Marvel Comics, 2016.

Tamaki, Mariko (w.), and Nico Leon (p.). "Deconstructed: Part Three," *Hulk* #3. New York: Marvel Comics, 2016.

Tamaki, Mariko (w.), and Nico Leon (p.). "Deconstructed: Part Five" *Hulk* #5. New York: Marvel Comics, 2016.

Tamaki, Mariko (w.), and Nico Leon (p.). "Deconstructed: Part Six" *Hulk* #6. New York: Marvel Comics, 2016.

Taylor, Tom (w.), and Jorge Molina (a.). *Generations: Wolverine & All-New Wolverine*. New York: Marvel Comics, 2017.

9

MALE AUTHORITY AGAINST FEMALE BODIES
Gender, Sexuality and Violence in Comics

ELISABETTA DI MINICO

This project has received funding from the European Union's Horizon 2020 research and innovation program under the Marie Skłodowska-Curie grant agreement No 847635.

The depiction of women in comics is a complicated issue because female characters' representation is not univocal and fixed, neither temporally nor geographically, neither physically nor conceptually. Women can be strong and indomitable as well as hypersexualized. They can be relegated into domesticity, dreaming of a perfect married life, or they can occupy position of power. Women can be damsels in distress, sidekicks, superheroines, girlfriends, wives, lovers, and villains. They can be what they want or what men want them to be. Or they can be in the middle, fighting to find their place and their voices in their stories. This essay briefly analyzes how gender issues and violence against women are presented in superhero comics.

Comics devoted to superheroes are one of the most popular genres of the ninth art and they describe realities where heroic characters, thanks to superpowers such as "extraordinary abilities, advanced technology, or highly developed physical, mental, or mystical skills" (Coogan 30), pursue fundamental and selfless missions against vicious and heartless villains. These worlds are extremely exaggerated and theatrical: reshaping "ancient myths and folklore" (Gavaler 15), superheroes and villains (of which, according to Amanda Shendruk, almost 80 percent are male) maximize human emotions, ideals, and faults, often showing epic battles between good and evil, between light and darkness. In this scenario, violent events and accidents resulting from these fights are generally central and inevitable elements of the plot and, whether weak, enhanced, discordant, obedient, or rebellious, the characters have to deal with this violence, bear it, overcome it, or succumb to it.

Comics' fictional social portraits are also compelling from a gender studies perspective because these realities defined by overemphasized violence, superhumanism, and hypermasculinity unavoidably influence and damage the construction of women's identity, images, and roles in society. In fiction and in daily life, women can be subjected to several kinds of violence: if psychophysical abuse, rape, and femicide are the most blatant, tangible, and dangerous examples, there are many other common and only apparently less striking methods and tendencies that support misogynistic and patriarchal systems, such as sexist language and humor, sexual objectification, aesthetic prejudices, conservative moral order, control, humiliation, depreciation, domestication, and bias. With the hope of also reflecting on these prejudices, I analyze the rhetoric, and the actions promoting the marginalization of and abuse against women in reality, as well as the linguistic, cultural, sexual, and physical representation of women in comics, by focusing on suitable and prominent titles, mostly from the two major comic books publishers, Marvel and DC, including *Avengers*, *Batman*, *Green Lantern*, *Spider-Man*, *Watchmen*, *Wonder Woman*, and *X-Men*, among others.

BETWEEN REVEALING COSTUMES, INDOMITABLE POWERS AND DIMINISHING PREJUDICES: WOMEN IN COMICS

It is not true that women in comics only occupy supporting roles or that they are only stereotyped and objectified. Women represent just 15 to 25 percent of comic characters (Shendruk), but, in this small percentage, there are many superheroines and female figures who are perfectly able to compete in strength, courage, intelligence, and determination with their male counterparts.

Just think about the most celebrated woman in comics history and one of the most impressive feminist icons of popular culture: Wonder Woman. A mighty Amazon and the daughter of Queen Hippolyta, Diana was created by psychologist William Moulton Marston and artist Harry G. Peter in the 1940s. In a time when many women's rights were still to be recognized, Marston imagined a strong, independent, resourceful, and educated female superhero, communicating to American society new gender roles and attacking patriarchal themes and systems. According to Marston, quoted by Jill Lepore, Diana is "a psychological propaganda for the new type of woman who should, I believe, rule the world" (VII). Promoting gender equality in real life while fighting villains in fictional worlds, Wonder Woman was and still is a concrete sociopolitical *medium* for emancipation, as Lepore suggests: "Wonder Woman was a product of the suffragist, feminist, and birth control movements of the 1900s and 1910s and became a source of the women's liberation and feminist movements of the 1960s and 1970s" (296). She supports justice and rights and, paraphrasing Simone de Beauvoir, rejects the idea that women are simply sexual and submissive objects, an inessential "other" compared to the "subject" and the "absolute" represented by men (6). Despite controversial details, such as the bondage cliché, the hypersexualization, and the occasional depowering of her body,[1] Diana is a princess that doesn't need to be saved. On the contrary, she often saves her lover, Army officer Steve Trevor, and many women from dangerous and generally sexist incidents or menaces, trying to empower women to look after themselves and to discover their own physical, sociopolitical, and economic strengths. In *Wonder Woman* #5 (1943), for example, Mars, the war god, wants to stop the emancipation that women are reaching during World War II and uses mad scientist Dr. Psycho's deception to spread misogynistic speeches against women's freedom. According to the god, in fact, if women gain power, "*THEY'LL ESCAPE MAN'S DOMINATION COMPLETELY*," "*THEY WILL ACHIEVE A HORRIBLE INDEPENDENCE*," and "*PUT AN END TO WAR*" (2), not only showing gender equality as a threat to patriarchy, but also tracing a direct connection between war and hypermasculinity. Wonder Woman stops Dr. Psycho, who is also an abusive husband, and ultimately reminds women that man have no power except what women give them. "Girls" can fight against male domination and be independent, and, in wartime, they are even perfectly able to defend their nation: "*GET STRONG! EARN YOUR OWN LIVING—JOIN THE WAACS OR WAVES*[2] *AND FIGHTS FOR YOUR COUNTRY! REMEMBER THE BETTER YOU CAN FIGHT THE LESS YOU'LL HAVE TO!*" (16). In *Wonder Woman* #13 (1945), Diana helps the Daughters of Venus, a female community living in Eveland, a sunken Garden of Eden beneath Antarctica, to defeat the brutal Seal Men, eager to enslave them. In the end, the women thank Wonder Woman for saving them, but the superheroine proudly responds: "YOU SAVED YOURSELVES. I ONLY SHOW THAT YOU COULD" (11). As Mitra Emad notices, "The fate of most women in comics was dependent upon the male heroes not only to rescue them, but to give them a sense of purpose. They were powerless without a man" (996). Wonder Woman, instead, shows readers that women are not simply men's commodities or subordinates. They are naturally strong. They can oppose violence, submission, and prejudices, and demand sociopolitical, economic, and cultural equality. Diana's wonderful abilities are divine, but the superheroine teaches us that every woman possesses indomitable powers. According to Gloria Steinem, Wonder Woman's lesson is "that each of us might have unknown powers within us, if we only believe and practice them" (7).

Diana is not alone: she is one of the many powerful women in the comics world, such as Marla Drake, Mary Batson, Kara Zor-El, Barbara Gordon, Jean Grey, Natasha Romanoff, and Carol Danvers. First appearing in 1941, Sunday newspaper comic strip character Miss Fury, alter ego of Marla Drake, fearlessly opposes criminals, including mad scientist Diman Saraf and evil Nazis, as Erika von Kampf. Miss Fury is a crucial character for the history of female superheroes because she is one of the first female fighters of the ninth art and also the first superheroine created, written, and drawn by a woman, cartoonist June "Tarpé" Mills, who published her work under a "sexually ambiguous name" (Madrid 10) to suggest that the author was a man. Not only did the Miss Fury character have a secret identity, but Miss Fury's creator in real life was initially forced to hide herself to avoid misogynistic prejudice against the title. Appearing for the first time in *Captain Marvel Adventures* #18 (1942), Mary Batson, also known as Mary Marvel, is the twin sister of Billy Batson, aka Shazam/Captain Marvel,[3] and one of the first female counterparts of a tremendously popular superhero. Kara Zor-El, aka Supergirl, is a Kryptonian and invulnerable superheroine who first appeared in *Supeman* #123 (1958) and who can compete in power and skills with her cousin, the Man of Steel himself. Many fearless women have worn the Batgirl costume, including Betty Kane, Cassandra Cain, and Stephanie Brown. The most popular and iconic alter ego of the renowned superheroine is Barbara Gordon, who held this role from 1967 to 1988. A brilliant "librarian with a PhD and without superstrength, relying on her brain, martial arts training, and gadgetry to fight crime" (Cocca 17), Barbara Gordon perfectly embodies empowerment and feminist values and was ranked seventeenth in the "Top 100 Comic Book Heroes" of the ING chart. First appearing in *X-Men* #1 (1963), Jean Grey, the first woman on the X-Men team, possesses outstanding telekinetic and telepathic powers, and is one of the strongest mutants in the world, while former Russian spy and later S.H.I.E.L.D. agent and member of the Avengers, the Black Widow, alter ego of Natasha Romanoff, is biotechnologically enhanced and extremely intelligent. First appeared in *Tales of Suspense* #52 (1964), she is an expert martial artist and tactician, agile, cold-blooded, and lethal. An officer in the US Air Force, Carol Danvers, who made her first appearance in *Marvel Super-Heroes* #13 (1968), has her most notable alter egos in Ms. Marvel and Capitan Marvel. She is one of the most powerful Avengers, and possibly the strongest Marvel superheroine: she can fly, she has superhuman strength and speed, she can absorb and release energy, and she possesses a "seventh sense," a sort of precognitive ability.

Moreover, several female superheroes are extremely significant not only for being powerful women but also because they embrace racial, ethnic, and sexual otherness and points of view. "X-Woman" Ororo Monroe, aka Storm, who first appeared in *Giant Size X-Men* #1 (1975), is a Kenyan American mutant able to control weather, and is one of the first female and Black leaders of comics history: she charismatically incarnates antipatriarchal and antiracist values. Shapeshifter Mystique, whose first appearance was in *Ms. Marvel* #16 (1978), is a conflicted character, often represented as a mutant supervillain, who embodies queerness and gender fluidity. Sexually free and aware, she can become a man, she is bisexual and, together with her lover Destiny, she raised another strong superhero: Rogue. First appeared in *Vengeance* #1 (2011), America Chavez, aka Miss America, can fly and travel through multiverse and other realities, has superhuman strength and speed, and can project a devastating star blast. Moreover, she is also the first Latin American female and lesbian character to have her own series. Pakistani American Kamala Khan, who first appeared in *Captain Marvel* #14 (2013), is the new Ms. Marvel. As a smart and adventurous teenager, a geek, and a religious person in her own way, she can be considered a young but promising Muslim feminist (Gibson 23–45): Kamala respects her family and her family's values and legacy, but she is also eager to write her own path, supporting dialogue and inclusion between different realities and traditions.

This short list shows extraordinary and resourceful female superheroes, incarnations of otherness and freedom that are normally resilient, independent, and emancipated. But even the strongest and the mightiest ones can be subjected to hypersexualization, commodification, disempowerment, and diminishment, reflecting masculine canons of beauty and serving male power interests. In the darkest backgrounds, women and superheroines have to face not only brutal enemies, but also limiting stereotypes, sexist oppression, and gender-based violence. In comics and, sadly, in reality, abuse doesn't directly start from physical harassment, but originates from cultural and linguistic domination of masculine myths and from distorted, idealized, and sexualized representation of women's identities and bodies. Public commodification and private stigmatization and repression of female figures are in themselves forms of societal and psychological violence, and they also represent a dangerous substratum from which physical abuse and aggression toward women can be developed.

Language and feminine beauty ideals (clearly based on heteronormative views) can become patriarchal power structures employed to support the (de)construction of female gender, indoctrinating individuals and imposing and justifying the control of women and their marginalization though the repetition of misogynistic and sexist stereotypes and actions until they are accepted by the majority of the population, even by the oppressed subjects. In fact, when the process is achieved, women too are forced to speak and interiorize the dominant language and the cultural tendencies that prescribe they be beautiful and caring sexual objects, that primarily describes them as wives and mothers, that presents them as less powerful and intelligent than men, less able to fulfill some tasks. Many comics display feminine clichés, where women and superwomen occupy subordinate roles and predetermined spaces, performing stereotyped jobs and talking or worrying about love, beauty, and fashion. Almighty Wonder Women, for example, joyfully accepts her position as the secretary of the Justice Society of America in *All-Star Comics* #13 (1942), while, in the first years of the *X-Men* series, Jean Grey is often showed cooking, nursing, or sewing, despite being Charles Xavier's most trusted and powerful pupil.

While superheroes often avoid serious relationships, many superheroes' love interests are almost obsessed with love and marriage. Owl Girl, Bulletgirl, Rocketgirl, Doll Girl, and many characters from the Golden Age of Comics, which went from the 1930s to the 1950s, even oppose crime and evil not for a sense of justice but to "prove their love for their boyfriends" (Madrid 14). Sometimes, female characters directly quarrel and fight to gain the affection of their beloved superheroes, as Lois Lane and Lana Lang do in order to attract Superman's attention and feelings during the 1950s and 1960s. According to Anthony Mills, sweet and docile Lana Lang was created in 1950 "to serve primarily as Lois's rival.... By November 1960, the sole motivation for Lois and Lana was to show which of them could be a better housewife for Superman" (35). When superheroines challenge each other for love, they also forget their missions. In *The Brave and the Bold* #78 (1955), Wonder Woman and Batgirl try to win Batman's heart with embarrassing declarations, grand gestures, and blatant competition, sculpting the Dark Knight's statues, and offending each other with mean insults such as "MASKED SORCERESS," "MUSCLE-BOUND WITCH," and "UNHIP CHICK" (6). After Marston's death in 1947, even Wonder Woman, a liberating icon for both sexes who, in the 1940s, fostered the success of other strong and smart female characters such as Miss Fury, Mysta of the Moon, and Liberty Bell, lost her revolutionary traits for decades, becoming a more submissive, fragile, and, for a time, depowered character. From the late 1940s into the 1950s, real patriarchal power attacked the independence that women obtained during the war years, and comics too corroborated their return into domesticity by presenting "more strictly binary, unequal, and supposedly 'natural' gender roles" (Cocca 8).

During the Silver Age, until the late 1960s, women didn't reach a real space for empowerment and autonomy in the comics narrative. It is sadly ironic, for example, that the only woman of the Fantastic Four,[4] Sue Storm, possesses the power of invisibility. For years after the creation of the team in 1961, she was relegated to the role of the beautiful and nurturing subordinate with a preference for domestic work. In *The Fantastic Four* #14 (1963), for example, the group leader and Sue's future husband Reed Richards, aka Mister Fantastic, asks Sue to silently do the housecleaning, for which she has just volunteered. In the meantime, he is lying on the couch and is surrounded by a sleepy Thing and curled up Torch.

During the Bronze Age of Comics from the 1970s to the 1980s, things started to change, largely thanks to the protests of 1968 and the second wave of feminism. Reflecting the sociopolitical changes of the time, during the 1970s minorities and women were substantially empowered in the comics world, as proved, for example, by Chris Claremont's new and renewed female mutant characters, such as, just to quote few names, Rogue, Kitty Pryde, Psylocke, Phoenix, Rachel Summers, and Mystique. These figures, often also expressions of racial, cultural, sexual, and economic otherness, smashed the limited and stereotyped portrayal of women in comics and supported the diffusion of strong female characters that can face and bear any enemy and any task. During the Dark Age or Modern Age of comics from the late 1980s to 2000s, there was a revival of the "binary representation on gender," with "hypermuscular man and hypersexualized women" (Cocca 11). Violence was visually and conceptually exalted, and sex and sexuality were deeply spectacularized. Superwomen were both powerful and objectified. Supported by new feminist waves and sociopolitical movements, the last two decades are witnessing an always more positive characterization not only of women, but also of sexual, racial/ethnic, religious, and physical diversity, as the characters Kamala Khan and America Chavez embody, and a "decrease in the underrepresentation, sexualization, and objectification of female characters" (Cocca 14). Nevertheless, decrease doesn't mean erasure, and many disturbing issues still remain unsolved, such as the dominance of male and white protagonists, and the latent eroticization, debasement, and stereotyping of women: despite being strong and bright superheroines who dynamically fight crime, women can still be depowered and demeaned by male and patronizing authority.

According to Shendruk, who analyzes the gender representation of 34,476 comic book characters, superheroines are "more often given non-physical, thought-induced abilities," such as intellect, telepathy, precognition, and emotion control. While male superheroes tend to possess physical powers as strength, stamina, and invulnerability, female superheroes have more light capacities, such as agility or flight. To make matters worse, even gendered code names show a sexist tendency: while 30.9 percent of superheroes have the word "man" in their names and only 5.1 percent "boy," 12.6 percent of superheorines are called the minimizing term "girl," and just 5.7 percent of them are "woman" (Shendruk).

The male gaze dominates comic world, and not only on the inked pages. Most of the workers in comics are male, most of the readers of superhero comics are men,[5] and the majority of the portrayed characters are men. Thus, the visual representation of women's bodies is tendentially based on male fantasies and fears. Men are not generally depicted as sexual objects. It is true that most superheroes and villains are hypermuscular and dressed in close-fitting suits, but even the handsomest are rarely portrayed in explicit and eroticized ways or positions. Moreover, there are also many overweight, beastly, repulsive, gigantic, disfigured, or unpleasant male characters that do not reflect the classical aesthetic canons of beauty, proportion, and harmony, such as Kingpin, Hulk, the Thing, Hellboy, Beak, Beast, Nightcrawler, Deadpool, Doctor Doom, Penguin, Two-Face, Thanos, Toad, and Colossus. Instead, women in comics, especially superheroines, are regularly depicted as beautiful, thin, tall, and busty figures with "anatomically impossible proportions" (Cocca 11). There are, of course, relevant exceptions, including Aunt May, Cassandra Nova, Big Bertha, Faith, Atom Eve, Callisto, Sin, Dorothy Spinner, and Elastic Girl, but the general trend is to create idealized female figures that do not recognize and reflect women's diversity, and that propose unrealistic models of female physicality.

The costumes of many superheroines leave almost nothing to imagination: they often wear leotards with deep necklines, very short skirts, tight pants, tops that look more like bras, and high heels. Emma Frost's white lingerie, Psylocke's ninja bathing suit, Catwoman's leather catsuit, and Power Girl's costume with a big hole right on her chest are iconic and yet disturbing examples of this tendency. Besides revealing clothes, superwomen are also constantly presented in sensual and sexist points of view or poses. Describing their anomalous postures, Carolyn Cocca uses the expression "broke back pose": women are frequently showed "unnaturally twisted and arched to display all of their curves in front and back simultaneously. One's back would have to be broken to contort in such a way" (12). Anatomy takes second place behind the necessity to eroticize the female figure for the pleasure of the male gaze. Just to report one awful example, when gigantic mutant villain Blob eats size-shifting superheroine Wasp in *Ultimatum* #2 (2009), the body of the woman is showed from a strange angle that still emphasizes her breasts.

To underline this deceptive representation of women, a satirical Tumblr page called *The Hawkeye Initiative* was created in 2012, thanks to the support and instruction of comic artists Noelle Stevenson and Blue: its aim is to replace female characters in extremely contorted or sexy poses with fan art of the male superhero Hawkeye doing the same thing, usually with the same dress. The result is that the strict contrast between male and female treatment is distinctly visible and risible. While it appears clear that the male superhero is in a strange, almost ridiculous position, for women superheroes it seems ordinary and can even go unnoticed, because we are accustomed to these portrayals that modeling female subjects as sexual objects.

Analyzing the visual pleasure in cinema, Laura Mulvey explains that women are generally "displayed as sexual objects" (809), and that "the image of woman as (passive) raw material for the (active) gaze of man" (815) reinforces patriarchal ideology and conservative fantasies of domination. The inaccurate and sometimes outrageous treatment of female bodies shows us that women are objectified and diminished not only for the male gaze, but also because of the male authority. Women are generally eroticized, even when not necessary, and narratives featuring women are obsessed with female shapes, stereotypes, and sexuality. Female characters can be abused and humiliated, but they usually still need to "produce" beauty, sensuality, and excitement. Despite their repression, female bodies are vehicles of erotic and social power: controlling them is a way to limit men's fear of castration and the threat of male authority debasement correlated to it. This is the reason why superwomen, regardless of their wonderful abilities, are still often constructed as sexual fantasies: shaping their bodies as sensual mirages makes the female characters appear less threatening to manhood and comfortingly useful from an erotic point of view. The gaze of male creators, readers, and fictional characters controls the female body to the point of transforming it into fetish, and, as Mulvey affirms, fetish is something "reassuring rather than dangerous" (811). This approach to eroticism also negatively influences women's sexual liberation and awareness because women remain chained to male desire and expectation without actually experimenting and emphasizing the strength of their bodies, a strength that could also come from sexual consciousness and independence. While generally superheroines are not shown as very sexually active and they do not exploit their bodies to manipulate enemies, villainesses such as Emma Frost and Mystique are often characterized by extreme sexual freedom or by an explicit use of their appearance to control their opponents. When Jean Grey goes mad and becomes Dark Phoenix in the eponymous 1980 saga, a progressive sexual awakening parallels her evil transformation. When men do not control female sexuality, female sexuality becomes dangerous. The problem, then, is not eroticism in itself, but the male control that it often implies.

FROM DISEMPOWERMENT TO VIOLENCE: TALES OF PATRIARCHAL METHODS AND SYSTEMS

As Judith Butler suggests, the body can be interpreted as a "passive medium on which cultural meanings are inscribed" (8): women's roles, images, and identities are not determined by nature or biology, but are subjected to culture, stereotypes, and tradition, constructed by social and political needs. This means that in societies with patriarchal tendencies, both fictional and real, women's lives are influenced and even affected by "masculinist domination" (Butler 141). In these contexts, women can be victims both of power as sociopolitical subjects representing otherness and of male oppression as sexual objects to conquer and submit.

The list of abused, traumatized, and murdered women in comics is long. The characterization of male figures, both good and evil, usually includes a hypermasculinity that exalts strength, control, power, and fantasies of submission and domination. Superheroes generally don't use brutal violence against women, but they are not immune to sexist language and behavior. Especially in the Golden and Silver Age of Comics, several superheroes diminish or even hit their female partners, and make jokes about women's bad habits and inferiority. Superman, for example, generally uses a paternalistic approach with Lois Lane, sometimes even employing harassing actions, which were not perceived as wrong in the 1960s: he erases Lois's memory with a kiss to cover up his super-identity, he gives her superpowers just to show how unbearable they are for a woman, and, in *Superman's Girlfriend, Lois Lane* #14 (1960), he punishes Lois with a "WELL-DESERVED SPANKING" (8) using a Superman robotic replica because the woman enters into the Fortress of Solitude, plotting to convince the "last son of Krypton" to marry her. In exceptional cases, superheroes can cross the line and commit reprehensible gender-based violence. In *Avengers* #213 (1981), for example, Dr. Hank Pym, under the identity of Yellowjacket,[6] ferociously slaps his wife Janet van Dyne, aka the Wasp. Writer Mark Millar exaggerated his violent behavior in *The Ultimates* #6 (2002): Pym, during an argument, psychophysically abuses Jan and even tries to kill his shrunken wife in horrific scenes using bug spray and an army of ants. And while the insects are ready to assault Jan, he says to his frightened wife, "You shouldn't have made me look ***small***," justifying his actions with a twisted excuse that recalls the fear of castration discussed above. Jan's independence and her firmness in the discussion are interpreted by Pym as an attack against his masculinity, as an attempt to undermine his power and his control, generating an unstoppable desire of destruction, "because destruction is the most reassuring form of possession" (Battaglia 182).

When they deal with women, villains often interpret the glorification of their forcefulness as sexual subjugation and assault. Sometimes, their actions also show the desire to punish a male superhero by killing or brutalizing "his" woman, as though she is a male possession. This trend affects the comic world with what Gail Simone called "Women in Refrigerators Syndrome." According to Simone, there is a dangerous exploitation of death, rape, or injury of female characters in stories starring superheroes and, even for such conflicting worlds, this treatment is to be considered unfairly patriarchal because gender-based violence is often exploited as a plot device to force the male protagonists to grow, to face their fears, to add new reasons to their fights, and to enhance their morale. Women can sadly be helpless narrative tools to be used to deepen the male superhero's story and mission.

Simone's provocative "illness" is inspired by the murder of Alex DeWitt, the girlfriend of Kyle Rayner/Green Lantern. In *Green Lantern* #54 (1994), the smart, independent, and combative photojournalist is killed, dismembered, and literally stuffed into a refrigerator by sadistic villain Major Force, for no other reason than to hurt the superhero.

Alex is a notable name in a long list of killed and abused girlfriends, wives, and love interests that also includes Gwen Stacy, the girlfriend of Spider-Man/Peter Parker. His archenemy Green Goblin kills Stacy in *The Amazing Spider-Man* #121 (1973), kidnapping her and throwing her off a bridge. Spider-Man tries to save Gwen, but it is not simply too late: according to Gerry Conway, the author of this dramatic story arc, the superhero is "partly responsible for her death" (3), since he inadvertently causes a mortal neck injury to his girlfriend while stopping her with his webs. Gwen's murder is a traumatic and painful moment for Peter. Until this point, despite the many tragedies and the many obstacles in his life, Spider-Man has always faced evil with a smile. Now, he is brokenhearted and wishes for a bloody revenge. Saying goodbye to Gwen is an indelible wound and the grief forces Peter to mature and become more adult, transforming a story about adolescent alienation into "a mirror to a generation confronting its unspoken fear of life's futility" (Conway 4). This tragedy was a pivotal moment in comics history, "the end of innocence for the series and the superhero genre in general, a time when a defeated hero could not save the girl, when fantasy merged uncomfortably with reality, and mortality finally visited the world of comics"

(Blumberg). Conway directly links this fictional loss of innocence with "the loss of innocence in society as a whole" (4): superheroes have their limits, like US national power. Gwen became the allegory of this innocence, the sacrificial lamb that accidentally fostered the passage between the lighthearted Silver Age and the more conflicted and sociopolitically aware Bronze Age, also reflecting the real tumultuous historical background in which America faced the Vietnam War, Watergate, atomic nightmares, and severe social contrasts. The most disturbing detail of this story arc is that the reasons behind Gwen's death were partially misogynistic. Gwen is a good, smart, and educated young woman, and the only possible end for her relationship with Peter would have been marriage, but the creators didn't believe that this path would have been right for the superhero's characterization (Blumberg) as they wanted new love adventures for Spider-Man. Thus, they decided to kill Gwen off. Because it was not the right time to be a wife, she had to die.

Another surprising and upsetting episode of violence against women is perpetrated on Barbara Gordon, daughter of Commissioner Gordon, by Joker in *Batman: The Killing Joke* (1988). Joker wants to prove that "ALL IT TAKES IS **ONE BAD DAY** TO REDUCE THE **SANEST MAN ALIVE** TO LUNACY." He shoots Barbara, leaving her paralyzed, and, while she is still in pain, undresses her and takes nude pictures of her. It is disturbing that "the whole point of what is done to Barbara is to explore how her father and Batman react to it and feel about it" (Cocca 65). She is just a *medium*. Similar to what happened to Gwen Stacy, Barbara's suffering and abuse are justified only in the perspective of exalting the moral firmness of the male characters.

The sexualized violence against Barbara reminds us that many comics also depict the sensitive issue of sexual abuse and rape, and that several villains or antiheroes are rapists or harassers. In the Wonder Woman universe, Amazons are raped and enslaved by Hercules and his men. Like many other women and men, Jessica Jones is mind-controlled by Purple Man. Psychologically tortured for months and initially unable to resist the manipulation of the villain, she is sexually abused and forced to have intercourse against her will in *Alias* #24–28 (2003). Felicia Hardy/Black Cat is raped by her college boyfriend Ryan and drugged and abused by Garrison Klum, a disturbed and perverse mutant and drug dealer in *Spider-Man/Black Cat: The Evil That Men Do* (2002–2006). One of the most shocking episodes of violence against women is the attempted rape of Sally Jupiter/Silk Spectre by Edward Morgan Blake/the Comedian in *Watchmen* #2 (1986). Silk Spectre and the Comedian are teammates: they are both part of the Minutemen, the principal superheroes group of the 1940s in the *Watchmen* timeline. As with many other Alan Moore's characters, the Comedian is not an impeccable superhero; he is presented more as a negative hero/antihero: violent, rude, and broken. The scene in which he tries to rape Sally is visually brutal and linguistically misogynistic. The Comedian beats the woman and justifies his actions through victim blaming and rape myths: since she is wearing a sensual and revealing costume, Sally is asking for sex, and her refusal secretly means that she wants it but is playing hard to get. For the offender, no means yes. Silk Spectre is saved by fellow Minuteman Hooded Justice, but neither is her helper compassionate. After ruthlessly pushing the Comedian away, Hooded Justice commands Sally to "GET UP . . . AND, FOR GOD'S SAKE, **COVER**" herself (8), implying that her bloodstained and forcibly undressed body is shameful. In *Watchmen* #1 (1986), even vigilante Rorschach judges Comedian's crimes, including Sally's attempted rape, as "MORAL LAPSES" (21), suggesting that "one bad deed, no matter how heinous, can't remove one's status as a moral agent" (Held 31), without taking into account the rights and the feelings of the victim. This is a cruel example of the cult of masculinity and the purity myth that aims to limit or nullify female sexuality and sexual awareness, strengthening a rape culture in which "men are expected to be sexually aggressive and women passive" (Phillips 11). In this way, as Jessica Valenti argues, sex is transformed into an act of persuasion and domination: "When women's sexuality is imagined to be passive or dirty, it also means that men's sexuality is automatically positioned as aggressive and right—no matter what form it takes. And when one of the conditions of masculinity, a concept that is already so fragile in men's minds, is that men dissociate from women and prove their manliness through aggression, we're encouraging a culture of violence and sexuality that's detrimental to both men and women" (172).

In this vision, feminine bodies are like territories to be invaded, governed, and exploited to prove attackers' supremacy against women and/or the enmity they symbolize. Aggressors exploit sexual abuse in order to impose oppressive gender roles and to exalt patriarchal dominion on bodies that are perceived as discordant, not obedient, or threatening. The aim of violence is to hurt, humiliate, and break individuals, as Felicia Hardy says to Matt Murdock in *Spider-Man/Black Cat: The Evil That Men Do* #4 (2006), giving an incisive explanation of rape and its reasons:

I'M TALKING ABOUT SOMEONE WHO **FORCES** HIMSELF INTO YOU, AGAINST YOUR **WILL**. AND THE WHOLE TIME, YOU KNOW HE'S NOT DOING IT BECAUSE HE **WANTS** YOU. HE'S DOING IT TO **HURT** YOU. HE'S DOING IT BECAUSE HE WANTS YOU TO KNOW HOW **POWERLESS** YOU ARE.

HE'S DOING IT TO TAKE AWAY EVERYTHING GOOD AND POSITIVE YOU EVER FELT ABOUT YOURSELF. HE'S DOING IT TO **HUMILIATE** YOU. HE'S DOING IT TO BREAK YOU.

To make things worse, at times victims also have to deal with the diminishment of their trauma. Besides an aged and lonely Silk Spectre that minimizes her trauma because it happened decades ago, another example of this tendency is in *Avengers* #200 (1980). To celebrate the milestone, it was decided that Ms. Marvel would have a baby, but the imagined story arc for this special issue is absurdly heinous. Carol is abducted, brought to Limbo, brainwashed, and impregnated by Marcus Immortus, the unhappy son of Avengers' archenemy Immortus. Back on Earth, an oblivious Ms. Marvel suddenly gives birth to a baby boy after a three-day pregnancy. The newborn rapidly grows into an adult man, and we discover that he is the conscious reincarnation of his rapist father who wanted to escape from Limbo, implanting his essence into Ms. Marvel. After causing a catastrophe that threatens to destroy time and space on the planet, Marcus decides to return to his hellish confinement and save the world from its collapse. A confused and still manipulated Ms. Marvel accompanies him in the other dimension, talking about the unexpected strong (and incestuous) feelings she has for her child/father-of-the-child/rapist. The Avengers say goodbye to Carol, wishing her to live "HAPPILY EVER AFTER" and completely ignoring the heavy implications of such an event. Rape, conditioning, and forced pregnancy are not clearly recognized as abuse and are presented more as plot devices to catch the audience's attention. Ms. Marvel is traumatized and violated. She has control of neither her body nor her other feelings, and no choice about giving birth. Motherhood is presented as something natural, a gift, no matter what the conditions are, and it is implied that maternal love could also overcome violent impregnation and oppressive personal relations. Wasp even congratulates "THE PROUD PARENT" of the baby. Carol can only reply that she has been used and she doesn't feel any connection with the newborn, only to strangely change her mind a few pages after.

RESILIENCE AND RESISTANCE: THE ANSWER OF SUPERWOMEN AGAINST VIOLENCE

As analyzed in these few examples, violence has several meanings and implications. It can be physical or psychological, or both. It can hurt people for sociopolitical reasons or for disturbed fantasies of supremacy and sexual control. It can materialize the worst nightmares of patriarchy or misogyny. It can be influenced (but never justified) by culture, tradition, and economy. The treatment of female characters in comics reflects the treatment of underrepresented, hypersexualized, diminished, discriminated, and/or violated women in real life. Whether they are corporeal or fictional, survivors of violence have to deal with difficult traumas and problems, including behavioral disorders, relationship and sexual difficulties, depression, anxiety, insomnia, and rage. They have to learn how to endure and not give up.

Despite the clichés, the objectification, and the revealing costumes, this is exactly what female superheroes show us at the end of the day: how to endure and not give up. They embody resistance and resiliency. The Amazons ultimately defeat Hercules and his warriors, and in so doing they smash the toxic conception that interprets gender-based violence as a behavior that supports and validates male power (Reid-Cunningham 284). Jessica Jones learns how to fight back Purple Man. Barbara Gordon is no longer Batgirl (at least for a long while), but she keeps fighting crime, becoming Oracle, "the genre's most developed disabled hero" (Alaniz 292). Felicia Hardy doesn't give up on love and trust, also inviting other victims to face trauma, to go to therapy, and to report abuse. She remembers readers that victims are never to blame, aggressors are, always. In one way or another, (super)women who survive violence take control of their bodies back, reaffirm their power and their rights, and raise their voices.

The present-day comics industry is extremely different from the past eras, but there are still problems in depicting superheroines and female characters. In order to propose more inclusive and realistic models of femininity and diversity, publishers, writers, and artists should increase the normalization of the hypersexualized and artificial representation of women, the limitation of the sexist language, and the challenge to gender roles, beauty standards, and racial/ethnic prejudices, among others. The less the focus is on female appearance, the more women's role in comics will be really empowered, emancipated, and sexually liberated. Giving voice to real women's issues, superheroines are an extraordinary medium of education, culture, and promotion of feminist values, fictional symbols able to fight against patriarchal myths, misogynistic actions, and sexist discourses in reality. Superheroines can encourage little girls to reach for the stars and not to watch the sky from the tower of a castle. Superheroines can help us teach and foster peace, respect, resistance, inclusion, and equality in a world where women are still and too often silenced, abused, and killed just because of their gender.

Notes

1. Published since the 1940s, the history of *Wonder Woman* is extremely complex and contradictory, especially for the bondage cliché and the occasional disempowering events. Wonder Woman is one of the first superheroines, and she is independent from major male superheroes, symbolizing a new and empowered femininity. Even when submitted and humiliated, Wonder Woman ends up defeating her enemies, their bonds, and the patriarchal stereotypes that they embody. Moreover, she is also capable of binding opponents with her lasso, submitting them to her will and forcing them to tell the truth. Nevertheless, the constant references to bondage in the storytelling (especially during Marston's run) and the hypersexualization of her shapes and dress tend to show Diana as a "sexual fetish" reflecting male fantasies of female domination and submission. Wonder Woman and many other female characters are often seen "chained, bound, gagged, lassoed, tied, fettered, and manacled" (Lepore 246) for the pleasure of male villains and, consequently, of male readers. After Marston's death in 1947, the new writers and artists slowly transform Wonder Woman into a more domestic and romantic character that thinks more about marriage and fashion and less about her heroic missions. Sometimes she is also depowered. In *Wonder Woman* #179 (1969), for example, she refuses to follow her mother and the Amazons to another dimension to renew their force in order to remain on Earth with Steve Trevor and loses all her powers. From the 1970s and the 1980s, also through the work of Gloria Steinem and George Perez, she returns to epitomize feminism and to popularize woman-empowering messages.

2. The WAACS (Women's Army Auxiliary Corps) and the WAVES (Women Accepted for Volunteer Emergency Service) were women's branchs of, respectively, the United States Army and the United States Naval Reserve established in 1942, during World War II.

3. Comics history has witnessed the appearance of several characters called Captain Marvel. The first one is Billy Batson, a young boy able to transform himself into an adult hypermuscular superhero by shouting the magic word "Shazam." Created by C. C. Beck and Bill Parker in 1939 for Fawcett Comics and owned by DC from the 1970s, Batson changed his superhero name to Shazam in 1972 in order to not originate trademark conflicts with Marvel Comics and its homonym character Captain Marvel. In the Marvel universe, this name is, at first, associated with Mar-Vell, an alien military high officer of the Kree Imperial Militia created in 1967 by Stan Lee and Gene Colan. The second Captain Marvel is the human Monica Rambeau. Appeared for the first time in *The Amazing Spider-Man Annual* #16 (1982), the superheroine is an African American police lieutenant able to generate, absorb, and manipulate energy. After many changes, the current character to use the name Captain Marvel is indomitable Carol Danvers, known as Ms. Marvel until 2012.

4. The Fantastic Four is a Marvel superhero team created in 1961 by Stan Lee and Jack Kirby. The superheroes, who received their powers after a space accident and exposure to cosmic rays, are Reed Richards/Mister Fantastic, Sue Storm/Invisible Girl (later Invisible Woman), Johnny Storm/Human Torch, and Ben Grimm/The Thing. Reed is the leader of the group and a brilliant scientist able to stretch his body, while Sue has the power of invisibility and, since 1964, can also project invisible force fields and make other people and objects invisible. Johnny is Sue's youngest reckless brother. He can fly, control fire, and completely torch his body. Bulky, grumpy, but funny, Ben possesses an impenetrable rock-like skin and, unlike his teammates, cannot change his appearance.

5. According to Tim Hanley, in the second half of 2018, DC creators were 3,476, of which 2,877 male, 597 female, and 2 nonbinary. In the same period, Marvel creators were 4,781, of which 4,002 male, 777 female, and 2 nonbinary. Thus, the percentage of female creators in Marvel and DC was less than 17 percent. Regarding the percentage of male and female readers of superheroes comics, as Noah Berlatsky reports, there are many statistics with different results, mainly because it is very complicated to analyze so much data. In any case, the majority of surveys reveal that superheroes comics are preferred by males, with female readership percentages that range from 5 to 45 percent.

6. Created by Jack Kirby, Stan Lee, and Larry Lieber in 1962, Dr. Henry "Hank" Pym is a biochemist who discovers a size-altering serum that allows him to alter his dimensions, shifting from microscopic to gigantic measures. Pym's most famous superhero identity is Ant-Man, a powerful and insect-sized fighter, but he also assumes other alter egos, such as Giant-Man, Goliath, and Yellowjacket, who first appears in *Avengers* #59 (1968). Under the Yellowjacket identity, Pym generally reveals a psychological disturbed and aggressive personality.

Works Cited

Alaniz, José. *Death, Disability, and the Superhero: The Silver Age and Beyond*. Jackson: University Press of Mississippi, 2014.

Battaglia, Beatrice. *Nostalgia e Mito nella Distopia Inglese*. Ravenna, IT: Longo, 1998.

Bendis, Brian Michael, and Michael Gaydos. *Alias* #24–28. New York: Marvel Comics, 2003.

Berlatsky, Noah. "The Female Thor and the Female Comic-Book Reader." *The Atlantic*, 2014. www.theatlantic.com/entertainment/archive/2014/07/just-how-many-women-read-comic-books/374736/. Accessed Dec. 23, 2019.

Binder, Otto, and Dick Sprang. *Superman* #123. Burbank: DC Comics, 1958.

Binder, Otto, and Kurt Schaffenberger. *Superman's Girlfriend, Lois Lane* #14. Burbank: DC Comics, 1960.

Binder, Otto, and Marc Swayze. *Captain Marvel Adventures* #18. Fawcett, 1942.

Butler, Judith. *Gender Trouble: Feminism and the Subversion of Identity*. New York: Routledge, 1990.

Casey, Joe, and Nick Dragotta. *Vengeance* #1. New York: Marvel Comics, 2011.

Claremont, Chris, and Jim Mooney. *Ms. Marvel* #16. New York: Marvel Comics, 1978.

Cocca, Carolyn. *Superwomen: Gender, Power, and Representation*. London: Bloomsbury, 2016.

Conway, Gerry. "Introduction." In *Webslinger: Unauthorized Essay on Your Friendly Neighborhood Spider-Man*, edited by Gerry Conway and Leah Wilson, 1–4. Dallas: BenBella, 2006.

Coogan, Peter. *Superhero. The Secret Origin of a Genre*. Austin: MonkeyBrain, 2006.

De Beauvoir, Simone. *The Second Sex: Tenth Anniversary Edition*. New York: Routledge, 1999.

DeConnick, Kelly Sue, Scott Hepburn, and Gerardo Sandoval. *Captain Marvel* #14. New York: Marvel Comics, 2013.

Emad, Mitra. "Reading Wonder Woman's Body: Mythologies of Gender and Nation." *Journal of Popular Culture* 39, no. 6 (2006): 954–84.

Fox, Gardner, et al., *All-Star Comics* #13. Burbank: DC Comics, 1942.

Gavaler, Chris. *Superhero Comics*. London: Bloomsbury Academic, 2018.
Gibson, Mel. "Yeah, I Think There Is Still Hope: Youth, Ethnicity, Faith, Feminism and Fandom in Ms. Marvel." In *Gender and the Superhero Narrative*, edited by Michael Goodrum, Tara Prescott, and Philip Smith, 23–44. Jackson: University Press of Mississippi, 2018.
Haney, Bob, and Bob Brown. *The Brave and the Bold* #78. Burbank: DC Comics, 1968.
Hanley, Tim. "Women in Comics, by the Numbers: Summer and Fall 2018." Comicsbeat, Feb. 15, 2019. www.comicsbeat.com/women-in-comics-by-the-numbers-summer-and-fall-2018/. Accessed Dec. 23, 2019.
Held, Jacob. "Can We Steer This Rudderless World? Kant, Rorschach, Retributivism, and Honor." In *Watchmen and Philosophy*, edited by Mark D. White, 19–32. New York: John Wiley & Sons, 2009.
"ING's TOP 100 COMIC BOOK HEROES." ING, 2011. www.ing.com/lists/comic-book-heroes. Accessed Jan.10, 2020.
Lee, Stan, and Jack Kirby. *The Fantastic Four* #14. New York: Marvel Comics, 1963.
Lee, Stan, and Jack Kirby. *X-Men* #1. New York: Marvel Comics, 1963.
Lee, Stan, N. Korok, and Don Heck. *Tales of Suspence* #52. New York: Marvel Comics, 1964.
Lepore, Jill. *The Secret History of Wonder Woman*. New York: Knopf Doubleday, 2014.
Loeb, Jeph, and David Finch. *Ultimatum* #2. New York: Marvel Comics, 2009.
Madrid, Mike. *The Supergirls: Feminism, Fantasy, and the History of Comic Book Heroines*. Minneapolis: Exterminating Angel Press, 2016.
Marston, William, and Harry G. Peter. *Wonder Woman* #5. Burbank: DC Comics, 1943.
Marston, William, and Harry G. Peter. *Wonder Woman* #13. Burbank: DC Comics, 1945.
Millar, Mark, and Brian Hitch. *The Ultimates #6: Giant Man vs The Wasp*. New York: Marvel Comics, 2002.
Mills, Anthony. *American Theology, Superhero Comics, and Cinema*. London: Routledge, 2013.
Moore, Alan, and Dave Gibbons. *Watchmen* #1–2. Burbank: DC Comics, 1986.
Mulvey, Laura. "Visual Pleasure and Narrative Cinema." In *Film Theory and Criticism: Introductory Readings*, edited by Gerald Mast and Marshall Cohen, 803–16. Oxford: Oxford University Press, 1985.
Phillips, Nickie. *Beyond Blurred Lines: Rape Culture in Popular Media*. Lanham, MD: Rowman & Littlefield, 2016.
Reid-Cunningham, Allison Ruby. "Rape as Weapon of Genocide." *Genocide Studies and Prevention* 3, no. 3 (2008): 279–96.
Shendruk, Amanda. "Analyzing Gender Representation of 34,476 Comic Book Characters." *The Pudding*, 2017. www.pudding.cool/2017/07/comics/. Accessed Jan. 10, 2020.
Shooter, James, and Bob Hall. *Avengers* #213. New York: Marvel Comics, 1981.
Shooter, James, et al., *Avengers* #200. New York: Marvel Comics, 1980.
Smith, Kevin, and Terry Dodson. *Spider-Man/Black Cat: The Evil That Men Do* #1–6. New York: Marvel Comics, 2002–2006.
Steinem, Gloria. *Wonder Woman: Featuring Over Five Decades of Great Covers*. Burbank: DC Comics-Abbeville Press, 1995.
Thomas, Roy, and Gene Colan. *Marvel Super-Heroes* #13. New York: Marvel Comics, 1968.
Valenti, Jessica. *The Purity Myth*. New York: Seal Press, 2009.
Wein, Len, and Dave Cockrum. *Giant-Size X-Men* #1. New York: Marvel Comics, 1975.

10

"IT'S FOOTBALL, SIR. IT'S WORTH THE BLOOD"

Football and "The Violence That Finds Us" in Aaron and Latour's *Southern Bastards*

JIM COBY

In October of 2011, Peter Singer optimistically entitled his *New York Times* review of Steven Pinker's *The Better Angels of Our Nature* "Is Violence History?" Over the course of fifteen hundred words of so, Singer lauds Pinker's monolithic study, which factors everything from the Enlightenment thinking to better empathetic reasoning as a means of explaining why violence, as Pinker understands it, has been on the decline. Pinker's work has, understandably, drawn criticism and ire since its publication for, among other things, a somewhat limited definition of what specifically "violence" entails. Moreover, Pinker relies on the idea that, although violence is on the decline overall, you wouldn't know it from watching contemporary media. And it's at that particular crux—perception versus data—that so many have taken umbrage with Pinker's ideas. Because, if violence happens to be on the downward slope, you'd never know it to look at contemporary comics, especially if you happen to take a tour of Craw County, Alabama, the setting for Jason Aaron and Jason Latour's horrifying and mesmerizing series *Southern Bastards*.

Aaron and Latour's characters inhabit a swampy, crimson-tinged landscape rife with hyperrealistic and sensationalized violence alike—violence for revenge in the form of blood feuds and violence for entertainment in the form of football games and violence that resides at the intersections between these worlds. Aaron and Latour's violence doesn't exist purely to titillate our prurient desires, however (much as Frederick Wertham would likely argue it does), but rather to comment on embedded textures of violence throughout the US South's troubled tenure. As Baker and Nelson comment in their now classic essay "Preface: Violence, the Body, and 'the South,'" "In literature, music, film, popular culture, religious records, and studies by social scientists, we find bodies in jeopardy in the South—violence always in ascendance" (232). Indeed, what is the American South, whether as an idea or a region, but a product of the most violent conflict in United States history? That is, without the violence of the Civil War (and the violence of slavery that preceded it) the South would not exist as a historical fact or as a contemporary cultural product. While the historical significance of violence helps to frame our discussion, much of the violence in Aaron and Latour's text directly reacts to the violences of the contemporary South. If comics, as M. Thomas Inge has posited, "serve as revealing reflectors of popular attitudes, tastes, and mores" (xi), then it is worth considering what precisely Aaron and Latour believe to be the mores deeply embedded in contemporary southern culture. Moreover, it is likewise worth exploring the ways in which Aaron and Latour make readers complicit in the violences of Craw County by virtue of reading the texts themselves. As Hillary Chute explains, "Comics can be so powerful because it presents the texture of real-life disaster and war without sensationalizing the violence—and yet without turning away from it" (37). In short, much as Coach Euless Boss will force the denizens of Craw County to reflect on the horror they enabled when he publicly displays a murder weapon he used in a crime for which he will not be convicted, so too do Aaron and Latour force engagement and interaction with their readers—to compel them when they prefer to look away.

At its core, *Southern Bastards* is a work dedicated to consistently and ruthlessly upending reader expectations and dismantling cultural conventions. From killing off its alleged protagonist at the conclusion of its initial four issue run to Craw County football's mortifying homecoming loss, at every turn Aaron and Latour work to demonstrate that, for all readers might think they know about the South, it's a place far more nuanced, complicated, and violent than they could possibly imagine. Described by the authors as a "love letter/hate rant to the South" and "a dark version of the *Dukes of Hazard* if it was done by the Cohen Brothers" ("First Look"), *Southern Bastards* explores the physical and psychological toils of living in a hyperviolent and insular southern locale. Aaron and Latour's saga begins with Earl Tubbs's homecoming to Craw County, Alabama, where he intends to retrieve some belongings from his former home. The plot veers unexpectedly when, just four issues into the series, Tubb, our ostensible hero, winds up dead at the hands of the vindictive and mercenary high school football coach, Euless Boss. At this juncture, the narrative once more shifts, and Aaron and Latour spend several issues excavating Boss's past before bringing the plot once more to the present, when Boss's football team, and the pride of Craw County, are mercilessly routed in their homecoming game.

Violence permeates the very fabric of *Southern Bastards*. Readers fall victim to violence within even the first few pages of the first issue, as Tubbs, now an elderly man, silently visits locations from his childhood. Juxtaposed against the images set in present day are those of the past presented with a deep, red hue, as if to suggest that the very nature of Tubbs's past, much like that of the South itself, is one marred and hued by violence and bloodshed. As with many of the most powerful works of graphic narrative, the past and present here interplay and interact, signaling that the long-repressed traumas of Tubbs's early life may well be on the verge of spilling over into the present. As Faulkner famously penned in *Requiem for a Nun*, "The past is never dead. It's not even past" (73). And while much can and should be made of the violence within the BBQ restaurants, the streets, the woods, and the homes of Craw County, I am more immediately concerned with a very specific, deliberate even, type of violence that occurs on the gridiron. As one of the animating ideas of Aaron and Latour's series is how deeply embedded within southern culture violence is, likewise I am interested in the confluence between those two ideas as they relate to one of the most defining components of southern culture in the popular imagination—the obsession with football.

Introduced in the very first issue of the comic series, the coach of the Craw County Runnin' Rebels, Euless Boss, garners an almost mythical status, not from his intimidating presence, but rather from the threat and intimidation of violence perpetrated in his stead. An early scene in the first issue presents Earl Tubb, a former resident of Craw County who has returned to take care of his father's estate following his death, enjoying a plate of barbeque ribs at Boss BBQ, an establishment unsurprisingly owned and operated by Euless Boss. As Tubb enjoys his "good as hell" ribs (vol. 1, 14), a frantic and disheveled character named Dusty Tutwiler approaches him. Tutwiler, who mistakes Tubb for one of Boss's employees, breathlessly explains, "Look, just tell him I need to **talk**, okay? Tell him I can strengthen things out. I just gotta—" (vol. 1, 14). Tutwiler's entreaty goes unfinished as Tubb shortly interrupts him, but even in its brevity Tutwiler's words evince the terror he experiences when discussing Boss. Latour illustrates Tutwiler in a stance of supplication, his arms held close to his body, hands raised and palms out, as if to signal his lack of threat and terror. His mouth, too, formerly a long line with sharp canine-like teeth spilling from the upper lip, becomes comically small, as if Tutwiler can only barely manage to eke out his plea for grace. Most significant in this scene, however, is Jared K. Fletcher's lettering of Tutwiler's words. That Fletcher bolds the typeface of the word "talk" clues readers to the fact that verbal discourse and debate are atypical of Boss's character, and that physical aggression likely operates as the modus operandi for Boss. Without having seen the character, readers intuit the array of violences and fears promulgated by the barbeque magnate. As such, Aaron and Latour early in their series highlight the violence that permeates the very air of Craw County, Alabama. Indeed, Brian Massumi explains that "violence is not reducible to the punctual acts that bring it to full expression in bodily aggression. It can act in and as its own potential. Violence can be as oppressive in the way it looms over us as an unspoken threat" ("Histories of Violence: Affect, Power, Violence"). In effect, without having leveled any sort of physical aggression—at least not yet—Euless Boss fosters a type of mental and social violence in the ambient threat his very presence places about the town. It would be easy enough, then, to write Boss off completely as unequivocal evil, but Aaron and Latour refuse such easy pigeonholing. Inasmuch as the United States South itself embodies a complicated region full of both prejudices and celebrations of diversity, so too does Boss encapsulate both ferocious evil and opportunity.

Aaron and Latour provide the origin story for the series' primary antagonist in a run of four issues entitled "Gridiron." It is in these issues that Aaron and Latour present us the history of the series's antagonist, Euless Boss, and ask us to, if not explicitly empathize, then to at least understand the myriad confluences of violence that catalyze Boss's later mania. In these issues they grapple with the implications of legacies of violence in a young person's life and how those tendencies might ultimately manifest themselves. The first panels of "Gridiron" showcase a breathless, teenage Euless Boss on his knees, staring at a row of tackling dummies on a football practice field hours after practice has ended as the team's coach towers over him, chiding "You want a little piece of advice? Quit" (vol. 2, 1). After receiving several additional taunts about his diminutive stature and dearth of athleticism, Boss turns his masked face upwards to the coach and coughs, "It's football, sir. It's worth the blood" (vol. 2, 2). Because football has never really been about the game, not really. At its heart, football unearths the innermost desires for brutality toward oneself and one's fellow man; it engages with all manners of class and racial distinctions; it provides an outlet for aggressions, but packages them as a pastime, as something near admirable. (Little wonder then that Stephen Crane watched football games in preparation for writing of Civil War conflicts in *The Red Badge of Courage*. Little wonder, too, that Aaron and Latour find themselves so endlessly engaging with the sport.) If football acts as a metonym for aggressions and social tensions, then what better fulcrum on which to hinge their explorations of the violence inherent to much southern culture. Andrew Doyle argues that the ascendance of collegiate and high school football's popularity in the South directly correlates with a perceived surfeit of opportunity. He writes that popular rhetoric surrounding the sport preached "it as a means of teaching the meritocratic and technocratic values of modernity to southerners" and that "football violence ... was a means of instilling masculine aggressiveness necessary to compete in the Darwinians world" (192). And so what Aaron and Latour ultimately unearth in Boss's pyric quest toward inclusion on his high school's football team is the potential the sport and its concomitant violence ostensibly offer to young men of lesser means.

In an attempt to comprehend and rationalize the self-destructive tendencies that many poor white southerners often exhibit, Harry Crews, the "Grit Lit" laureate, once offered a list of troublesome questions: "Are you plagued with sourceless anxiety? Do you worry about God and the order of the universe? Or do you worry about the existence of God and whether or not there *is* order to the universe? Are you unhappy for no apparent reason? Do you obsess over the future of your children?" (3). Reluctant to allow for ambiguity with his answers, Crews offers a definitive solution. He writes, "If the answer to any of the above is yes, *then go and get your ass kicked*. You will be purified and holy.... Nose-to-nose combat is better than a psychiatrist, is never as humiliating and is not nearly so expensive" (3). Crews's offers gut-wrenching but frequently sardonic advice. Interviews reveal him to have a far gentler soul than his gruff appearance and ferocious writing style might indicate. Nonetheless, his essay indeed strikes at the heart of a very particular type of southern masculine posturing—one typically white, rural, and born out of desperation (the complaint about the expense of therapy implies far more about the economic concerns of the speaker than it does about the profession as a whole). Indeed, W. J. Cash in his landmark treatise *The Mind of the South* found a similarly pernicious propensity toward violence embedded in the southern psyche. "However careful they might be to walk softly," Cash writes, "such men as these of the South were bound to come into conflict" (43). In *Southern Bastards*, Aaron and Latour interrupt conventional and popular understandings of the American South, and their target for the disruption of white southern masculinity, the logical conclusion of the type of man who takes Crews's words not as parodic, but as gospel. The enlivening capacity of violence Crews highlights becomes somewhat vexing when contrasted against the title of his essay: "The Violence That Finds Us." While the content of Crews's essay suggests a predatory approach to violence, the title insists that textures of violence permeate the very fabric of southern life, at least for certain populations. Moreover, a type of baptismal effect may accompany the moments of pain and torment. To feel physically and mentally assaulted by your own volition, suggests Crews, is to be reborn. If true, then to focus on America's most violent pastime—football—would well serve as an outlet for Boss's pent-up aggressions and anxieties.

Boss's need for acceptance on the gridiron becomes most appreciable when Aaron and Latour provide a glimpse of his home life in the following issue. After a particularly brutal practice, Boss cycles home to the decrepit trailer that he shares with his father. Overstuffed garbage bags litter the yard. Couches and old tires form something like a barrier to entry to the property. And Christmas lights remain strung, despite them clearly being out of season. While the detritus in the front yard certainly indicates a lack of care toward the physical property, it is once Boss opens his front door that the true measure of abuse and lack of care becomes clear. A panel providing a point-of-view shot from the interior of the trailer shows Boss entering the home; shadows from within the trailer land of Boss's face, allowing only his teeth to shine through, and resembling nothing as much as a skull, highlighting how deadening Boss's own home is to him. "**Who the fuck's there?**" demands an unseen character who is holding a pistol aimed directly at the teenage Boss's chest. "Shit. Daddy, it's me," Boss whimpers (vol. 2, 31). As startling and unsettling as this initial encounter is, the true horror show awaits both readers and Boss on the following page where Latour lays out a splash page chronicling a tableau of debauchery: naked figures writhe across the page, liquor and beer bottles cover every available source, and, of all things, cages and live chickens run around the trailer's interior, crowding all of the humans into a Bruegelesque scene. At the forefront of the madness stands Boss's father, naked except for an open bathrobe, one hand on his genitals, the other on the pistol. "Don't know no 'me,'" he grunts at his son, "Get the fuck out" (vol. 2, 32). The panels following present Boss's father kicking his teenage son down a short flight of stairs and into the dirt outside of the trailer and finally Boss crawling into the family's car in an attempt to get some sleep before school the following day. What underscores this cavalcade of violence and vice is the notion of surprise. By requiring readers to flip the page from Boss's face to the full vision of what is happening within the walls of the trailer, Aaron and Latour catch their audience completely off guard. Whatever we may have been expecting from Boss's homelife, it certainly wasn't an orgy accompanied by livestock. Because although football possesses an obvious participatory aspect, there is also something of the sacrificial about the ways in which young men are allowed—if not outright encouraged—to offer their bodies as potential fodder for destruction in order to entertain and placate their parents and community members. As Girard notes, there is necessarily a sacrificial component of ritualized violence; the rub, however, is how "to 'purify' violence; that is, to 'trick' violence into spending itself on victims whose death will provoke no reprisals" (221). While death remains an unlikely outcome for football players, Girard's comments remain relevant in their concern over how egregious acts might be made palatable to nonparticipants. The same obviously holds true for Boss. Having experienced demoralization and humiliation from a coach who tells Boss he won't make the team only to return to his home and find no safe haven, to be further denied refuge from the people and locales that should provide him with some degree of comfort and safety only further destabilizes Boss's world. And so faced with a homelife that perpetuates horrors and violences beyond Boss's control, he seeks refuge in the one type of violence that he can fully understand—the participatory violence of the football field—by making a promise to himself that he will become a member of the team at all costs.

With Boss's eventual success on the football field, his expected scholarship to the University of Alabama to play for Bear Bryant's Crimson Tide, and the healthiest relationship he has ever experienced coming from the training of his mentor, the winds of change begin to seemingly blow in Euless Boss's direction for once. Echoing Harry Crews's belief that some sort of redemptive, illustrative, if not wholly euphoric epiphanies might come from self-inflicted engagements with seemingly controlled violence on the gridiron, Eric Bain-Selbo writes in *Game Day and God: Football, Faith, and Politics in the American South,* "We might not always want to know of our violent and aggressive selves, but at least some cultural creations can turn that violence and aggression into something that has some merit and some beauty. Football, perhaps, is such a thing" (68). Bain-Selbo's optimism notwithstanding, he rightly points out the act of participation and creativity involved with football. The "beauty" of the game reveals potential for Boss, but it is potential shortly denied him. Following his final game, Boss returns to his high school in the hopes of landing a coaching position. Insisting that he would best serve as a position coach, Boss explains, "I'm one of the best linebackers who ever played at this school" (vol. 2, 69). His explanation is met initially with ambivalence and then malice, as his former coach chides, "If you was so good, then how come you ain't playin' college ball, huh? Oh wait. Might be because I told everybody who called me what grade-A pieces of shit you and your whole damn family was" (vol. 2, 69). In that moment Boss gains an awareness that the redemptive power of football, and the potentially therapeutic act of physical violence, can easily be eclipsed by the overwhelming power of spite. Boss's former coach effectively shutters Boss's chances of escaping a life of poverty and unwanted physical violence. Instead of a generative and potentially redemptive type of violence, Boss here slips into a psychic chasm occupied only by madness, in which he will reveal his truest nature—that of a man hellbent on achieving his aims regardless of the cost. In effect, what we witness here amalgamates two different types of violence—the immediate and explosive violence of bodies colliding on a football field and a more long-term manifestation called "slow violence." Conceptualizations of what specifically "violence" entails have experienced a dramatic shift over the past several years. No longer conceived of as singular moments of physical trauma, violence might well now include the physical and psychological effects of corrosive and toxic language, economic destitution, or systematic oppression. Chief among those on the forefront of rethinking through the concept of violence is Rob Nixon, whose 2011 work *Slow Violence and the Environmentalism of the Poor* helped to usher in a new understanding of not just the act of violence itself but the temporal span of the violent act. Nixon explains, "By slow violence I mean a violence that occurs gradually and out of sight, a violence of delayed destruction that is dispersed across time and space, an attritional violence that is not typically viewed as violence at all" (2). Given the previous discussion of football in this essay, the obvious point of slow violence would be the traumatic and lingering long-term injuries associated with playing football competitively. Undoubtedly, Boss suffers from the catastrophic injuries he suffered at the hands of his father, but he equally wears the psychic wounds of a lifetime of mental torment and anguish from both his home and his school.

Despite a number of setbacks, not limited to being hobbled by a gunshot and denied information about a potential athletic scholarship to the University of Alabama, Boss emerges from the physical and psychological violence he experiences throughout his adolescence by proving himself equally, if not more, capable of destructive acts. Through acts of intimidation, the creation of a makeshift gang willing to carry out his bidding, and ruthless opportunism, Boss emerges not only as the preeminent restaurateur of Craw County, but also the coach of its illustrious high school football team. With his meteoric rise comes the respect commonly bestowed on football coaches in the American South. We need only remember the (widely ridiculed) slogan of the NCAA football's Southeastern Conference, "It just means more" ("About"), to understand the type of emphasis and valor bestowed on coaches. That is, bestowed on football coaches *who win*. The series' thirteenth issue, "Fourth and Goal," revolves around a fiercely contested game between Craw County and the Wetumpka Warriors, and the depths to which Euless Boss has descended.

"Fourth and Goal" succinctly highlights the cyclical violence to which Boss has confined himself in its representation of a football game and the concomitant aftermath. The issue begins with a closeup of Boss's face pressed near the helmet of one of his players. Thin white lines indicating a fierce rainstorm dapple the page, and the effect clearly indicates the Runnin' Rebs are behind. Boss growls at his player, "Bleed it you to! Break you fucking bones if that's what it takes! But do not give these mother fuckers another. Goddamn. Inch!" (vol. 3, 93). The intensity of Boss's rhetoric no doubt inculcates fear in his players, and his demands for self-sacrifice highlight the violence he demands of his players. Notable, however, are the words that follow, in which Boss thinks, "I don't ask nothing' of my players I didn't ask of myself when I was their age" (vol. 3, 93). This moment of self-reflection highlights that Boss remains totally in control of faculties and understands completely the type of cyclical violence that he asks of his players. That is to say, aware of how his own life evinces the impact of the various types of violence to which he has been exposed, he has no qualms about assigning the same kind of future to his young players. As it becomes increasingly clear that the Runnin' Rebs will not pull out the game, Esaw, the team's defensive coordinator and Boss's henchman, suggests an attack on an especially productive Wetumpka player. "Next play that kid gets the ball," Esaw suggests, "Let me send in a couple boys divin' at his knees. We'll get his ass outta that game right quick" (vol. 3, 109). While Boss is, of course, no stranger to unceremonious acts of violence, Esaw's suggestion upsets his moral calculus. Boss furiously responds, "Around here, we win football games by playin' football" (vol. 3, 109). Esaw's suggestion rejected, the Runnin' Rebs go on to lose their homecoming game. Boss's code of violence, however, prohibits him accepting the loss and thinking about the next game. Instead, Boss swallows a fifth of bourbon and locates a Wetumpka player at a postgame party who gave the Rebs a particularly difficult time. As he staggers toward the young man, Boss growls, "Either you run through me, boy. Or I'm gonna go through you" (vol. 3, 114). The player charges at Boss, only for Boss to charge and end up breaking the young man's knee. Effectively, Boss institutes Esaw's game time plan, but waits until he is off the field to do so. As a result, Boss finds himself an active participant in the cycles of violence he experienced himself as a young man, both on and off the field. The elation and lucidity that Crews suggests is possible through occasional violent entanglements disappears, replaced by an ever-present violence. The respites for Boss are not the violent interludes, but rather the peaceful ones.

Taylor Hagood recently suggested that "to observe that the popularity of American football is concomitant with the power of television" and that the act of witness is integral to viewership. (277). Within the context of *Southern Bastards*, additional elements of southern culture become intertwined with football. What Hagood finds rote in this comparison becomes more vexing when one considers the violence inherent to the sport. The inexorable violence in football and other high-impact sports becomes somewhat negated by its ephemerality; the sack may be brutal, but it's over quickly. Certainly, the rise of online video-sharing services and (arguably) overreliance on instant replay allow for viewers who failed to witness the moment of impact the opportunity to relive it, but the fact remains that a large part of the appeal of sports is its liveness, its "once-in-a-lifetime-ness." That is, those who didn't witness the event in the moment don't hold the same level of experience that those present possess. Comics change that. With a comic strip, the moments of impact are frozen. The brutal collisions, the cracking of bones, the crashing of helmets, and accompanying sound effects stand still. As a result the violence, so quick to pass in a televised event, becomes ingrained and made static. Of course, the physicality of the violence and the physiological resonances are not the only violences present in the text. Indeed, the slow violence present expands beyond the confines of the game itself, and football becomes a metonym for the insidious problems throughout the US South.

What Aaron and Latour ask readers of their comic to tackle is nothing less than the scope and sweep of public southern history. By couching their discussions of systemic class distinctions in the context of the participatory violence of football, their comic, too, suggests just how easy it is for the casual fan to fall into a mindless complicity for the sake of entertainment. The reviews that *Southern Bastards* have received speak to its enormous influence in contemporary southern discourse. Joshua Rivera argues that *Southern Bastards* is "a comic that understands the wide range of sentiments held regarding the South and cuts through them all with the humanity of its story, the pathos lurking underneath all the ugliness" ("This Beautifully Brutal"). And indeed, Aaron and Latour consistently ask their readers to acknowledge both the intensely violent and viscerally upsetting aspects of Coach Boss's life, while also appreciating the deleterious circumstances that so warped his mind. Moreover, however, a single theme emerges time and again when readers are asked to contemplate their reaction to the series. When considering what he finds so *real* about Aaron and Latour's series, novelist Tom Franklin responded, "The violence, the landscape, the religion, the ignorance, the poverty, and, above all, the FOOTBALL" (319). Franklin here rightly notes how football, and its attendant participatory violence, undergirds so much of the decisions (and the concomitant aspects he notes earlier in his appraisal) that catalyze future legacies of violence in Aaron and Latour's series.

Works Cited

Aaron, Jason, and Jason Latour. *Southern Bastards, Volume 1: Here Was a Man*. Portland: Image Comics, 2014.

Aaron, Jason, and Jason Latour. *Southern Bastards, Volume 2: Gridiron*. Portland: Image Comics, 2015.

Aaron, Jason, and Jason Latour. *Southern Bastards, Volume 3: Homecoming*. Portland: Image Comics, 2016.

"About." It Just Means More. https://itjustmeansmore.com/about. Accessed Dec. 12, 2021.

Bain-Selbo, Eric. *Game Day and God: Football, Faith, and Politics in the American South*. Macon, GA: Mercer University Press, 2012.

Baker, Houston A., and Dana D. Nelson, "Preface: Violence, the Body, and 'The South,'" *American Literature* 73, no. 2 (2001): 231–44.

Cash, W. J. *The Mind of the South*. New York: Vintage, 1991.

Chute, Hillary. *Why Comics? From Underground to Everywhere*. New York: HarperCollins, 2017.

Crews, Harry. "The Violence that Finds Us." In *2 By Crews*. Northridge, CA: Lord John Press, 1984.

Doyle, Andrew. "On the Cusp of Modernity: The Southern Sporting World in the Twentieth Century." In *The American South in the Twentieth Century*, edited by Craig S. Pascoe, Karen Trahan Leathem, and Andy Ambrose, 188–208. Athens, GA: University Press of Georgia, 2005.

Evans, Brad. "Histories of Violence: Affect, Power, Violence—The Political Is Not Personal," *Los Angeles Review of Books*, Nov. 13, 2017. https://lareviewofbooks.org/article/histories-of-violence-affect-power-violence-the-political-is-not-personal/.

Faulkner, William. *Requiem for a Nun*. New York: Vintage, 2011.

Franklin, Tom. "On Comics, Crime, and Football: A Conversation with Jason Aaron and Jason Latour." *Southwest Review* 104, no. 4 (2019): 319–29.

Girard, Rene. *Violence and the Sacred*. Baltimore: Johns Hopkins University Press, 1972.

Hagood, Taylor. "Football, the South, and the Spatiality of Television." In *Small Screen Souths: Region, Identity, and the Cultural Politics of Television*, edited by Lisa Hinrichsen, Gina Caison, and Stephanie Rountree, 277–93. Baton Rouge: Louisiana State University Press, 2018.

Inge, M. Thomas. *Comics as Culture*. Jackson: University Press of Mississippi, 1990.

Nixon, Rob. *Slow Violence and the Environmentalism of the Poor*. Cambridge, MA: Harvard University Press, 2011.

Rivera, Josh. "This Beautifully Brutal Comic Gave Me a New Appreciation of the South." *Business Insider*, June 30, 2015. https://www.businessinsider.com/southern-bastards-comic-review-2015-6. Accessed Nov. 20, 2019.

Truitt, Brian. "First Look: Creators Walk Tall with 'Southern Bastards.'" *USA Today*, Jan. 16, 2014. https://www.usatoday.com/story/life/2014/01/16/southern-bastards-comic-book-series-first-look/4504377/. Accessed 20 Nov. 2019.

11

COMPLEX COMICS, COMPLEX TRAUMA

Registration of Traumatized Childhood in the "Autographics" of Phoebe Gloeckner

PARTHA BHATTACHARJEE AND PRIYANKA TRIPATHI

I

Confronting the truth of one's life with regard to both childhood abuse and a traumatized "girlhood" conveys an unforeseen dark side of violence. It is incomprehensible and difficult for the author to reminisce about the episodes of violence. Recollecting episodes of violence on the "body" and representing it in a verbal-visual medium where readers need "to respond through body and affect" (Hirsch 1211) is an arduous task. Phoebe Gloeckner marks her prominent position as an underground comix artist during the 1990s with her strategic engagement with trauma, violence, and sexual abuse.

Gloeckner presents her emotions, encounters, and experiences through her autobiographical alter ego, Minnie Goetze. In this chapter we extend our inquiry to a detailing of the physical and psychological wounds of the protagonist Minnie. Gloeckner's first volume, *A Child's Life and Other Stories* (1998), is a narrative representation of sexual violence forced on the child Minnie. Gloeckner's second installment, *The Diary of a Teenage Girl: An Account in Words and Pictures* (2002), is a journey of Minnie's growth through her many epiphanic moments. Written with a combination of words, standalone illustrations, and episodic comics, the text raises questions about complex relations, incestuous abuse, and violation of the body. The word "account" in the subtitle of the second memoir denotes a position from which an author can write about an experienced self. Gloeckner distances herself from Minnie, but the hints or resemblances in the illustrations cannot hide the fact that the illustrations reference her life. While commenting on *The Diary of a Teenage Girl*, Whitney Joiner notes it to be "one of the most brutally honest, shocking, tender and beautiful portrayals of growing up female in America." Quite appropriately then, in the context of Gloeckner, the body becomes a site of violence.

While creating a definition of her own version of the diary, Gloeckner follows the strategy of Phillipe Lejeune: "A diary is a history of thought, event, and emotion, whose creation is a consecutive recording of an individual life. It is an artifact that asks for no redaction" (xv). The inclusion of the term "diary" in her comic often forces readers to dissolve the separate personas of Minnie and Phoebe. It is via the readers' perspectives that readers come to see Phoebe's life through Minnie's in *The Diary of a Teenage Girl*. Rebecca Hogan points out,

> If we consider the diary from the point of view of the writer, we can see its ability to entertain multiple purposes and intentions, often contradictory. If we think about the diary in terms of the reader, we can see that it has a wide range of audiences on a continuum from a confidante for the private self to the wider audience of a published diary. (97)

Kylie Cardell (2014) argues, "Like other autobiographical modes, the *diary* is an *icon* of confessional culture, the embodiment of *a* widespread fascination for the lives of others and a signifier of powerful desires for contact *with a* literary 'real'" (5). While she was in her twenties, Gloeckner started writing her diary in a confessional mode in which the text metaphorically becomes a representation of her bruised mind and traumatized body.[1] She took up writing on subjects that were taboo even then—female sexuality, virginity, nudity, drawing naked illustrations of genitals. When asked if *The Diary of a Teenage Girl* was an autobiographical text, Gloeckner denied it, yet emphasized that she had taken incidents from her diary while writing the narrative.

Gloeckner passionately inscribes her experiences in her diary, as the diary contains ignominious incidents, harrowing experiences, and disturbing elements. It acts as the form of a semiautobiographical comic in the genre of "autobiofictionalography," a term used by Lynda Barry for her graphic narrative *One! Hundred! Demons!* in which she states that there is always a tinge of "truth-claiming" or a quest for an "autobiographical pact," (Lejeune 3) in the words of Philippe Lejeune. The semiautobiographical graphic narrative is a disjunctive encounter between experiencing (phenomenal or empirical) and understanding (thoughtful naming, in which words replace things or their images) (Hartman 540). Considering the traumatic experiences Gloeckner shares, the graphic narratives are more than "life-testimony" as they go beyond the private life and the act of "'writing' is constantly tied up with the act of 'bearing witness'" (Felman and Laub 2).

II

Gloeckner's first memoir, *A Child's Life and Other Stories*, explores childhood trauma, violence, and incestuous abuse. Crafted intermittently in black-and-white and color comics, Gloeckner divides the narrative into five sections: "A Child's Life," "Other Childish Stories," "Teen Stories," "Grown-up Stories," and "Paintings, Drawings, & Etchings." Through nonlinear and fragmentary vignettes, these sections revisit and register different dimensions of abuse that the protagonist Minnie and other girls suffer in their childhood days. In between the foreword and introduction, there is a black and white illustration of the artist titled "Self Portrait with Pemphigus Vulgaris, 1987." As a medical illustrator, Gloeckner understood the pain of bullae on the skin and associates it with the pangs of an abused survivor in the illustration. She reimagines the violence and pain of abuse and represents it metaphorically through the physically diseased body. A zoomed-in focus shows the decomposition underneath the cell, which implicates the bruised psychology of a growing child.

The first section of *A Child's Life* comprising seven narratives shows Minnie's family members: her mother, her sister, and her would-be stepfather. The narrative reveals that her mother is timid and her would-be stepfather, Pascal, is short-tempered and responds brutally to Minnie and her sister. Minnie is likely bothered by her alcoholic mother's careless attitude towards her, for she gives Pascal too much room to intervene in Minnie's personal space, as he attempts to take a toll of her tender instincts with a luring eye on her body. The rendering of Pascal indicates that he is sexually prone towards Minnie as he was found with a disproportionately large erect penis. Pascal's response towards the girls, while masturbating, is an allusion to the objectification of the female body where the female body is framed as available to a "sexual spectator" (Michael 351). Gloeckner's realistic style of drawing adds to the nature of both characters. Minnie is drawn as a girl with dark-eyes and pampered affect, attached to her family members and a bit possessive of them, whereas Pascal is drawn as a man who speaks inappropriately and in an unsuitable manner to Minnie, asking her if she has begun to develop breasts and asking Charlotte for an open marriage in front of the girls. Pascal's words are also full of sexual innuendos. In a three-page vignette, titled "Hommage à Duchamp," Minnie and her sister see Pascal masturbating through the broken frame of the bathroom door. Gloeckner represents the naked male body and genitals as a source of symbolic trauma, like her over-impressive anatomical cross-sections of female body parts, in order to deconstruct the oppressive and obsessive power of voyeuristic consumption of the male gaze on women's bodies. In this representation Gloeckner makes plain the consequences of an abusive dynamic on children by deploying the tools of memory "appropriate for the therapeutic representation of traumatic memories" (Køhlert 129).

The panels in the first two pages feature only one panel, while the last page features three panels with standard gutters. The first page shows dark-eyed Minnie and her sister near the bathroom door, curiously peeping through the broken glass. Her sister's face is in a confused and messy state, which also signifies the weight of the familial disturbances in her psyche. The second page shows the right eye of Minnie gazing at Pascal's penis and the third page consists of three panels where Minnie and her sister run away to escape the situation. Later, Minnie, now ten years old, recollects the shocking moment when with an experienced eye she revisualizes the memory of a man masturbating after seeing a child. And yet the haunting memory remains. Cathy Caruth, in her text *Trauma: Explorations in Memory*, rightly points out that "the problem arises not only in regard to those who listen to the traumatized, not knowing how to establish the reality of their hallucinations and dreams; it occurs rather and most disturbingly often within the very knowledge and experience of the traumatized themselves" (5). As young girls, Minnie and her sister were shocked by the premature exposure they had, for it was "a frightening event outside of ordinary human experience" (172). In the last panel of the final page, Minnie asks her sister, "Do you think he saw us? What do you think he was doing?" Her sister replies in confusion, "Maybe he was washing his penis" (Gloeckner 29).

A clear comparison can be drawn between Pascal masturbating in the bathroom and the masturbation of Monroe, Minnie's mother's boyfriend (28, 73). Olga Michael (2018) notes, "Growing up in an environment where she is sexualized by Pascal as a child, Minnie (or Gloeckner's other autobiographical alter ego) has sex for the first time with Monroe at the age of 15" (9). Despite Minnie's confession of having sex with her stepfather for the first time she is extremely passive, whereas Pascal is shown sweating and utterly repulsive. By showing Pascal's violent act of having sex with a child, the panel makes it clear that for Minnie sexual violence is pervasive. As Minnie ventures into her memory, she visualizes a moment in her traumatized past when Pascal would frequently pick Gretel up from the chair and wrestle her to the ground. In one harrowing scene, set at 3:00 a.m., as Gretel screamed in pain, Pascal spit a mouthful of wine into her mouth. This is a haunting recurrence for Minnie, as she is forced to watch her sister be constantly bullied by Pascal while her mother remains a mute and helpless spectator to the scene. As Minnie remembers, "Mommy would usually just sit in the kitchen and drink + cry during such episodes" (68).

Gloeckner reveals the stories of other children who have also experienced sexual trauma. In that way, she might be seen to move beyond her own painful experience and create a world of fictional stories based on her personal choice and voice. "Other Childish Stories," the second chapter of *A Child's Life*, is a nonlinear narrative that diverts the readers to another location outside of Gloeckner's, but where other children also experience psychological and sexual trauma. The nonlinear panel structures might provide relief to readers who find themselves overwhelmed by Minnie's pathos-laden experiences. "Other Childish Stories" introduces the adolescent female character Magda. In the first section of this chapter, "Magda Meets the Little Men in the Woods," Magda comes across unknown little men who misbehave with their girlfriends and torture them psychologically in the woods. In one of these panels, very much in a fairytale structure, Magda is fully clothed and surrounded by naked men. One of them remarks, "I'm going to get drunk with my friends + I won't come home until 3.00 AM!! You'll be crying and I'll try to have sex with you!!" (Gloeckner 56). The story of Magda is a clear reference to Minnie's experience, given that she had sexual intercourse with Pascal and witnesses his spitting the wine into her sister's mouth at 3:00 a.m. These are meant to be seen as parallel forms of (s)exploitation.

In another panel, Magda meets a naked man who is having sex in a bird's nest with several women. He tells her that he is going to be her husband in the next thirteen years and they will have an "<u>Open Marriage</u>!" which she fails to understand (underline in original; 56). Upon enquiring, the man informs her that he will establish his "love by sleeping with other women but always coming back to" (56) her in a near similar way to Pascal's description of open marriage with Charlotte (Gloeckner 23) in *A Child's Life*. The man in the nest further remarks that Magda does not know how to discipline the children and he will have to take care of that, similar to what Pascal says earlier to Minnie: "Poor thing! If your real father won't care for you, I will!" (Gloeckner 34). Magda also meets a man with a glass who says, "I'm gonna be your boyfriend in 17 years!" (57). He holds Magda's legs intending to reach her genitals. His left leg has come out of the panel, suggesting a visibly clear sexual implication. In the third panel, Magda punches the man in his belly, and the intensity of the punch is shown with three strike marks making the sound "POW." With this act Magda represents an attempt at resistance and self-defense against sexual abuse.

The last three panels show Magda taking refuge in her mother's lap fearing the loss of her innocence: "Mommy! I don't ever want to grow up!" (57). While analyzing Magda's harrowing experience, which is similar to that of Minnie's, we find that Gloeckner plays a major role in making comics unearth the truest sense and essence of traumatic truths. There are two dimensions: firstly, the little men in the wood are abusers metaphorically presented in a fairy-tale narrative, and secondly, Magda's experiences are linked to those of Minnie described in "Minnie's 3rd Love, Or: Nightmare on Polk Street," a collection of vignettes from "Teen Stories."

The first narrative from "Teen Stories" also refers to Minnie's mother's alcoholism. (73). "Teen Stories" includes characters such as Mary, a teenager with alcoholism and an incestuous affair, and Ann, who thinks Mary a prostitute. "Minnie's 3rd Love, Or: Nightmare on Polk Street" begins with a drug addict named Tabatha who incidentally tells her story to Minnie. She also has a drug addicted mother who does not protect her child from sexual abuse or incest but rather pushed her into "porno films when she was small child" (72). Tabatha sells her body and in return, she takes drugs from the dealers. The illustration on page seventy-five shows Tabatha busy watching TV with her drug dealer while Minnie is lying naked on the bed. With an erection, an unnamed man has spread Minnie's legs and holds a used tampon that he has just removed from Minnie's vagina. The image juxtaposes Minnie's experience of sexual trauma against her physical coming-of-age; Minnie must confront her growing sense of her own sexuality at the same time she learns to navigate adolescent bodily and psychological changes. Peggy Orenstein observed in the *New York Times Magazine,* "[t]he Minnie stories describe adolescence that is at once traumatic and picaresque. They explore the power a girl feels in her emerging sexuality as well as the damage inflicted by those who prey upon it." Another narrative from this section, "The Girl from a Different World," includes two characters: Penny and Walter. They fall in love with each other but the sudden revelation of the harsh truth that Penny's stepfather had an affair and sex with her when she was thirteen shatters his romantic view of her, in which "all innocence was collapsing before me [Penny]" (91). This narrative corresponds to Gloeckner's earlier narratives depicting troubled childhood and adolescence driven by the haunting reality of sexual trauma.

The last section of the book, "Paintings, Drawings, & Etchings," contains several untitled illustrations, each of which connotes a sense of the effects of abuse. As a medical artist, not only does Gloeckner show the impact at the physical level, but she also points out how it leaves a scar on someone's psyche through illustrations, sketches, and paintings. The first two pages (134–35), drawn with a careful pencil-sketch, portray the dissection of the pelvic girdle, including several parts of the penis, uterus, and vagina. A box on page 135, highlighted with a white background, shows the diagram of "posterior dislocation of left tibia," which we read as evidence of extensive sexual abuse.

III

The Diary of a Teenage Girl was published in 2002 and was later revised in 2015 with a cover consisting of illustrations of a teenage Minnie. This graphic narrative uniquely blends comics and prose and is formatted as a diary. Hilary Chute's (2010) analysis of the narrative goes beyond narrative modes and analyzes the text's representational modes:

> *Diary* uses four representational modes: diary entries composed by Gloeckner or Gloeckner's alter-ego character, Minnie; archival comic strips that the author drew during the years of the action of the diary (1976–1977); comic strip narratives that sweep in and periodically substitute for text, composed from an older, wiser narratorial perspective (there are seventeen of these); and twenty-seven full-page and fifty-six in-text illustrations. (74)

The Diary of a Teenage Girl accommodates manifold dimensions of Minnie's wounds, be they inflicted by her mother, Pascal, or even Monroe, so that the diary almost becomes a *body* itself as the letters, lexicons, and the wounds are interspersed with each other. Chute (2010) remarks that "Minnie's diary is synecdochically *her*: *she* has been wounded by her mother's lack of recognition and care, and yet she refers to her *diary* as wounded. She is wounded—injured and reinjured by the indifference to her trauma—and thus addresses her story itself as wounded: its integrity is ignored" (85). In that way, the diary also becomes a symbol of Minnie's wounded self and a means of articulating pain and suffocating existence. She finds a source of healing in her diary by expressing her trauma and reaching out to her readers.

Careful anthrological readings reveal careless mother-figures in both *A Child's Life* and *The Diary of a Teenage Girl*. The reference to her mother in the first narrative resonates with the way it is referred to in its sequel. She writes, "I don't remember being born. I was a very ugly child. My appearance has not improved so I guess it was a lucky break when he was attracted by my youthfulness" (2). The diary of a fifteen-year-old Minnie Goetze begins in 1970s San Francisco and represents her struggling with her premature sexuality and troubled identity.

Gloeckner represents a bitter moment in her life when Minnie says, "My real Dad still lives in Philadelphia, but even when I lived there, I didn't see him much, only once or twice a year" (15). Here we see Minnie's yearning for paternal affection as she is going through an adolescent phase during which time there can be a flickering obsession with the self. She wishes to be admired by the experienced "male, but Minnie doesn't come across any man who 'looked' at her, despite having a 'fairly evenly' proportioned body, with 'broad shoulders and broad hips'" (3). She also has a sexual inclination for her mother's boyfriend, Monroe, but she longs for someone to tell her not to look at herself even objectively for it traumatizes her. In her own words, "Sometimes I feel incapable of love. I have a little feeling that I'm doing something wrong" (15). The illustration of Minnie and Gretel inadvertently suggests her discomfort and disenchantment with herself.

Minnie's sense of betrayal from Monroe emerges out of lurking ambush when she writes a short letter to Monroe: "Did you really take advantage of me? That wasn't very nice" (35). The duality in Monroe's nature lies in the fact that he used to care and treat Minnie as his own child in front of her mother, and then turns her into an object when her mother is not around. Gloeckner illustrates on page 79 the idea of the male gaze, denouncing the domineering Monroe. The illustration is captioned "*He said he didn't like stupid little chicks like me trying to manipulate him*" (79; italics in original). Both of them were drunk, and Minnie confessed that after sex she refused to put her clothes on. In the illustration one finds three images: there are three Coors beer cans and Monroe's glass on the table with a messed-up tablecloth; a side view of naked Monroe with his testicles visible from behind; and Minnie pointing her middle finger to Monroe in a clear sign of hatred and disgust. She is puzzled by the idea of finding a loving partner and registers in her diary that "both Monroe and my mom date other people but they still sleep together. I don't understand their relationship or what it means to me but I'm not allowed to talk to Monroe about it" (102). Once she completes her comics, entitled "Identity Crisis," (182) she finds herself mentally deteriorating and ends up writing a poem to supplement it:

> and from this wretched body I speak
> Saying it will be different when I die
> When I cross the Nile to the west
> . . .
> When I die I would like to die by
> Drownation in the Ganges River . . . (186)

This refers to Minnie's disgust for Monroe, who is a deceitful character; on one hand, he shows sympathy towards Minnie and on the other, he plays her emotions and abuses and distorts her perception about others. Minnie finds that it is better to live with Tabatha because "Monroe is such a bastard" (211). Despair in Minnie's eyes prompts an epiphanic disclosure from her—"Everything is so loveless and mediocre" (212)—shaping her wounds in the diary.

However, her hatred is shifted altogether from Monroe to Pascal when she hears Pascal insulting her to Charlotte. Minnie eavesdrops on a conversation between Charlotte and Pascal, and hears him say, "There seems to be something sexual about Minnie's need for physical contact with you, Charlotte" (84). Though Pascal sends her letters, Christmas cards, and birthday wishes containing the words "I LOVE YOU" in upper case, Minnie does not respond to any of them out of utter disgust. The title of the third section, "My Junior Year: I wallow in a state of despair, but by and by, I am befriended by a girl named Tabatha," also suggests the same, and ends with Minnie's own words and her own revelation to herself:

> I hate Pascal. I'm glad I saved all his letters. I can look at them with new eyes now . . . One that seduces you with false concern as he makes you believe he's accepted you in his pretentious exclusive inner circle. He's just like Monroe but more evil because he's smarter and understands his own intent. He's a liar through and through and I thought he loved me like a father. (278)

The last dialogue balloon in a way summarizes her disgust towards her family, friends, love life, and herself. The image features a silhouetted figure and carries a deep connotation of how much a troubled and traumatic childhood and adolescence can ruin a person's life. This motif reverberates through the pages of the comic.

IV

While dealing with child abuse and trauma in literature, Judith Herman (1992) comments that "chronic childhood abuse takes place in a familial climate of pervasive terror, in which ordinary caretaking relationships have been profoundly disrupted" (98). In this study of Gloeckner's comics, we have analyzed the role of the autobiographical eye and the "I" that experiences psychological pain and, thereby, trauma. It reaches to the core of the heart of a child whose blooming petals of childhood are hurt and plucked before she reaches a status to handle the intensity and continuity of the abuse. These harrowing experiences are never eradicated from the memory of the victims.

Note

1. Body here does not denote the physical body only, but it also includes the site of violence. Be it physical or psychological, a body is hurt or bruised in terms of internal and external exploitations.

Works Cited

Cardell, Kylie. *Dear World: Contemporary Uses of the Diary*. Madison: University of Wisconsin Press, 2014.

Caruth, Cathy. *Trauma: Explorations in Memory*. Baltimore: Johns Hopkins University Press, 1995.

Chute, Hillary. "Comics as Literature? Reading Graphic Narrative." *PMLA* 123, no. 2 (2008): 452–65.

Chute, Hillary. *Graphic Women: Life Narrative and Contemporary Comics*. New York: Columbia University Press, 2010.

Felman, Shoshana, and Dori Laub. *Testimony: Crises of Witnessing in Literature, Psychoanalysis and History*. New York: Routledge, 1992.

Hartman, Geoffrey H. "On Traumatic Knowledge and Literary Studies." *New Literary History* 26, no. 3 (1995): 537–63.

Herman, Judith. *Trauma and Recovery: The Aftermath of Violence—From Domestic Abuse to Political Terror*. New York: Basic Books, 1992.

Hirsch, Marianne. "Editor's Column: Collateral Damage." *PMLA* 119, no. 5 (2004): 1209–15.

Hogan, Rebecca. "Engendered Autobiographies: The Diary as a Feminine Form." *Prose Studies* 14, no. 2 (1991): 95–107.

Køhlert, Frederik Byrn. "Working It Through: Trauma and Autobiography in Phoebe Gloeckner's *A Child's Life* and *The Diary of a Teenage Girl*." *South Central Review* 32, no. 3 (2015): 124–42.

Lejeune, Philippe. *On Autobiography*. Edited by Paul John Eakin. Translated Katherine M. Leary. Minneapolis: University of Minnesota Press, 1989.

Lejeune, Philippe. *On Diary*. Honolulu: University of Hawai'i Press, 2009.

Merry, Bruce. "The Literary Diary as a Genre." *Maynooth Review / Revieú Mhá Nuad* 5, no. 1 (1979): 3–19.

Michael, Olga. "The Other Narratives of Sexual Violence in Phoebe Gloeckner's *A Child's Life and Other Stories*." *Journal of Graphic Novels and Comics* 9, no. 3 (2018): 229–50. DOI: 10.1080/21504857.2018.1462223.

Michael, Olga. "Reading Phoebe Gloeckner's *A Child's Life and Other Stories* at the Time of #MeToo." *Life Writing* 16, no. 3 (2019): 345–67.

Nietzsche, Friedrich. *Beyond Good and Evil*. Coradella Collegiate Bookshelf, 2004.

Whitehead, Anne. *Trauma Fiction*. Edinburgh: Edinburgh University Press, 2004.

12

#BLACKLIVESMATTER AND CARTOONING RACIAL VIOLENCE

VINCENT HADDAD

While cell phones, dash cams, and social media have enabled the mass circulation of images of racial violence and police brutality over the past decade, how viewers consume these images is not so straightforward. Some people may struggle to justify looking at one more act of horrific violence committed against Black victims, while others watch and rewatch these videos frame-by-frame, share them, and debate them. Questions of whether these images facilitate or mobilize political action or if they desensitize viewers to the acts of violence themselves complicate the fact that the putative truthfulness of these images in practice routinely fails to secure convictions, or even indictments, of guilty officers. Within this context, I analyze a remixed superhero story, *Black* (2017), an antihero superhero story, *Genius* (2014), and a YA graphic novel, *I Am Alfonso Jones* (2018). Each of these examples represents scenes of police violence against Black men, women, and children, though with varying stylistic fidelity to the "real." In this survey, I put pressure on the effectiveness or appropriateness of these cartoon images of racial violence. What is the function of these images? Does genre impact these functions? What about narrative? Or style?

From archival photography to smartphone videos disseminated online, scholars and activists weigh skepticism over these spectacular images of violence with their potential to hold power accountable. In her study of photographs of violence against African Americans, Courtney R. Baker argues, "We who look from a safe distance at the pain and death of others have been challenged by the motivations and exploitations that are involved in this peculiar visual dynamic. There are troubling consequences set up by this looking scenario in which a spectator seems to hold power over an exposed victim" (1). Focusing on images of the Black Lives Matter (BLM) movement, these "motivations and exploitations" so often manifest in the form of bad faith retorts ("All Lives Matter"), victim-blaming ("just follow orders"), and fearmongering about organizers and protesters as so-called "terrorists." Applying a similar lens to the ethics of racialized images of violence on Twitter, Wendy Sung describes a new form of "anticipatory nonspectatorship" wherein "Twitter users register a deep suspicion of the photographic and the premise/promise of indexicality, as well as its uses, refusing the spectacle of racial violence's visual form and instead highlighting its ubiquitous and quotidian nature by asserting themselves into their own scenes of visual failure and death" (17–18). The mixed effects and ethical implications of the saturation of these images only intensify as they become more prevalent in the fictional realm: in television, movies, novels, and a growing number of BLM-inspired comics. Like photography, images in comics exist in a frame; unlike photography, comics artists and writers build a network of other panels and images that shape how the reader looks at the image. Moreover, like Sung's concept of "anticipatory nonspectatorship," comics rely on an imaginative act of closure and self-assertion between these panels to produce the narrative and its literary effects.

Comics have attracted several theorists interested in representations of historical and personal trauma, ranging from natural disasters and genocide to sexual violence and assault, because of the effectiveness of the form in producing empathy. In *Ethics in the Gutter*, Kate Polack explains,

> [While] reading accounts of violence who experienced it firsthand, we *don't* actually experience what they did. Graphic narratives, because of the createdness of the page and the interplay of text and image, draw our attention to that distance. . . . [The] very constructedness that makes the reader aware of the gulf between his own experience and that which is depicted also cues the reader into an engagement more ethically nuanced than he might have had otherwise. The relative "truth" of a particular account of genocide, for example, is not something most caring, compassionate human beings are inclined to question. Discussions of audience or stylistic choices can, in the case of survivor testimony, feel positively sacrilegious. The comics form, however, frees the reader to discuss *choices* made about representation and thus engage more deeply in the ethical project of cultural memory. (14)

However true this assessment of the form may be, the BLM movement and the bad faith cultural and political responses to it put pressure on its every assumption. The inclination to question the victimhood of Black Americans killed by officers has been validated over and over by our legal system, and, as the rhetoric of the Trump administration has made clear, sacrilege is perhaps our new political currency when it comes to violence against people of color in the US. Even following the summer of 2020, featuring the national and international multiracial protests of the murders of George Floyd in Minneapolis and a growing awareness of systemic transformations such as defunding and abolishing the police, I still hesitate, drawing on Baker and Sung's insightful critiques of the visual culture of racialized violence, to adopt Polack's assumptions about "caring, compassionate human beings" and the stylistic freedoms in cartooning violence and trauma those readers might afford in the context of BLM-related comics.

Not only do these exigent factors of overt racism require more careful consideration of how cartoon violence is used in narratives that claim a relation to the BLM movement, but so do the unconscious biases that affect even generous readers of historical and racial trauma. According to a recent psychology study, white Americans are susceptible to believing Black Americans have superhuman qualities, or "mental and physical qualities that are supernatural (transcending the laws of nature), extrasensory (transcending the bounds of normal human perception), and magical (influencing of manipulating the natural world through symbolic or ritualistic means) or simply put others as '*beyond* human'" (Evans). Another study considered why Black Americans were treated less frequently with pain medication by doctors and asserts a connection to the false beliefs held by not only white lay persons but also medical students and professionals about biological differences between Blacks and whites, such as that "blacks have thicker skin than do white people or that black people's blood coagulates more quickly than white people's blood" (Hoffman et. al 4297). For stories that trade on the ability to understand the difference between the constructedness of fictional comic narratives and reality, it is important to recognize that images that evoke racial violence are vulnerable not only to being misinterpreted, but to confirming existing biases.

The political potential Polak and others attribute to comics is because the power of looking does not belong solely to the individual images, but to their connection to other panels across the gutters and their context in the narratives they are used to tell. Unfortunately, in a survey of comics that represent or adapt the BLM movement, many of these narratives yield mixed and damaging results. Perhaps no genre has included more references to the BLM movement, and done so more problematically, than the superhero genre. Superhero narratives are inseparable from the logics of criminality and "law and order."[1] Yet, even when the mere presence of superheroes proves the inadequacies of policing to address social conflicts and inequalities, contemporary superhero narratives display the lingering if latent legacy of the Comics Code Authority's prohibition of presenting "policeman, judges, government officials, and respected institutions . . . in such a way as to create disrespect for established authority." Black superheroes in particular have long struggled to overcome their mostly white creators and their added burden of confronting racial politics.[2] Though big publishers such as Marvel often capitalize on topical content like the BLM movement, they can tend towards the most conservative reactions to the movement, such as a plot in which an all-Black superhero team led by Black Panther literally beats up emotionally vulnerable BLM protesters who are thus being easily manipulated by the supervillain.[3] A recent group of BLM-inspired comics from independent publishers seem to lend a more radical shape and form to our cultural imagination for alternatives to a policing system linked to racial bias and violence against Black communities. Yet, by tracing cartoon violence in these texts—who is an appropriate target of this violence and who is an inappropriate target of this violence—my aim is to assess whether these narratives offer readers more nuanced and ethical relations to the BLM movement and what political potential they offer.

In *Black*, writers Kwanza Osajyefo and Tim Smith 3 with artist Jamal Igle invent a storyworld where the only people with superpowers in the entire world are Black—a concept that propelled this book from Kickstarter to a forthcoming Warner Brothers feature film. Khary Randolph's arresting and radical cover art deserves its own critical attention for its articulation of the continuous material, linguistic, and visual legacy of American policing from slavery to its modern-day iteration. His cover for Issue 3, for example, features a police lineup of four young Black men from different historical eras holding placards that mirror what Anthony Neal refers to as the connotative struggle of "The Naming": the placard "slave" is held by an enslaved person chained with an iron neck ring, "negro" by a Civil War–era soldier, "colored" by a man in a suit and suggestive of a participant in the civil rights movement, and "thug" held by a tattooed man. *Black* offers a nuanced critique of the superhero genre and its complicated representations of race, but also reproduces many of the problems characteristic of such power fantasies. The first issue opens with an overt example of racial profiling from police who "patrol the places, but don't know the places" (3). Teenager Kareem Jenkins and his friends are walking home when police officers looking for "black males, 20s, in basketball shorts and t-shirts" confront them with guns drawn. (3) After his friend turns to flee out of fear, the officer opens fire; the conventional comic sound effect "Pop!" and cartoon splashes of blood obscure the all-too-familiar scene of a violent encounter between police and unarmed Black children assumed to be both older and guiltier than they are. This exaggerated use of comic violence draws attention to the fictionality of the image and the story more broadly, as the event reveals the fictional conceit of the story: Kareem has superheroic healing abilities. The empowering image of a young Black man who cannot be destroyed by bullets is a certainly an attractive route for superhero narratives, as can be seen in the television shows *Luke Cage* and *Black Lightning*. However, one problem with this setup is, as Jordan X. Evans argues, that officers like Darren Wilson describe victims like Michael Brown in almost identical terms in order to legally justify their actions, and "[African Americans] cannot don a hoodie, be shot 16 times like Luke Cage, and walk away unscathed; instead when [African Americans] are perceived as a bulked out Hulk it can mean [their] death" (Evans). As the genre perhaps demands, the comic values its singular hero, his unique abilities, and his subsequent journey, over the very nonsuperheroic people this image might empower; his friends, presumably dead, are forgotten, hardly mentioned or mourned in the rest of the narrative arc.

Despite the limited reach of its empathic treatment of cartoon violence, *Black* volume 1 does use the genre to develop a compelling critique of policing and mass incarceration. After showing his abilities, Kareem is immediately recruited by "the Project," charged with tracking down and helping other Black people who exhibit superheroic abilities. However, when Kareem discovers that this team simply reconstitutes the very police order that first shot him, arresting and incarcerating those whom they decide are too aggressively seeking retribution for the racism they've faced, he runs away. Kareem ultimately finds himself caught between the Project seeking to enforce a peaceful pathway to racial progress and a militant Black superhero team led by O, who is willing to kill for their cause. The superhero genre, with its dependency on cartoon violence to propel its plots forward, seems to gravitate toward constructing such reductive and confused analogs to the debates between Martin Luther King Jr. and Malcom X over the path to Black liberation.[4] Kareem's healing ability is meant to provide a synthesis between the two as they confront the villain: a white man whose "family has been managing these people longer than our great country has existed" and who seeks to control their powers for his profits (100).

In the narrative's climax, the two teams battle each other to determine whether to kill or arrest the villain, who taunts, with the bald-faced hypocrisy readers have come to expect in certain segments of the public sphere, "Ugh! These violent liberals . . . are being radicalized by Black Lives Matter" (136). The violence these Black superheroes wage against one another in this battle fills page after page. Yet, when Kareem finally reaches the white villain, violence becomes a point of philosophical debate. Kareem argues, "With all these powers we don't have to start a war, we can be better than—," to which O interrupts, "*tch* are you dumb? That we're better is precisely why they kill us, and you want to help in this deception" (141). Although the narrative suggests an affinity towards and ultimately depends on O's radicalism—he has secretly been broadcasting the battle, revealing the superpowers of Black people to the world—Kareem is trapped in the contradictions set by the narrative's use of exaggerated cartoon violence, wherein any exercise of violence in the pursuit of liberation is a red line. When the villain launches into another diatribe, Kareem breaks the tension with an apparent compromise to both teams, connecting a nonfatal left hook, "Whop!" as he rebuts, "Lemme put some 'spect on that name" (141). Yet, the cartoonish representation of violence—stars and planets circle the villain's stupefied head—allows Kareem to step back and affirm his separation from O's ideology.

Ultimately, the story ends without any clear sense of what violence is appropriate to a comics frame and what is politically and ethically inappropriate. Kareem adopts the name "X" and explains a muddled vision of his politics: "[The Project] wants Emancipation, O wants retaliation . . . I think people need somethin' else . . . someone to represent. I'ma be a'ight . . . I'm their worst nightmare . . . a nigga they can't kill" (148). A full departure from The Project's work towards emancipation may be surprising to some readers, but Kareem is acutely aware of the misalignment of what Rinaldo Walcott calls the "long emancipation" and Black freedom, wherein "emancipation is a legal process and term that . . . marks continued unfreedom, not the freedom it supposedly ushered in" (1). One could read Kareem's solution "to represent" alongside Polak's emphasis on the importance of representation in comics and its relation to developing a more ethically nuanced reader. Yet, by identifying representation as separate and apart from either emancipation or retaliation, Kareem also exemplifies Gayatri Chakravorty Spivak's argument about the meaning of representation as dual and oppositional: "The complicity of *vertreten* [to speak for] and *darstellen* [to depict], their identity-in-difference as the place of practice . . . can only be appreciated if they are not conflated by a sleight of hand" (260). The narrative seems to link Kareem's desire to speak for his community and the comic's own power to facilitate a mode of representation apart from traditional superhero comics. In this sense, the narrative echoes Tavia Nyong'o's claim that, by viewing this duality of representation as coherent, power becomes "naturalized as a mode of political authority" (Nyong'o 72). Just as Kareem is set above and beyond his friends killed in the first issue, the reader is ultimately left with little confidence that he can or will imagine any political leadership that does not also set him apart, singularly charged with the capacity to both speak for and depict those vulnerable to cartoon violence.

This theme is extended in what appears to be one of the most radical comics about policing and Black liberation: *Genius* written by Marc Bernardin and Adam Freeman with artist Afua Richardson. The story follows a young Black woman, Destiny, who, fed up with the police violence in her community, decides to use her military genius to wrest control of Compton from the police. Through its related uses of gender and cartoon violence, *Genius* performs a certain vision of radicalism as it dangerously affirms right-wing caricatures of Black collective organizing.

It should not be surprising that, among a survey of BLM-inspired comics, *Genius* stands out for having a Black female protagonist—and the narrative plays on this fact. A seemingly impartial police detective, whose words frame the first page and who is guided only by data "dissected, analyzed, catalogued, and cross-referenced," conarrates the story with Destiny. In the second issue, he explains the life story that would have created someone capable of organizing the slaughter of forty police officers, his predictions accompanying the corresponding images from Destiny's life, such as when she witnesses police kill her parents at the age of ten (10). As he accurately documents her motivating events and traumas, the officer repeatedly, here and throughout the first issues, assumes the masculine identity of his "suspect zero" (10). Her backstory plays out against the ironic contrast of the detective, explaining,

> Alpha's rise to power can happen in a number of ways, in a pack or primitive tribe it will most likely be through sheer physical prowess. But in higher-functioning civilizations, they may first become the beta male. A trusted confidant of the current alpha male. If he was out to prove his dick was bigger, he would have popped up on our radar a long time ago. (40–41)

This emphasis draws our attention to not only the comic centering a Black female protagonist in a medium and genre that so often marginalizes them, but also to the fundamental role of Black women in organizing Black liberation movements—in particular Alicia Garza, Patrisse Khan-Cullors, and Opal Tometi who founded the BLM movement.[5] In Barbara Ransby's authoritative history of the coalition of Black activist groups that constitute the Movement for Black Lives, she documents how "the most coherent, consistent and resolute political voices to emerge over the years since 2012 have been Black feminist voices, or Black feminist-influenced voices" (59).

However, if the repeated misgendering of Destiny is meant to draw our attention to the progressive bonafides of the narrative and the rightness of its protagonist, it does so by actualizing the obvious fabrications that were so often told about these women and the movement itself: that they were "terrorists." In a continuation of the long history of the US government labeling Black activists as "terrorists" and violent—not least a leaked FBI report that warned of "an emergent domestic terror threat sweeping the nation and threatening the lives of law enforcement officers: the 'Black Identity Extremist' ('B.I.E.') movement"—*Genius* can be read as validating these harmful fabrications about the movement itself, especially in its depictions of violence against police officers (Beydoun and Hansford). Although, like we see in *Black*, cartooning violence can function as the language of radicalism and shock value in comics, it is not the actual language of Black radicalism. As I move to analyze the comic's use of cartoon violence, I want to pause to underscore the movement's policy and philosophy grounded in nonviolence, and thus, even as cartoon representations, that Destiny bears no ideological relation to the movement itself.

The comic opens provocatively with a full-page splash image of a Black officer being shot and a voice-over provided by the narrator-detective, "What I'm trying to tell you, sir . . . is that we're sitting on a powder keg, just waiting to explode" (7). This image is set against an abstract background of mathematical equations. We might read this as an invitation for the reader to consider the author's calculation in opening the book in this fashion, recalling Polak's argument that comics allow, more than other mediums, the possibility to "discuss *choices* made about representation"—among which the officer's race stands out. This fact recalls some of the debates that emerged in the case of the death of Freddie Gray in Baltimore, in which three of the officers charged, including the one with the most serious charges, as well as many of the other local authorities, were African American. Activists in Baltimore developed a systemic critique of racism that responded to both bad-faith responses, such as that the race of the officers meant that no racial bias played part in the event, and even well-intentioned but inadequate calls for police reform, like that simply increasing the diversity of police departments would help solve the problem of racial bias in policing. As Ransby points out, "BLMM/M4BL organizers indicted the system in Baltimore as racist, emphasizing the structural nature of the problems that persisted, irrespective of which individuals were carrying out policy" (xi). The complicity of Black elites across various positions of governance, including Black officers, has been a central feature of many works of scholarship on the BLM movement, most notably *Democracy in Black* by Eddie S. Glaude Jr.,

From *#BlackLivesMatter to Black Liberation* by Keeanga-Yamahtta Taylor, and *Locking Up Our Own* by James Forman Jr. Is this image an attempted continuation of these critiques? Or, is it simply another example of cartoon violence being easier to apply to a Black character within a fictional plot than a white character, especially a white police officer? Perhaps, in this storyworld, these equations suggest Destiny's calculations of what violence, even against Black people, are necessary for her vision of Black liberation.

We receive a potential answer just a few short pages later when Destiny makes her coup of the neighborhood known to the rest of the police force, saying: "Now, you listen here ... bitch. I'ma let you pick up your meat, here, and crawl the fuck back from where you came. And when they ass' you what happened, you tell 'em that this here belongs to me" (9). Echoing the horrific mistreatment of Michael Brown's body left for hours in the streets of Ferguson, the reader glimpses that Destiny's use of violence may be more reactionary than liberatory. If the goal of *Genius* is to enact a fantasy of Black liberation based in the community, it remains bound to the structures of power and violence that devalue Black life, and these structures will inform her very treatment of her community. Following the "might makes right" paradigm historically embedded in the superhero genre, Destiny proceeds to "declare martial law in this motherfucker," ultimately revealing the comic's limited imagination for a world without a militarized police force (12).

Following this logic, the narrative ultimately crystallizes around a justification of the carceral state, rather than using its imaginative potential to explore any of the actual proposals of transformative justice that BLM/M4BL activists developed.[6] As the violence spirals out of Destiny's control, she disguises herself as Internal Affairs and confronts her conarrator. While the detective ponders why someone would do this violence, Destiny shifts the conversation from her actions as a symptom of her experiences, thinks to herself "fuck it," and confesses: "Maybe there isn't a why ... Only that she's very good at breaking things. What if you were so good at a thing that had no application in a civilized world? Wouldn't that frustrate you to the point where you'd orchestrate your life to find some way to satisfy that?" (112). Narratively, Destiny learns from this interaction that the National Guard has been called in, and she needs to do anything she can to protect her neighborhood. But this introspection on her inherent appetite for violence, a justification in itself for over-policing and militarized force, foreshadows her solution: to turn herself in and go to prison. In the fictional realm of *Genius*, her expertise in violence qualifies her for a secret military program. And, though the promise of her returning to her community with even more military knowledge lingers, the story can avoid entirely reckoning with the carceral state, as BLM has effectively critiqued, as an ineffective vehicle for either justice or rehabilitation.

As perhaps the most provocative and promising examples of BLM-inspired superhero comics, these two texts illustrate the contradictions and pitfalls of racialized cartoon violence, which in some cases serve to desensitize readers to the state violence exercised against Black communities. However, when narratively well-supported, images of racial violence can be quite effective, as they are in the YA graphic novel *I Am Alfonso Jones* by Tony Medina with artists Stacey Robinson and John Jennings. Set against the backdrop of their high school's performance of *Hamlet*, Alfonso is killed by an officer when he and his friend Danetta are shopping for his suit for the homecoming dance. The narrative then develops this encounter in the "real" world, where friends and family must reckon with its aftermath, and in the afterlife, where Alfonso as a ghost listens to the stories of other Black victims of racial terror and state violence across history.

The reader follows Alfonso in the final week of his life and then as his family and friends struggle to reckon with his death, the court proceedings, and the BLM protests that follow. In this space, each of the bad faith arguments that would call the truthfulness of the images of his fatal encounter with police into question are raised by various characters, and rebutted unapologetically and forcefully by teachers, parents, and activists who educate their kids (and the reader) about systemic racism. In one scene, the students begin debating what conclusions about policing and racism they might make from Alfonso's death. A white female student becomes incensed, asserting that her uncle is a cop and "we are protected by the police." The students engage in a high-level debate over community policing, diversity in the makeup of police departments, and who falls under the category "we" when, in Danetta's experience, their role is to protect "*their* neighborhoods—or stores! And shoot us and kill us like Alfonso!" The one student remains unconvinced, repeating over and over again "there are good cops." Rather than end the scene in this disagreement, Medina stages a full splash page of the teacher explaining:

> I'm sick of the phrase, "But there are some good cops," too. It makes it seem that when people speak out against police violence, they're automatically judging all police. We are all very hurt and angry about what has happened to Alfonso . . . But we can't allow our anger to turn us into what we loathe the most. Natasha is right. We cannot stereotype all cops. But there's something deeply wrong with policing and that's where we should focus our energies. (90)

Across all the seemingly radical BLM comics I have surveyed—seemingly radical in the images of violence they deploy and plots they imagine—this is by far the most radical scene. With the stylistic emphasis constructed around this teacher, a reader of *I Am Alfonso Jones* comes closer to the work of BLM activists than in any of the prior examples of representations of violence.

This commitment to the actual concerns and platforms of the movement for Black Lives is buoyed by the fictionality of the story and the constructedness of the page. In the literary tradition of novels such as Toni Morrison's *Beloved* and Jesmyn Ward's *Sing, Unburied, Sing*, Alfonso haunts the narrative as a ghost. He travels on the NY subway with a host of other Black victims of police violence whose stories educate Alfonso that he is but one in a long history of state-sanctioned racial terror. Periodically interrupting the main story, the reader learns alongside Alfonso each of these ghosts' stories, as they relive the feelings and experiences of their deaths. As Mama Eleanor, the first ghost, begins her story, "My God! What did those savages do to you! Baby, what happened? Were you lynched? . . . Do you remember how that felt? They got you looking like a colander. I remember how they did me. Remember it like it was yesterday . . . As clear as you are sittin' here all big-headed and bug-eyed" (25). In addition to the image of Alfonso appearing in the afterlife with a hangar wrapped around his neck, the reference to lynching prepares the reader for a historical reckoning of Alfonso's death. The layered structure of the story situates the individuated tragedy of Alfonso Jones into a long history of racial atrocities. By doing so, *I Am Alfonso Jones* educates its readers that, just like real images of racial terror, images of cartoonish racial violence are in a network of other competing images and narratives that seek to call it fictional. These images do not alone produce empathy, nor do they necessarily mobilize readers to political action; in fact, they may do the opposite. Instead, they require stronger networks of images and well-crafted narratives to support them: narratives that sharpen readers' capacities to not be led astray by simple and bad faith rhetorical detours, and narratives that use fictionality to highlight the violence against Black communities are not contained by single images, but sustained and felt across a long history of racial terror.

Notes

1. Thomas Giddens, "Crime, Justice, and Anglo-American Comics," *Oxford Research Encyclopedia of Criminology*, https://oxfordre.com/criminology/view/10.1093/acrefore/9780190264079.001.0001/acrefore-9780190264079-e-50.

2. *White Scripts and Black Supermen*. Produced, directed, and written by Jonathan Gayles, Wolfman Productions, 2012.

3. Vincent Haddad, "Can Superheroes Be Woke?: Black Liberation and Black Panther," *Black Perspectives*, Feb. 24, 2018, https://www.aaihs.org/can-superheroes-be-woke-black-liberation-and-the-black-panther/.

4. Prince Shakur, "'Black Panther' Mirrors the Duality of Martin Luther King, Jr. and Malcolm X," *Teen Vogue*, March 10, 2018, https://www.latimes.com/archives/la-xpm-1986-07-05-ca-20403-story.html.

5. Keisha N. Blain, "The Black Women Who Paved the Way for This Moment," *The Atlantic*, June 9, 2020. https://www.theatlantic.com/ideas/archive/2020/06/pioneering-black-women-who-paved-way-moment/612838/.

6. Mariame Kaba, *We Do This 'Til We Free Us* (Chicago: Haymarket Books, 2021).

Works Cited

Baker, Courtney R. *Humane Insight*. Champaign: University of Illinois Press, 2015.

Bernardin, Marc, Adam Freeman, and Afua Richardson. *Genius*, vol. 1. Portland: Image Comics, 2015.

Beydoun, Khaled A., and Justin Hansford. "The FBI's Dangerous Crackdown on 'Black Identity Extremists.'" *New York Times*, Nov. 15, 2017. https://www.nytimes.com/2017/11/15/opinion/black-identity-extremism-fbi-trump.html.

Evans, Jordan X. "Superhumanization." *Nursing Clio*, Jan. 3, 2018. https://nursingclio.org/2018/01/03/superhumanization/.

Hoffman, Kelly M., Sophie Trawalter, Jordan R. Axt, and M. Norman Oliver. "Racial Bias in Pain Assessment and Treatment Recommendations, and False Beliefs about Biological Differences between Blacks and Whites." *PNAS* 113, no. 16 (2016): 4296–301.

Khan-Cullors, Patrisse, and Asha Bandele. *When They Call You a Terrorist*. New York: St. Martin's Press, 2018.

McCloud, Scott. *Understanding Comics*. New York: HarperCollins, 1993.

Medina, Tony, Stacey Robinson, and John Jennings. *I Am Alfonso Jones*. New York: Tu Books, 2017.

Neal, Anthony. "The Naming: A Conceptualization of an African American Connotative Struggle." *Journal of Black Studies* 34, no. 1 (2001): 50–65.

Nyong'o, Tavia. "Unburdening Representation." *Black Scholar* 44, no. 2 (2014): 70–80.

Osajyefo, Kwanza, Tim Smith 3, and Jamal Igle. *Black*, vol. 1. Los Angeles: Black Mask Studios, 2017.

Polak, Kate. *Ethics in the Gutter*. Columbus: Ohio State University Press, 2017.

Ransby, Barbara. *Making All Black Lives Matter*. Oakland: University of California Press, 2018.

Spivak, Gayatri Chakravorty. *A Critique of Postcolonial Reason*. Cambridge, MA: Harvard University Press, 1999.

Sung, Wendy. "In the Wake of Visual Failure: Twitter, Sandra Bland, and an Anticipatory Nonspectatorship." *Social Text* 39, no. 2 (2021): 1–23.

Taylor, Keeanga-Yamahtta. *From #BlackLivesMatter to Black Liberation*. Chicago: Haymarket Books, 2016.

Walcott, Rinaldo. *The Long Emancipation*. Durham, NC: Duke University Press, 2021.

13

RADICAL EMPATHY IN *MARCH*

LEAH MILNE

In the first of his graphic novel trilogy, *March: Book One*, Congressman John Lewis recounts how, as a child, he shirked his farm duties by hiding under the porch and then rushing off to school when the bus arrived. He remembers that his sharecropper father would scold him, but "deep inside I think he knew there was no stopping me. This was a life decision I had made, and it was near-impossible to turn me away from it" (13). This devotion to study would serve Lewis well in his nonviolent struggle for equality. And perhaps most appropriate for this chapter, Lewis's dogged devotion to study and reflection is a pedagogical model for how to broach conversations about learning how to better practice empathy, both in and beyond the classroom. Lewis frames his own journey towards understanding empathy historically, and specifically through a nonviolent lens: the *March* trilogy depicts several historical events including Bloody Sunday in Selma, the actions of the Freedom Riders, and the Nashville sit-ins, and their foundation in the systematic practice of nonviolence. Fundamentally, Lewis, who died of pancreatic cancer in 2020 at the age of eighty, seated his philosophy in a deeply felt sense of nonviolent empathy, specifically an active form of protest and radical empathy that he often referred to in speeches, books, interviews, and even on his Twitter account as "good trouble" (Meacham 248). The *March* trilogy makes a case for this form of nonviolent empathy as requiring study, disciplined practice, and relentless vigilance. By causing good trouble—that is, by getting in the way and forcing others to contend with his humanity, Lewis believes that he and his fellow protesters have the best chance of bringing about positive change toward equality. His nuanced approach to empathy affords a valuable opportunity in the classroom (and elsewhere) to discuss what is truly involved in the work of positive change.

Empathy involves taking on the feelings and perspectives of another, and the act of "feeling with" someone comes much more naturally than the higher orders of empathy involving an attempt to imagine and understand someone's thoughts and emotions (Batson 4). In many ways, empathy is fundamental not only to Lewis's comics but to the comic medium in general. Kate Polak highlights that "the formal qualities of graphic narratives . . . [prompt] readers to consider their emotional and ethical relationships to the text" (2), making them complicit collaborators in the work of reading and interpretation. When I teach *March* in my Introduction to Literature, African American Literature, and Young Adult Literature courses, we talk about the choice of the graphic memoir to tell this story and the work that readers are asked to do as they engage with the text. When asked how a graphic memoir of Lewis's life may differ from one without images or even from, say, a documentary or set of archival photographs, students immediately make the connection to empathy. They note the inability to turn away from or lessen the intensity of images of violence perpetrated against the story's hero, and the relative control that the authors and artist have in imparting their message. "You really connect with John [Lewis]," wrote a student in an essay. "The way he and the artist tell his story inspires young adults today to stand up and embrace what they believe in. Anyone can read a history book. However, when they read a book such as *March*, the meaning becomes more special." Following the zigzags of panels and gutters, when present, and then turning the page to encounter a scene of chaos or a full-page profile of a historical figure further creates a unique experience that encourages empathetic and involved reading.

As a class, we also discuss how the connections between empathy and comics highlight the limits of our ability to fully empathize with those whose appearance and historical experiences differ from our own. As Hillary Chute writes, comics "has evolved as an instrument for commenting on and re-visioning experience and history. Drawing today still enters the public sphere as a form of witness that takes shape as marks and lines because no other technology could record what it depicts" (265). Unlike a cartoon-like face that would incline us towards identification and universality (McCloud 36), *March*'s style thrives in near-photographic specificity, proving, as Chute notes, how comics expands and forces us to consider "what it means to document, to archive, to inscribe" (7). My students match up archival footage of Hosea Williams, Amelia Boynton, Lewis, and the other marchers on Bloody Sunday, and even recognize depictions of coauthor Andrew Aydin by comparing certain panels to his photograph at the back of the book. There is thus no direct way for students to project themselves fully onto the trilogy's large cast of characters. The comic deliberately does not do the work of empathy for us. But we quickly learn that the distance the students and I must bridge to begin to understand what Lewis, Diane Nash, and others went through is part of the point.

Students also consider narrative choices within the trilogy and how they relate to empathy. For instance, the violent events that Lewis endures are made slightly less frightening by the nonlinear structure of the story itself. In a cinematically styled cold open, *Book One* of the trilogy presents a breathtaking set of scenes on March 7, 1965, or Bloody Sunday, where Lewis, alongside Hosea Williams and hundreds of fellow marchers, crosses the Edmund Pettus Bridge and is subsequently attacked by police and community members. The book interrupts the chaos with a two-page title spread featuring a serene overhead view of the National Mall in Washington, DC, followed by Lewis preparing to go to his office on January 20, 2009. Lewis's encounter with a mother and her two young boys in his office set up the frame of the narrative, where Lewis begins to tell the children his story of how he and the country were brought to this moment, the inauguration of the country's first Black president.

While empathy may seem easier to understand in a more linear form of storytelling that does not disrupt scenes of violence, students acknowledge that the structure actually *aids* empathy; knowing that Lewis not only survived the dangers of the civil rights movement but that he then became a revered member of Congress helps them to better engage with the stories that Lewis shared without the distraction of fearing for his life. I concede that all readers—especially younger ones—can get wrapped up in feelings of fear and hope that Lewis expresses in the books, despite knowing that he ultimately survives. However, I am more inclined to believe that the narrative structure better responds to the attention span of readers, myself included, who are becoming increasingly accustomed to the nonlinear storylines of books, TV shows, and movies and that this, combined with Nate Powell's absorbing artwork, is what helps bridge the gap between reader and subject.

In fact, as a class, we also discuss how Lewis, Aydin, and Powell's other authorial and pictorial choices add to our interpretation of the text and to our ability to connect to its real-life characters. For students who are not as familiar with more traditional superhero comics, I bring in examples of Captain America punching Hitler on the cover of the comic's debut issue and a Black man in *Green Lantern* #76 questioning the comic's hero for helping blue and orange skins on other planets while "never bother[ing] with . . . the black skins" on his own planet. We discuss how and why *March* diverges from these comics in style, format, and storytelling approaches. The first distinction that usually gets brought up is always related to the choice to use black-and-white instead of full color. While we also discuss considerations of publishing house style and cost related to this fact, someone is always quick to point out that the country was indeed—and in many ways still is—mired in racial issues of black and white, making the choice clear. Students also point out that the lack of orderly rectangular panels, and even the frequent omission of gutters altogether, is a subtle way to draw attention to how Lewis and his friends were also traversing boundaries in their fight against segregation, expanding the law to make it more encompassing and inclusive. In other words, Lewis's good trouble refuses to stay within the lines.

And finally, there is the language of the texts themselves. While some dialog balloons are deliberately unreadable, representing the chaos of the era, others capture the fear and hope of the movement in enrapturing ways. The frame story of *Book One* sets up the conversational tone of the captions, leading readers to feel, just as the mother and her two sons at the beginning of the trilogy, that Lewis is inviting them to a friendly chat, a chance to get to know him better. Lewis explains how, as a child aspiring to be a preacher, he practiced sermonizing to his chickens. Paired with Powell's striking images seen through a child's perspective, Lewis describes the wide expanse of the 110 acres of farmland of his youth, bought by his father "in the spring of 1940 for $300. Cash" (*Book One* 20). He contrasts this with the magic of the candy store and the tall and crowded buildings of Buffalo where he visits his uncle's family and witnesses with disbelief that "they had white people living next door to them. On both sides" (*Book One* 43). Without much explanation, readers intuit the ways that these events shaped Lewis's life. Even students who are uncertain that they would make the same choices as Lewis are nevertheless able to empathize with the frustration he feels when he learns of the lesser quality of his schools compared to white students, and when he realizes that the law, which promised an end to such disparity, never works as quickly or effectively as he would like. By the time we get to *Book Three* and learn of the Birmingham church bombings, Lewis's simply worded question deeply resonates: "How could our quest for human dignity spawn such *evil*?" (16). And, by the time Lewis first hears Martin Luther King Jr.'s "social gospel" on the radio and then joins Jim Lawson in his nonviolent workshops, these events thus appear part of a natural progression (*Book One* 56, 65), a superhero origin story that would almost seem contrived were it not actually true. By this point, students recognize that Lewis's personal history is part of the larger public history of all Americans, fueling empathy in the process.

In fact, even before it would go on to be the first graphic novel ever to win the National Book Award and the Robert F. Kennedy Book Award, the story of how the *March* trilogy came about has itself become the stuff of legends. Professed comic aficionado Andrew Aydin had been working as one of Lewis's congressional staffers for less than a year when Lewis began to tell him about a comic book that greatly influenced him. Written by Alfred Hassler and Benton Resnik, *Martin Luther King and the Montgomery Story* (1957) relates how King, Rosa Parks, and others, in a year of nonviolent boycotts and negotiations, integrated the city's public transportation. Aydin's enthusiasm eventually led to a promise to coauthor *March* with Lewis, alongside artist Nate Powell. Through his graduate thesis, Aydin would also write the first extensive study on Hassler and Resnik's comic, prompting the discovery of its previously uncredited artist, Sy Barry. The publication of *The Montgomery Story* was itself radical, created in the age of McCarthyism when many churches, schools, libraries, and government subcommittees believed that comics were linked to juvenile delinquency and moral decay (Aydin 14). Published by the Fellowship of Reconciliation (FoR), the comic was a tool that people such as FoR field secretary Jim Lawson used in nonviolence workshops and seminars, inspiring Ezell Blair and the rest of the Greensboro Four, as well as the young seminary student John Lewis. (The comic was, as WBUR and other news outlets point out, even passed around in the 2010–2012 protests collectively known as the Arab Spring.)

One of the earliest attendees of the FoR workshops, Lewis had been long frustrated about how segregation, though deemed unconstitutional, held sway over his life. On a page of *March: Book One* that also includes an image of *Martin Luther King and the Montgomery Story*, Lewis sits in a near-empty church in downtown Nashville, alone in a pew with his hand raised, poised to ask Lawson a question. Across the aisle sits Nash, whom he would later join at lunch counter sit-ins as part of the Student Nonviolent Coordinating Committee (SNCC). Through Lawson, Lewis learns how to use nonviolence as King did, to face racism, poverty, and war. Lawson emphasized that these evils—represented in the book by a hand holding a noose, another shaking with hunger, and a third amputated in battle—could all be addressed through nonviolent action. Lewis states, "Jim Lawson conveyed the urgency of developing our philosophy, our discipline, our understanding. His words liberated me. I thought, this is it . . . this is the way out" (77–78). This "way out" becomes ingrained in Lewis's civil rights struggle, so much so that, just before marching on the Edmund Pettus Bridge many years later, volunteers are instructed, "If you *can't* be nonviolent, *don't* get in here. If you can't accept blows without retaliating, *don't* get in the line" (*Book Three* 213). It is through these workshops that the connection between radical empathy and nonviolence, or Lewis's "good trouble," first becomes clear to readers of the trilogy.

Classroom conversations about empathy become especially animated when discussing the inclination to more easily empathize with those who resemble you in looks or experience, what Martin Hoffman calls "similarity bias" (208). The repeated exercises that Lawson, Lewis, Nash, and the student activists and volunteers practice throughout *March* directly confront similarity bias (or familiarity-similarity bias), the inclination to favor and be drawn to those who are like you or who confirm experiences and behaviors with which you are comfortable. Of course, this bias also affects how and with whom we empathize. Lewis recalls in *Book One* how, in the workshops, "everyone plays the roles of protesters, the instigators, and the resistance. There may be a Black person playing the role of a white person, or vice versa. We each tried to do everything we could to test ourselves, to break each other's spirits. We tried to dehumanize each other" (80). One panel shows a Black female student harassing a Black male student, calling him the n-word. In the next panel, the students' roles are reversed, and the mild stoicism of the man's face in the previous panel is replaced with rage as he takes on the role of the white harasser (*Book One* 80). The two students, like other workshop participants, are pushed to the limits of their empathy in extreme ways, asked to understand even the stance of those who might wish them harm. Lawson seemed to suggest that if one cannot empathize with those whose views and looks are opposite one's own, then the work of truly addressing racist violence will never be fully addressed.

SNCC leader Bob Moses, who like many of the SNCC members wore overalls to help increase empathy toward the rural groups they worked with, particularly emphasized the need for white volunteers to address similarity bias, warning that they would be treated much more harshly by white instigators: "Don't come to Mississippi this summer to save the Mississippi Negro," he admonished. "Only come if you understand—really understand—that his freedom and yours are *one*" (*Book Three* 43, 67). In other words, Moses, Lawson, and others pushed for empathy that moved beyond the simplicity of fellow feeling. Instead, this "good trouble" required sustained and repeated practice, hard lessons, and a changed mindset that included the very belief that empathy was neither natural nor easy. As witnesses to this struggle, readers also absorb the intent behind these values, their historical weight, and their applicability to their present lives and experiences. As a teacher witnessing my own students' struggles with this topic, I sense that this form of radical empathy sometimes even challenges generational preoccupations with how one expends emotional labor, and for and with whom. Moses's example of the discipline of preparing one's internal mindset for this empathy work thus remains vital and relevant.

The biggest challenge I've encountered with students examining empathy through *March* comes when they read how Lewis's encounters with violence put the workshops and the philosophy behind them to the test. Practicing the principles of nonviolence gleaned from King and Lawson, as well as James Farmer, Gandhi, and Jesus Christ, Lewis joins the Congress of Racial Equality (CORE) Freedom Riders, knowing the life-threatening dangers of practicing empathy and protest in this way. Lewis and his fellow riders even wrote wills before getting on the bus. Questioned by reporters in *Book Two*, Farmer lays down the rules they will follow: "If there is an arrest, we will accept that arrest, and if there is violence we will accept that violence without responding in kind. We will not pay fines because we feel that, by paying money to a segregated state, we would help it perpetuate segregation" (36). Several pages later, the pages turn black and the gutters disappear. *Book Two* features a bus in flames, with freedom riders fleeing not only the firebombed vehicle but also an Alabama mob wielding crowbars and guns just beyond the wreckage (44–45). At this point, even Farmer wants to call off the Freedom Rides, but Diane Nash, determined to continue, declares, "We can't let them stop us with violence. If we do, the movement is dead" (50). Farmer's hesitation is neither the first nor the last time that Lewis's belief in good trouble comes up against the fear of losing lives, and provides—at least in the classroom—one of the more grave consequences of radical empathy.

Students have found something of an answer to this challenge in realizing that not everyone is cut out for this work. For some, fighting the urge to not defend oneself when faced with violence also becomes too much to bear. In *Book One*, a workshop volunteer named Charles decides that he is unable to restrain himself, even when those spitting on him and calling him names are his friends helping him prepare for real scenes of violence. Covered in a drink someone has thrown at him, Charles raises his hands and declares, "I don't think I can do it. I just can't. Maybe I can bring signs, or make them. Maybe I can drive people to the site. But I can't take it. I *can't* be nonviolent. I *cannot*" (81). Seeing the limits of empathy is as important for readers as seeing when it is successful; these examples of struggling toward and even failing at empathy make it more apparent that this radical form of empathy requires strength and constraint. Possibly even more significant is the depiction of King's hesitation and eventual reversal on their second march to Selma. Though some read betrayal in what was later known as Turnaround Tuesday, Lewis realizes "there comes a time when you must retreat, and come back to fight another day" (*Book Three* 216). Finally, in *Book Three*, Lewis himself recalls the closest he came to being violent when, during the planning stages of the march on Selma to gain voting rights, a man broke into the crowd to punch Martin Luther King Jr. Amid the chaotic struggle, Lewis remembers he did not hit the attacker, "though I may have thought about it for a split-second . . .

I found out that day, even I have limits" (153). Seeing where nonviolence fails and how one's empathy is pushed to the threshold is as important to readers of *March* as is seeing the fallibility of any comic hero.

Lewis thus works to expand his capacity to empathize even with those unable or unwilling to practice his philosophy. *Book Two*, for instance, devotes a full-page panel to Malcolm X. Lewis finds commonality in their shared belief that the fight for equality had to happen in both the courts and on the streets, but X's inclination toward violence was where Lewis drew the line. Nevertheless, he admits that he "could understand [Malcolm X's] appeal, and the feelings of restlessness that drove it" (149). Indeed, despite their differences, it was clear that Malcolm X also believed in the power of empathy, though his version veered more towards an emphasis on class rather than race (*Book Three* 136). In *Book Three*, while touring Nairobi with his friend Don Harris, Lewis meets Malcolm X for what would be the last time. He instructs them to expand the national focus of their empathy, telling them that "we have to *identify* with the people of Africa, and that they must identify with us. The struggle in Africa is *inseparable* from our struggle in America" (135). Lewis explains that "Malcolm was saying, in effect, that it is a struggle for the *poor*—for those who have been left out and left behind—and that it *transcends* race" (136). Malcolm X's emphasis on class may very well have had to do with his own understanding of the workings of similarity bias, and may be why Lewis devotes so many pages of his trilogy to his ideas. For Malcolm X, the unifying factor that could bring about change was less in similarities of skin color or nationality and more in the fact that, as he states in *Book Three*, class inequality "was the root of our problems, not just in America, but all over the world" (136). He suggests here that addressing poverty may help those who would otherwise cross the inherent barriers of empathy based on similarity bias.

By the time policemen and others attack marchers on the Edmund Pettus Bridge in the event that became known as Bloody Sunday, Lewis was joined by a diverse group of protesters that included men, women, and children. Most were Black, some white, and others were Latinx or Asian American, representing different spiritual denominations and nationalities. The marchers' practice of getting into good trouble had gained national attention, especially since a week earlier, white minister James Reeb died of head injuries inflicted by the KKK. In a wide panel without dialogue, Lewis and Hosea Williams lead the marchers, who are all kneeling in prayer, as the Alabama state troopers prepare to advance. On the following pages, Powell highlights the marching feet of the policemen and the faces covered in gas masks before the scene erupts into disorder. Lewis is beaten on the head with a billy club while others in the background are also attacked. As Lewis passes out, the page fades to black, with the words "I thought I was going to die" floating in the darkness (*Book Three* 202). Fighting for consciousness, Lewis makes his way back to the Brown Chapel AME church amidst chaotic lines left deliberately unfinished by Powell's hand. Later, when Lewis awakens in the hospital, he confirms the power of the image to incite empathy, noting the impact of the television footage of Bloody Sunday. He states, "Something about that day touched a nerve deeper than *anything* that had come before. People just couldn't believe this was happening in America" (*Book Three* 209). In some cases for the first time, Americans were seeing their own people, some of whom looked like them, getting beaten in the name of voters' rights and equality.

The trilogy thus highlights the importance of acknowledging and addressing the various biases that others have to bring a definitive end to the violence. When he finally arrives in Montgomery alongside King and Rosa Parks, Lewis makes clear the work that they have done and the risk involved, declaring in a speech,

> "We are involved in a nonviolent war—we are involved in a nonviolent *revolution*. We don't have guns. We don't have missiles. We don't have tear gas. The only thing we have is our bodies—our tired feet. The same feet that brought us from Selma to Montgomery in our weary bodies—will take us to victory right here in the state of Alabama!" (*Book Three* 236)

Still, he and the others recognize putting their bodies on the line was not enough to stir the empathy of a nation. Lewis acknowledges the tension between Black SNCC volunteers who remained nameless and faceless on the news while their white allies were named and highlighted. Still, he realizes that "we were right to believe that the country would respond differently once young *white* people started dying alongside the countless Black activists who simply disappeared without a trace" (*Book Three* 53, 81). The murders of three CORE workers, James Chaney, Andrew Goodman, and Michael Schwerner, by Mississippi KKK members were notable to many in the country primarily because Goodman and Schwerner were white. At a convention shortly thereafter, one of the SNCC creators, Ella Baker, states her cause in terms of compassion: "Until the killing of black mothers' sons is as important as the killing of white mothers' sons—we must keep on" (*Book Three* 99). Baker's words echo that of the Black Lives Matter movement, and more specifically of Black mothers who have lost their children to police brutality and who demand justice and equality in society and before the law. Baker, Lewis, and others suggest that human dignity must begin with the ability to empathize with other humans, regardless of their skin color or other differences.

One of the turning points in the *March* trilogy is the passage of the Voting Rights Act of 1965, set into motion in a joint session of Congress, President Johnson's address being ultimately a plea for empathy. *Book Three* shows Lewis and Dr. King watching on television as Johnson makes his speech: "For, with a country as with a person, 'what is a man profited if he shall gain the whole world, and lose his own soul?' There is no Negro problem. There is no southern problem. There is no northern problem. There is only an American problem" (*Book Three* 223). Johnson asks Congress to see that what affects any one American is thus the problem of us all. Acknowledging the events of Bloody Sunday and the impetus behind the marches, Johnson continues by arguing that the African Americans' "cause must be our cause too. Because it's not just Negroes, but really it's all of us who must overcome the crippling legacy of bigotry and injustice. And we shall overcome" (*Book Three* 225). Lewis recalls that King had wiped away a tear when he heard the President quote this gospel and anthem of their movement (*Walking* 354). At that moment, Johnson signaled that he had absorbed King and Lewis's message of empathy and dignity.

In some courses where I teach *March*, I also teach excerpts from Lewis's *Across That Bridge*. In the 2017 memoir, Lewis states that his and the other protesters' willingness to endanger themselves through nonviolence demonstrated "that love had already overcome hate, that the pages of America's book had already been written, that this nation's destiny was already sealed in the moment it was founded, so every expression of evil, including segregation, could never stand" (21). Lewis's optimism was fueled not by denial but by the belief that a patient and disciplined devotion to nonviolence would ultimately triumph. In the years following *March*'s publication, the trilogy itself became an extension of Lewis's movement for nonviolence and empathy. Up until his death, he was a frequent attendee at comic conventions, where he spread his message to a growing number of young fans. In true comic con fashion, Lewis occasionally donned the "superhero costume" he wore half a century earlier on the Edmund Pettus Bridge—his white shirt, tie, khaki trench coat, and backpack—and led children in a march through the convention center. His message was simple: sometimes, the right thing to do is to get in the way and cause a little bit of good trouble.

Works Cited

Aydin, Andrew. "The Comic Book That Changed the World: Martin Luther King and the Montgomery Story's Vital Role in the Civil Rights Movement." *Creative Loafing* 42, no. 14 (2013): 14–19.

Batson, C. Daniel. "These Things Called Empathy: Eight Related but Distinct Phenomena." In *The Social Neuroscience of Empathy*, edited by Jean Decety and William Ickes, 3–15. Cambridge, MA: MIT Press, 2009.

Chute, Hillary L. *Disaster Drawn: Visual Witness, Comics, and Documentary Form.* Cambridge, MA: Belknap Press, 2016.

Hassler, Alfred (w.), Benton Resnik (w.), and Sy Barry (p.). *Martin Luther King and the Montgomery Story.* New York: Fellowship of Reconciliation (FoR USA), 1957.

Hoffman, Martin L. *Empathy and Moral Development: Implications for Caring and Justice.* Cambridge, UK: Cambridge University Press, 2000.

Lewis, John. *Across That Bridge: A Vision for Change and the Future of America.* New York: Hachette Books, 2012.

Lewis, John, and Andrew Aydin. *March: Book One.* Marietta, GA: Top Shelf Productions, 2013.

Lewis, John, and Andrew Aydin. *March: Book Three.* Marietta, GA: Top Shelf Productions, 2016.

Lewis, John, and Andrew Aydin. *March: Book Two.* Marietta, GA: Top Shelf Productions, 2015.

Lewis, John, and Michael D'Orso. *Walking with the Wind: A Memoir of the Movement.* New York: Simon & Schuster, 1998.

McCloud, Scott. *Understanding Comics: The Invisible Art.* New York: William Morrow, 1994.

Meacham, Jon, and John Lewis. *His Truth Is Marching On: John Lewis and the Power of Hope.* New York: Random House, 2020.

O'Neil, Dennis (w.), Neal Adams (p.), and Frank Giacoia (i.). "No Evil Shall Escape My Sight!" *Green Lantern* #76. Burbank: DC Comics, 1970.

Polak, Kate. *Ethics in the Gutter: Empathy and Historical Fiction in Comics.* Columbus: Ohio State University Press, 2017.

Simon, Joe (w), Jack Kirby (w,p), and Al Liederman (i). "Meet Captain America." *Captain America Comics* #1. New York: Marvel Comics, 1941.

WBUR. "Martin Luther King's Ideas Reverberate in Egypt." Accessed March 27, 2021. https://www.wbur.org/hereandnow/2012/01/16/egypt-cairo-comic.

14

PEACE BE WITH YOU
The Sheriff of Babylon and Violence in the "War on Terror"

LAWRENCE ABRAMS AND KALEB KNOBLAUCH

By March of 2004, after only one year of the American war in Iraq, some three hundred members of the Iraqi police forces had been murdered.[1] By the "official" end of the war in 2011 the body count for Iraqi security and police forces had risen to 10,125.[2] The ongoing violence against Iraqi police forces was emblematic of the failure of the American occupation to create a stable peace and the inconclusive outcomes of the war. But statistics and newsprint are no longer the only means by which people who participated in the invasion of Iraq share or reflect on those experiences. Set in post-Saddam Baghdad, from February to April 2004, *The Sheriff of Babylon*, created by Tom King and Mitch Gerads, follows an investigation into the murder of an Iraqi police trainee, and unravels the complex political, social, and even personal fallout of the American occupation of Iraq. This is a noir-style detective story and reliant on many of the same tropes and the cynicism of the genre. While it is a work of fiction, the verisimilitude of the series comes in part from King's own experiences in Iraq, where he worked as a counterintelligence officer for the CIA in 2004.

We argue in this chapter that *The Sheriff of Babylon* employs violence in several significant ways. First, violence is both valorized and interrogated as a necessary but inhumane reality of asymmetric warfare. Second, *Sheriff* depicts overt violence with ironic detachment—an emotional reaction to the perceived senseless and endless so-called "War on Terror." Violence in the series is also ultimately ineffective, reflective of the challenges of fighting an insurgency. Finally, violence in this comic is always racialized and gendered, but in ways that sometimes invert western readers' assumptions—violence is not just something done by dark-skinned people to white westerners. Violence in this series is a product of the ongoing American occupation; it became the language and tool of all sides to negotiate the struggle for power left by the absence of a strong Iraqi state.

While we will not summarize the entire series here, a brief synopsis is useful to understand the complexities of the plot. Christopher Henry, an American private military contractor in the Green Zone, has come to Baghdad to train the new Iraqi police forces. Chris assumes responsibility for a murder investigation, more or less by default, as no one else seems interested in the task.[3] During the course of the investigation the reader is introduced to Saffiya al-Aqani, a member of the Small Council for Iraq Reconstruction, whose grandfather was a founding member of the Ba'ath Party alongside Saddam Hussein; however, her entire family was murdered by the Hussein regime, and she spent most of her life in exile in the United States.[4] Saffiya introduces Chris to our third principle character Nassir al-Maghreb, a Shia Muslim and former police detective under the Saddam Hussein regime.[5] Each of these characters pursue their own individual and overlapping agendas, including solving the murder of the police trainee. Their pursuits lead to their involvement in a major counterterrorism operation against Jordanian-born American terrorist Abu Rahim who is pursuing jihad in Iraq. The principal trio of Chris, Saffiya, and Nassir must, over the course of the story, navigate a dangerous path through competing American interests, and layers of local Iraqi politics. In this essay, we address multiple forms of violence throughout the narrative and connect the events of the comic to the ways Americans and Iraqis used violence during the American occupation.

By questioning the moral legitimacy of the conflict and its uses of violence, King and Gerads engage with questions of western hegemony and American global sovereignty, thereby elevating the use of violence from the personal sphere to a political and strategic stage. This geopolitical view of violence, grounded in the personal violence of the titular "Sheriff's" story, questions the narratives of the war itself—couched as it was in terms of defending freedom and democracy. Such an interrogation of legitimate violence, virtuous justification, and western hegemonic power is central to studies of the use of force in counterinsurgency operations and asymmetric warfare.[6]

Violence is inextricable from the narrative of policing and control; however, before we continue our analysis of King and Gerads's text, it is worth defining what we mean by "violence" in the context of *The Sheriff of Babylon*. In 2002 the World Health Organization published the *World Report on Violence and Health*, which offered a comprehensive analysis of violence on the world stage, and defined violence as "the intentional use of physical force or power, threatened or actual, against oneself, another person, or against a group or community, that either results in or has a high likelihood of resulting in injury, death, psychological harm, maldevelopment or deprivation."[7] This definition provides a systematic typology of violence that we have used to categorize the different acts of violence depicted in the narrative of *The Sheriff of Babylon*; these include self-directed violence (self-harm and suicidal ideation); interpersonal violence (violence against family members and other intimates, between members of a community, and acts of child abuse, sexual assault, and violence in institutional settings, such as churches and schools); and collective violence (violence committed by states and institutions for social, political, or economic motivations). The predominant forms of violence in this story fall in the broad categories of interpersonal (community) and collective (both social and political). Most instances are physical in nature, though psychological violence is frequently present as well. As such, this chart serves as a useful baseline tool. However, it is not comprehensive enough to fully describe violence in the series.

Due to the multimodal nature of the graphic novel medium, we distinguish instances of violence by their method of representation. In this case violence can be represented visually through images, verbally through the text and dialogue, or in an implied auditory form via descriptive sound effects.[8] Violence in *The Sheriff of Babylon* is often explicit, in the case of viscera and flying bullets, but it is also often implicit or subtle in its strategic absence of one or more modes of comic book art and storytelling. Sometimes, wordless panels or a solitary onomatopoeia carry the emotional impact of a violent act, across the gutter or even across several pages. For instance, acts of violence are often sexualized but do not constitute sexual violence as this chart conceives them; there is an ambiguous grey area, specifically the portrayal of naked Iraqi bodies. The WHO report focuses on coercive and penetrative sexual acts; it has less to say about the kind of voyeurism and objectification present in the display of dead, naked Iraqi bodies.[9] We will address sexualized violence in greater detail later. Having now established a specific definition of violence for the purposes of this chapter, we will examine certain significant scenes in *The Sheriff of Babylon* that best demonstrate the uses of violence in this series.

The Sheriff of Babylon opens with a murder. The narrative of the war begins *in media res* in February of 2004, ten months after the fall of Baghdad to American occupying forces. The body of the murder victim, an Iraqi police trainee, is already cold and rests under the crossed Swords of Qadisiyah Victory Arch. A pair of American soldiers stand over the body, asking "What are we supposed to do with this . . . is this garbage?" They wonder whether their job of garbage disposal includes removing the body.[10] The juxtaposition of such a mundane but bloody task in a locale memorializing the victory of a bygone war is typical of *The Sheriff of Babylon*'s treatment of violence.[11] On the one hand, the location of this scene is emblematic of the valor of war—the Swords of Qadisiyah is Baghdad's most visible symbol of victory in warfare and of the defense of the country from foreign invasion. On the other hand, the cold detachment of the soldiers and their ambivalent characterization of the Iraqi body as garbage undercuts any sense of valor or purpose to the violence. This scene also centers race within the narrative. The Americans–one soldier is Black, one is white—are presented as essentially the same; it is the body of the dead Iraqi that is set apart. Furthermore, the presence of American occupiers under the shadow of the Victory Arch demonstrates the fleeting nature of victory in war. That said, this opening scene problematizes the perception of American supremacy, or even control, of the Iraqi capital.

The most significant aspect of *Sheriff*'s treatment of violence is an unwavering focus on the victims. King and Gerads have given several interviews about their process of creating this series, and in every case have been asked about the way they write and depict violence in a wartime setting. Though neither creator has said so explicitly, violence in *The Sheriff of Babylon* is clearly racialized and gendered. Firstly, and most obviously, the targets of violence in *Sheriff* are primarily Iraqis. The opening scene establishes the pattern for the series, and the mystery of who killed Ali al-Fahar haunts the narrative—even though his murder is largely forgotten by the principals through much of the second volume.[12] Though many Americans are put in harm's way, some even killed by principal characters in the story, *Sheriff* focuses the reader on the ways in which American occupation left physical scars on the wounded and dead bodies of Iraqi citizens.

Moreover, King and Gerads condemn the occupation for its dehumanization and depersonalization of victims like Ali al-Fahar. Using abstract language, such as "trash," dehumanizes al-Fahar, and the resolution of his murder becomes secondary to those charged with solving it. Chris tries to humanize al-Fahar, but in the context of the American occupation, al-Fahar cannot be fully human. This war cannot be waged against humans, so the only way to win is to remove humanity. Dehumanization of Iraqis, especially of dead Iraqis not only blunted the psychological impact of the war for the American soldiers of the occupation force but provided a safe psychological distance for Americans at home.[13] Psychological remove is nowhere more apparent than in the portrayal of gendered and sexualized violence.

The series repeatedly depicts sexual violence against Iraqi men and women. The point here is not that Americans were always sadistic in their treatment of Iraqis, but that the line between acceptable and unacceptable forms of violence was often blurred when it came to Iraqi bodies. The killing of an Iraqi girl—whose name we never learn—in a barracks mess hall is the first overt act of violence King and Gerads show in *Sheriff*. Chris enters the mess hall, which has been evacuated due to a potential suicide bomber, wherein he discovers a young girl, huddled in her clothes and sweating. Chris attempts to engage the girl in conversation, discussing a story from his grandfather about handing out chocolates to children in the Pacific in World War II. Chris is trying to deescalate the situation and assess whether the girl is a credible threat. His attempt is cut short on the following page with the first panel, a solid black square with the single onomatopoeic "Bang." and the girl's head is penetrated by a sniper round, mixing the allusion to penetrative sexual violence and the killing of this child.[14]

The episode in the mess hall shows how Gerads does not obscure every incident of violence in the series; he selectively reveals and obscures different instances of violence to illustrate different aspects of the American occupation. Throughout the series this violence is notably explicit in both verbal and visual form. Multiple attempts on the life of Saffiya drive elements of the plot, leading to a final confrontation between the woman and a notorious terrorist leader, who repeatedly insults the woman by referring to her as an "Iraqi whore! Shiite whore! American whore! Jewish whore!"[15] Nassir, following the killing of his wife by Americans (his daughters were also victims of an American bombing operation), is detained, stripped naked, and beaten when he lashes out at the Americans who are interrogating him.[16] Similar examples of degrading (not to mention illegal) treatment of Iraqi detainees were made most famous following the shocking revelations about prisoners in Abu Ghraib, and have been a part, albeit usually an unspoken one, of executing counterinsurgencies since the Algerian War for Independence.[17] Furthermore, the naked bodies of both this man and his dead wife are depicted with almost photographic realism, showing every wound, bruise, and damaged body part that suffered at the hands of American forces. It is not our intention to glorify or fetishize the acts of violence depicted in this scene by giving explicit description. However, these acts and their depictions are instructive in their brutality. The paradox of this violence is in its gendered specificity. Specific brutalization of genital areas, degrading the subject, even stripping the subject naked are meant to evoke a specific set of fears that are distinct from simply dehumanizing or killing a subject. Dehumanization depends on disinterest. Perverse as these acts are, they require an emotional investment and specific view of the subject as gendered and a target to be violated.

As in the real-world examples of Abu Ghraib or the Algerian War of Independence, vivid cases of sexualized violence are not an unintended consequence, but a deliberate feature of any counterinsurgency campaign. King and Gerads represent this gruesome feature of counterinsurgency with brutal realism. Despite these visceral depictions of violence, most of the significant acts of violence in *Sheriff* are hidden using creative techniques of comic book art such as the masking effect, blackout panels, obscured points of view, and perspective to create a sense of removal, even confusion, from the violent acts themselves.[18] These techniques contribute to another striking feature of *The Sheriff of Babylon*—its juxtaposition of dry humor and depictions of often gruesome violence in a wartime setting. These same techniques are displayed in a later scene where Chris and Nassir hunt and nearly kill a cat because of their fear and uncertainty, only to relax in relief at their error, despite the grim imagery of the cat eating a dead body.[19] The result of this mixture is a sense of ironic detachment from the horrors taking place around characters in the series. Detachment from acts or consequences of violence provides readers a sense of how these characters may have tried to cope with the almost daily traumas experienced during the occupation.

The Sheriff of Babylon also distances violence from the dialogue and panels of the comic. The most frequent technique in *Sheriff* to distance the reader from violence is the repeated use of blackout panels with onomatopoetic white text—e.g., Pop, Bang, Pow—interspersed across the panel grid. Likewise, the structure of these panes uses a classic 3 × 3 grid (King and Gerads rely on this layout in *Mister Miracle* and their other collaborations), such that the rigid structure of the grid amplifies the sense of mystery. The blackout panels hide that which readers most expect to see. The result of this technique is jarring, as the reader must then fill in the gory details of what happened behind the blackout. Violence often happens "off stage," distancing the reader from the overt act itself. Even when *Sheriff* presents violence directly, the frequently subtle—or background—depictions of violent acts, individual images or objects in a panel suggest the ongoing potential for violence. The result of these occluding techniques asks the reader to participate in the narrative through the phenomenon of closure and by deploying the very acts of violence Gerads deliberately attempted to obscure.[20]

Desensitization, as the text presents it, is a product of ubiquitous yet mundane and banal violence, which forms a backdrop to Iraqi politics and relations between Iraq and the United States. One scene explores this dynamic and is the first appearance of Saffiya. In this scene, bloody images of American soldiers are juxtaposed with an otherwise unremarkable meeting of the

Small Council.[21] Council members are debating "item #43," the discovery of three American soldiers who have been executed, as it turns out, by Nassir in retaliation for the loss of his daughters during an American bombing.[22] Saffiya serves the Iraqi government as a member of the Small Council, but this position is not the source of her real political power. It is her other job, as a fixer for the Americans and for various factions of Iraqi society, that demonstrates her importance to the occupation and highlights the role of sanctioned violence to undergird post-Saddam Iraqi society.

Sheriff occasionally drives detachment and desensitization to the point of absurdity, as shown in a later scene, in which Chris and Nassir, the first time that these two principal characters work together, are asked to identify a body of an Iraqi whose throat has been cut. The US troops making the request watch a video of an Iraqi man being executed, making a game of whether they can identify *this* body as the man in the video.[23] The video itself has the look of the kinds of bloody execution videos distributed by terror groups and broadcast (albeit heavily censored) in Western media.[24]

In an earlier scene, Saffiya is presented with a political problem by an American general. As she works to solve it, she encounters a series of political dominoes to which she responds with peremptory violence. The general complains that protestors are blocking the Assassin's Gate, and he wants them dispersed. Saffiya's investigation into the protest leads her to an Iraqi administrator, then to a tribal leader, and finally to a man who took the supplies (to feed his family) that set off the protests in the first place. Rather than negotiate, Saffiya has already preemptively murdered his family, except for his wife and children, who she declares "already [has] the truck."[25] She has the man executed, shot twice by her guard. Saffiya then takes her own weapon, and after "reassuring" the corpse that "at least [your family] did not have to watch it on the TV," she shoots him in the head a third time. We witness the conversations with the complaining political figures take place in reverse order, as Saffiya solves each of their problems in succession, garnering political capital in return.[26] We regard these scenes as examples of ironic detachment because the act of violence solves the various problems that take place before Saffiya ever sat down with the truck owner. The conversation was a sick joke; his family is already dead, Saffiya already has the truck and supplies, and she has already decided to kill this man, too. The conversation itself is superfluous; in fact, the only outcome of the conversation being the truck owner calling Saffiya "an American whore," which in turn seemed to motivate her to shoot *an already dead man* in the head. And this macabre scene allows the various players in Iraqi politics to continue with business as usual without personally dirtying their hands. Remember, no one asked Saffiya to kill anyone: she chose the most expedient route to resolving all these problems at once. And for the proverbial icing on the cake, Saffiya receives a lucrative telecom contract by the Americans for her quid pro quo.[27]

Using both creative techniques in text and visuals, particularly the use of blank panels and visual onomatopoeia, King and Gerads mask certain instances of violence while highlighting their emotional impact. In an interview with DC Comics, King explains, "I didn't want the focus of [*The Sheriff of Babylon*] to be the violence.... I've been in situations where bombs or guns are going off, and what's weird about it is that you don't really know what's going on when it happens.... It's in the aftermath, after you hear the shot, you look around and see what happened. You see the after effect. ... Once you hear the bang, whatever the bad stuff is that's happening has already happened."[28] This is not to say that violence is never depicted—we have repeatedly documented those instances in the series—but that overt depictions of violence tell us something else about the experience of the American occupation and the complex nature of counterinsurgency.

The complexity of asymmetric or counterinsurgent warfare often results in numerous agencies or military branches with conflicting definitions of acceptable violence. Chris, as a private contractor, repeatedly encounters individuals—usually American soldiers or other Defense Department agents—who have committed an act of violence that they insist was necessary and proper, according to their understanding of the situation or rules of engagement. The scenarios in which this violence occurs casts doubt on their assertions of necessity and demonstrates the inherent inhumanity of warfare and of the American occupation. For example, a character commits an act of violence in view of the reader and diners in a Mess Hall on base—when explosive ordnance technicians (EODs) storm the room and shoot a young girl who may or may not have been wearing a suicide vest—and immediately justifies the killing on procedural grounds. King's dialogue reflects the absurdity of the situation:

> EOD TECH: What the Hell you doing?! Get the Hell out of here! What're you thinking?
> CHRIS: She wasn't doing anything. You didn't have to.
> EOD TECH: You were in the room, man! We had to shoot with you there, man, what the Hell were you doing in there?
> CHRIS: Look, I was just trying to help. She was fine.
> EOD TECH: Help? Are you—Where do you think you are? Jesus Christ, man, get yourself together.[29]

Chris's attempt to defuse a potentially deadly situation—again, the reader never sees any definitive proof that the girl was wearing an explosive device—instigates a crisis response procedure that "requires" them to shoot to kill at a child. The narrative abruptly shifts to different characters on the next page and never addresses the morality of the rules of engagement, leaving the reader with only Chris's frustrated "Goddammit" as the final verdict on the chaos that just took place.[30]

Though Chris was obviously shaken by the killing of the Iraqi girl, and puzzled by the strict adherence to procedure, his own training compels him to react similarly to another situation involving a child later in the story. Chris has returned to the Victory Arch and encounters by a young boy hawking souvenirs to Americans who visit the site; he tries to question him whether he saw al-Fahar's body being placed in the plaza. The boy speaks little English—"Boo Saddam," "Yay America," and Fuck" comprise most of his vocabulary—and Chris bemoans his inability to communicate with the boy. But when the boy reaches quickly into his back pocket, Chris's hand jumps to his sidearm and asks the boy "**What** are you doing." He cautions the boy to move his hands slowly, but when the boy swings back around, Chris has his gun already drawn on him. The boy was not holding a weapon, but a pornographic magazine he wanted Chris to buy. King and Gerads address the psychological stresses that the Americans experience in their everyday encounters with Iraqis—in part the result of their inability to understand and communicate with the people they have occupied, in this scene the boy's English is largely limited to profanity and celebrity names—and in those moments of insecurity, real or perceived, violence and reliance on weapons is the first and last response.[31] In response to almost killing the boy, Chris could only impotently return to profanity.

In another jarring scene, Chris, Nassir, and Fatima engage in a tense and confused standoff, which results in a firefight where American forces kill Fatima, Nassir's wife. Agents of the Naval Criminal Investigative Service (NCIS) come to Chris's bunk to question Nassir about his potential involvement with a known terrorist recruiter. Men already have their hands on their weapons when Fatima steps out of the door of the bunk to ask her husband what is going on. As in the previous scene, communication is difficult between Americans and Iraqis, and in this case the NCIS agents speak in clunky, overly formal Arabic, and cannot understand Nassir and Fatima when they reply.[32] A soldier demands to see Fatima's hands from underneath her clothing, but of course she does not understand and is preoccupied with trying to determine whether her husband is about to be arrested or killed. Fatima thinks that the NCIS agents know about three Americans Nassir killed earlier in the story. She says to Nassir, "You will be Saddam to them. The **next Saddam** . . . They will take you as they took the girls!" The soldier demands to see her hands again, and then the lead NCIS agent shouts "GUN!" It is over for Fatima. The "rules of engagement" kick into gear and soldiers fire their weapons indiscriminately, despite Chris screaming to stop and trying to tackle the soldier. Another instance of the visual onomatopoeia—"Bang . . . Bang . . . Bang"—accompanies an image of Fatima riddled with bullets.[33] A panel on a later page shows at least ten distinct entry wounds in her torso and arms alone.[34] As in the Mess Hall, once the triggering event or word occurs, shoot to kill is the immediate and necessary consequence, and all the NCIS agent can think to say in response is "Why are there so many scarves?!"[35]

Violence in these scenes emphasizes the psychological stresses that result from an ongoing occupation and counterinsurgency, where death looms and the enemy could be anyone, at any time, in a place where they do not understand the culture, or even the language. To address uncertainty and threat, American forces rely on rote procedure and often sclerotic rules of engagement, which do not allow for recognition of cultural distinction or context. Only Chris managed to walk away from one such encounter without pulling the trigger, but he came perilously close and was the exception to demonstrate the necessary and inhumane rule. The theme of inhumane or bureaucratic violence is not simply meant to ground the reader in the visceral reality of the story, though it serves that purpose well. *Sheriff* deliberately uses representations of inhumanity to remind readers that violence accomplishes little and often leads to greater and deadlier acts of violence. These acts of violence are justified by the continuation of the occupation and the desire of American foreign policy for an ongoing presence in the Middle East, to continue its War on Terror. For example, the planning for an extended stay in the region by American forces was integral to the invasion plan from the very beginning.[36] *Sheriff* highlights this ongoing justification in several conversations between Chris and Fatima, and Chris and Nassir on the process of Americanizing Iraqis.[37] At one point Nassir points out to Chris that he should not be teaching the police trainees, and that Nassir should be training them instead. He continues, saying that what Chris is teaching them is good for their pay and understanding of Americans: "But then you must teach them to **not** be Iraqis. To be Americans."[38] Chris's response is telling; "Well what's the point of **anything** if you're not going to learn **that**?"[39] This process of Americanization, however, is emblematic of the ongoing lack of understanding of Iraqi culture and law on the part of American forces.

The lack of cultural understanding by occupying forces, historically a hallmark of warfare, directly contributed to the rise of a steady stream of insurgent activity and ongoing political and military blowback. While the term "blowback" originated in the CIA in the late 1980s to describe the consequences of covert actions being brought to light, it has since expanded to include the general costs and consequences of foreign policy or military actions.[40] Efforts to mitigate the known blowback effect of American activities abroad since the 1980s met with only limited success in Iraq. Despite some initial small successes in the early days of the occupation to 'win the hearts and minds' of Iraqis, centralized policy decisions which ignored local realities showed an increasing disregard for—or understanding of—the traditions of Iraqi culture, religion, law, or self-governance.[41]

The costs and consequences of both American ignorance and violence are brought to a head in *Sheriff* during an extended confrontation between Chris and Bob, the NCIS officer responsible for the shooting of Nassir's wife Fatima earlier in the story.[42] This scene encapsulates the narrative of the two volumes of *Sheriff* and reflects on many of the decisive moments of violence since the discovery of al-Fahar's body. Dialogue reflects the concept of "mission creep" and imagery throughout contradicts Bob's insistence of being "done" in Iraq.[43] Most telling are the moments in the scene where Bob reveals a simultaneous understanding of the political and religious fracture lines in Iraqi society, and a seeming incredulity as to why he might bear some responsibility for the consequences of his actions. Over the course of the scene, flashbacks reveal the fact Bob is, in fact, responsible for the death of Ali al-Fahar and set the entire story in motion. Bob had used Ali as an informant, which backfired spectacularly when bad intel led American forces to murder an Iraqi Christian family.[44] Bob all but murders Ali—a Sunni—by dropping him off in a militant Shia neighborhood and visibly paying him with wads of American dollars.[45]

This cynical manipulation of Iraqi culture contrasts Bob's naive denial of culpability in the death of Fatima, or any American fault in the shooting in the mess hall. When Chris asks Bob, "Whose fault is it?" Bob demonstrates a disregard for the local culture and denies fault even exists. Interestingly, while Bob continues to excuse his killing of Fatima, Chris begins to explain his interaction with the young girl in the Mess Hall; both men are talking past each other. Ultimately, the fruitless conversation is distilled into a comment from Bob that regardless of fault "you just can't take those risks."[46] It is worth noting that this final portion of the confrontation between Chris and Bob takes place largely with Chris standing behind Bob and without Bob knowing that Chris has drawn and aimed his gun at Bob's head. Likewise, the entire extended scene takes place simultaneously with the final confrontation between Saffiya, Nassir, and the terrorist Abu Rahim.[47] This parallel construction ends with Bob walking away unscathed as Chris handles his emotional shock, and both Abu Rahim and Saffiya's bodyguards being shot by American forces whose adherence to "procedure" blinds them from distinguishing between an armed friendly and a threatening terrorist.[48] Both of these scenes reveal much of the previously hidden underpinnings of the plot of *Sheriff* and leave the trio of principle characters with similar realizations regarding the futility and degrading effect of the earlier violence. The realization of the moral degradation and futility of violence by the end of the story is not simply our interpretation. Conveying the immorality and degradation of violence was one of the outright goals of the creative team behind *Sheriff*. In an interview with *GQ*, Mitch Gerads said of violence in this comic:

> I wanted to make it real. Not from an action movie standpoint, but I wanted to make something where people would read a book and see violence and cringe. Because I wanted them to feel that it's bad. No matter who you are, if you're a guy at home or a Navy Seal over there. Violence is bad. Nobody wants to do it. So I did some terrible research on that front, to try and get it as accurate as possible.[49]

The Sheriff of Babylon approaches violence from two distinct yet compatible directions. In the spirit of noir, individual acts of violence indicate broader patterns of social and political chaos—in this context, because of the American occupation. But this is only clear to the reader in hindsight. As King and Gerads unpack the events of the story in the final confrontations between Chris and Bob, and Saffiya, Nassir, and Abu Rahim, acts of violence gain a much more clearly elaborated cause and effect. Unlike earlier acts of violence, which are frequently masked using the techniques of flashback and visual onomatopoeia, the violence of the final scene presents a clear moral for the series. The murder of Ali al-Fahar was not simply a random or chaotic outburst born from the prevailing conditions of the occupation. Instead, the murder and subsequent violence are the direct outgrowth of a precipitating immoral act on the part of Bob and his fellows in the intelligence community.

In conclusion, *The Sheriff of Babylon* is ultimately a story of failure and a condemnation of the American occupation. Despite this condemnation *Sheriff* explicitly resists attempts to fit its characters into longstanding policy models. The sheer level of brutality and cynicism on display undercut the notion of the Iraq War as a just war. Nor is there a potential allegorical policy narrative that might lead from these warist principles to pacifist principles. Our lead characters are if anything more brutish, violent, inclined to violence, and cynical towards the possibility of peace by the end of the story.[50]

Some characters in *Sheriff* attempt to paint their actions in realist terms meant to minimize future conflicts. But such fig-leaf justifications are quickly dispensed with when the principal characters are faced with the choice of how to dispose with a final figure to be held responsible for the sequence of events that began the story.

The use of violence in the short term might advance concrete goals; however, in the long term, violence is destructive, self-defeating, and precludes any lasting peace. The final panels of *Sheriff* suggest that the story has ended exactly where it began: a body lies under the crossed swords of the Victory Arch. This time, it is not an Iraqi; it belongs to an American contractor we know only as "Jim from Ops." There is no mystery of who murdered Jim. His psychological torture and murder were committed by none other than Chris, Saffiya, and Nassir. Unable to lash out at those truly responsible for the pain and violence the trio have suffered throughout the course of the story, they abduct and murder the only conspirator they can effectively reach—a low level flunky whose entire role was to serve as a "gray hair" stalking horse to hide who is really in charge.[51] The protagonists' murder of Jim from Ops reinforces a conversation made at the start of the final chapter between Chris and Nassir about the state of their new crop of Iraqi police trainees as the people responsible for maintaining their new society. As Nassir points out "They do not get better. . . . You try I think. But they do not get better." Chris replies, "No, they don't."[52]

Notes

1. Mark Magnier and Sonni Efron, "Arrested Development on Iraqi Police Force," *Los Angeles Times*, March 31, 2004, articles.latimes.com/2004/mar/31/world/fg-cops31.

2. Michael E. O'Hanlon and Ian Livingston, *Iraq Index Tracking Variables of Reconstruction & Security in Post-Saddam Iraq*, Brookings Institute, Jan. 31, 2011, www.brookings.edu/wp-content/uploads/2016/07/index20120131.pdf.

3. Joshua Rivera, "Why the CIA Has to Read This Comic Before You Can," *GQ*, July 19, 2016, www.gq.com/story/sheriff-of-babylon-cia. King has said of the character Christopher, "In some way, he's supposed to represent those people who felt 9–11 happened to them personally. . . . I'm making it more of a metaphor with him where he's actually somewhat involved. He's trying to make up for that. He's saying he wants to be in this fight and affect some change, and he gets sent to Iraq, and he doesn't know how that impacts the way 9–11 affected him. How did he get from, 'I want to save the world from 9–11' to 'I'm fighting a war by training Iraqi police officers.' That impulse is based on myself and a lot of people I know."

4. Ibid. With the character of Saffiya, King said he wanted to explore "this generation of Iraqis that came back from Iraq on the heels of the Americans. I was in Iraq with them. There were a group of Iraqis who were outside Iraq that helped this effort and helped this country. I always found that kind of fascinating—these guys who would work with America to take

over a country that used to be theirs. I wanted to explore that.... In terms of making [Saffiya] a female, I knew some incredibly powerful women who were out there, who had been put in positions of authority because of the war. I found that to be very interesting—how much respect they could garner. So I wanted to explore both of those issues in one character."

5. The minoritarian rule of Sunni Muslims in the Ba'ath Party under the Hussein regime and the purges of the older Shia membership of the party are well documented. The tense relationships between Shia and Sunni Muslims in Iraq after the fall of that regime led to not only fraught relationships between the two groups, but also civil strife and ethnic cleansing. Saffiya al-Aqani and Nassir al-Maghreb are representative of the complexities of the relationships between these two groups in post-Saddam Iraq. It would be impossible to fully elaborate those complexities here, but readers should be aware of the added tension this history brings to the story. In short, our principal trio contain multiple and overlapping loyalties, interests, and identities that are often flattened in most depictions of Iraqi or Middle Eastern politics.

6. For example, see James Der Derian, *Virtuous War: Mapping the Military-Industrial-Media-Entertainment Network* (New York: Routledge, 2011); and Rupert Smith, *Utility of Force: The Art of War in the Modern World* (New York: Vintage Books, 2008).

7. Etienne G. Krug, Linda L. Dahlberg, James A. Mercy, Anthony B. Zwi and Rafael Lozano, eds. *World Report on Violence and Health* (Geneva: World Health Organization, 2002), 5.

8. We take our definition for this technique from Dave Gibbons and Tim Pilcher, *How Comics Work* (New York: Wellfleet Press, 2017), 121.

9. Ibid., *World Report on Violence and Health*, 149.

10. Tom King and Mitch Gerads, *The Sheriff of Babylon, the Deluxe Edition* (New York: Vertigo, 2018), 1.

11. The Swords of Qadisiyah Victory Arch commemorates the victory of Iraqi forces in the Iran-Iraq War. It also rests on the supposed site of the Muslim Arab victory over Persian forces in 636 CE.

12. *Sheriff*, 174.

13. Daoud Kuttab, "The Media and Iraq: A Bloodbath for and Gross Dehumanization of Iraqis," *International Review of the Red Cross* 89, 886–87, https://www.corteidh.or.cr/tablas/a21893.pdf.

14. *Sheriff*, 5–7.

15. *Sheriff*, 267.

16. *Sheriff*, 157–60, 164–65.

17. The AP first reported on the systematic abuse of Iraqi detainees in 2003. See Charles J. Hanley, "AP Enterprise: Former Iraqi Detainees Tell of Riots, Punishment in the Sun, Good Americans and Pitiless Ones," *San Diego Union-Tribune*, Nov. 1, 2003, http://legacy.sandiegouniontribune.com/news/world/iraq/20031101-0936-iraq-thecamps.html. Abuse of this nature in counterinsurgencies since the Algerian War of Independence, when they come to light, are powerfully recounted by victims. See Henri Alleg, *The Question*, University of Nebraska Press, 2006.

18. See *Sheriff*, 7, described in detail above for an example that contains nearly all the techniques we mention.

19. *Sheriff*, 49–54.

20. Scott McCloud, *Understanding Comics* (New York: William Morrow, 1994), 63–65. Closure, the phenomenon in which the mind fills in the gaps of the isolated panels or pages

is part of, as McCloud calls it, "the magic and mystery that are at the very heart of comics." It is a powerful technique in comics art and helps the reader make sense of, and connect narratively, the disparate images on the page.

21. *Sheriff*, 39–41.

22. *Sheriff*, 23–27.

23. Ultimately Nassir convinces the soldiers that it is a different man based on forensics evidence. He later confesses to Chris that he has no forensic knowledge, but that he can simply tell one Iraqi man from another.

24. *Sheriff*, 42–43.

25. *Sheriff*, 20.

26. *Sheriff*, 18–22.

27. *Sheriff*, 22.

28. Tim Beedle and Jason Inman, "Soldier to Soldier: Jason Inman Interviews the Sheriff of Babylon's Tom King," *DC*, Oct. 30, 2018. www.dccomics.com/blog/2018/10/30/soldier-to-soldier-jason-inman-interviews-the-sheriff-of-babylons-tom-king.

29. Formatting reflects the nature of dialogue scripted across multiple separated panels.

30. *Sheriff*, 16–17.

31. *Sheriff*, 87–88. Emphasis in the original.

32. Bob, the lead agent during the encounter, attempts to speak to Fatima, but his Arabic is comically formal. A change in typeface in the lettering shows the difference between his speech and all other dialogue. He says to Fatima, "Female, stayest thou there! Movest thou not now and soon!" (141). Of course she barely understands his garbled commands, adding to the confusion of the encounter.

33. *Sheriff*, 141–44. Emphasis in the original.

34. *Sheriff*, 147. Later on we see Nassir and Chris taking Fatima's body for burial wrapped in Superman bed sheets and a traditional Iraqi woven carpet. This hybrid burial shroud is indicative of the Americanization of every aspect of Iraqi culture.

35. *Sheriff*, 144.

36. Tom Engelhardt, "Iraq as a Pentagon Construction Site," *The Bases of Empire: The Global Struggle against U.S. Military Posts*, edited by Catherine Lutz (New York: NYU Press, 2009), 131–33.

37. *Sheriff*, 119–21, 129.

38. *Sheriff*, 129.

39. Ibid.

40. Chalmers Johnson, *Blowback: The Costs and Consequences of American Empire*, 2nd ed., Owl Books, Henry Holt, 2004, 8. The term is central to this and other arguments of Chalmers Johnson, whose later work on the blowback principle remains required reading for CIA operatives. See: Anonymous, "Intelligence in Recent Public Literature: The Intelligence Officer's Bookshelf," Central Intelligence Agency, March 29, 2011, www.cia.gov/library/center-for-the-study-of-intelligence/csi-publications/csi-studies/studies/vol.-55-no.-1/the-intelligence-officers-bookshelf.html.

41. Thomas E. Ricks, *Fiasco: The American Military Adventure in Iraq* (London: Penguin, 2006), 152–53, 155, 158–59. Among the notable issues to arise from lack of cultural understanding was the American central command producing acronyms like NIC (New Iraqi Corps), which sounded like the Iraqi slang for "fuck."

42. *Sheriff*, 214–65. This scene extends over several of the original issues of Volume 2.
43. *Sheriff*, 216, 226, 230, 237.
44. *Sheriff*, 240–46.
45. *Sheriff*, 254–56.
46. *Sheriff*, 264.
47. *Sheriff*, 220–70.
48. *Sheriff*, 269–70.
49. Rivera, "Why the CIA Has to Read This Comic Before You Can."
50. Duane Cady, *From Warism to Pacifism: A Moral Continuum* (Philadelphia: Temple University Press, 2010), xvii–xviii. *Sheriff* is relatively rare in Iraq War-set American comics for its lack of a just war narrative. But the degree to which it cynically rejects alternative policy narratives makes it virtually unique.
51. *Sheriff*, 287.
52. *Sheriff*, 273.

15

VIOLENCE FOR THE CAUSE
Social Justice and the Need for Representations of Violence

RITA COSTELLO

Censorship is an act of violence, a means of securing control for the powerful by silencing the marginalized. As in the iconic Act Up poster, *Silence = Death* (Finkelstein), efforts to erase violence from comics enact the same equation; silencing violence can literally erase women, people of color, LGBTQ peoples, and the disabled, among others. While the Comics Code of 1954 purported to curb violence, some rules are explicit about erasure and quelling unrest. The very first rule seems straightforward—"Crimes shall never be presented in such a way as to create sympathy for the criminal" (quoted in Nyberg 166)—but marginalized people are often criminalized. For example, the Supreme Court did not strike down laws criminalizing homosexuality until 2003. Regardless of criminalization, several rules eradicate LGBTQ people: "Illicit sex relations are neither to be hinted at nor portrayed. . . . sexual abnormalities are unacceptable"; "The treatment of love-romance stories shall emphasize the value of the home and the sanctity of marriage"; "Sex perversion or any inference to same is strictly forbidden" (quoted in Nyberg 168). In other words, Comics Code rules effectively equate LGBTQ *existence* with violence and corruption. The Code silences other ostracized and marginalized groups not openly criminalized as well; consider what the third rule truly says during the civil rights era: "Policemen, judges, Government officials and respected institutions shall never be presented in such a way as to create disrespect for established authority" (quoted in Nyberg 166). This rule becomes official the same year as *Brown v. Board of Education*, the year *before* Rosa Parks holds her seat, nearly a decade *before* the church bombing in Birmingham. In 1954, "established authority" kills citizens; to say comics cannot portray government officials or institutions in a way that "create[s] disrespect for established authority" is to say African American experience is not welcome and there is no room for protest. "Established authority" often oppresses marginalized groups of all types; these rules teach comic book readers their place and make sure comics strive to keep them in that place. This is not a side-effect of comics censorship, but rather a feature.

The expert witness against comics in the Senate Subcommittee on Juvenile Delinquency hearings, Dr. Fredric Wertham, alleged comics engender "race hatred" and that Hitler was "a beginner compared to the comic book industry" (Senate Subcommittee, 1:04:06–1:04:27). However, it is worth noting the first (and, for over a decade, only) incident of a publisher standing up to the Comics Code Authority (CCA)—William Gaines, the expert witness on behalf of comics—later exposed racism in how the code was applied. When Gaines, the original publisher of Al Feldstein and Joe Orlando's "Judgment Day" (1953), planned a postcode reprint in 1956, the Head of the CCA, Judge Charles Murphy, refused CCA approval.[1] The story follows a space-suited Earth man visiting a "planet of mechanical life" to evaluate if they are evolved enough to join a federation. He finds that the orange robots have subjugated the blue robots based on the color of their metal. The story ends with the official telling the robots they are not ready—but giving hope for progress by referencing Earth's history—and, once off the planet, removing his helmet in the final frame to reveal the protagonist as a Black man. Violence does not need to be depicted to be perceived. Murphy refused approval due to the final frame, telling Gaines "Judgment Day" could not be published with a Black astronaut, implying it inspires violence even without showing it. After Gaines threatened to sue, the request was greatly lessened to removing beads of sweat from the astronaut, but Gaines refused and published without revision (Von Bernewitz and Geissman 88). The precode publication had received positive responses including a letter from Ray Bradbury, who proclaimed the story "should be required reading for every man, woman, and child in the United States"—a message obviously anathema to the goals of the CCA.

Though Wertham may have ostensibly been antiracist, his approach to gender and sexuality reads more sinister. His book, *Seduction of the Innocent*, classifies superhero comics as crime comics and claims they literally seduce children by flipping "the short circuit which connects violence with sex ... slumbering in all people" (179). Girls learn "identification of sex with violence and torture [which may cause] actual frigidity" (185) and "homosexual childhood prostitution, especially in boys, is often associated with stealing and violence. For all of these activities children are softened up by comic books" (187).[2] These topics were raised when Wertham testified and his testimony before the Senate Subcommittee forms the basis for much of the CCA code.

Erasure ensues in creators as well as characters. As Betsy Gomez remarks in *She Changed Comics*, prior to CCA there was "something resembling gender parity" in comics but with the code came "a long period of near-erasure." When comics came under attack, Trina Robbins notes "as with any industry, the first fired were women" (117) and by 1974 "there were exactly two women artists left working for mainstream comic[s]" (118). Women forced out of the mainstream "turned to underground comix, alternative comics, and webcomics" (Gomez) or "left the industry" (Robbins 115–16). Since the demise of the code, however, "women comics creators are dominating the mainstream" (Gomez).

The CCA industry-created censorship—purportedly to limit violence in the pages of comic books (and designed to head off governmental censorship)—cultivated violence outside of those pages. Looking at the CCA rules alongside of the works that violated and eventually brought them down (fully defunct as of 2011) illuminates an interlocking violence of erasure and silencing most acutely visible in the areas of race, gender, and sexuality.

I. ESCAPING THE TRAP

It is no accident that underground comix became an intensifying movement in 1960s America—quick on the heels of congressional infringement threatening external censorship, which led to formation of the CCA's internal censorship, underground comix emerged as a response to these pressures. The system is a quiet violence of erasure—*do as I say or else*—and comix were *underground* precisely because they refused self- and industry-imposed censorship against violence and sex. As such, comix might be more aptly explained as the punk music of the comic book industry—comix are DIY, antiestablishment, intent on exposing what polite society hides. Mainstream comics censorship relies on the fallacious packaging of comics as juvenile—a model that would later prove useful for the Parents Music Resource Center—by way of pretending comics are both aimed solely at children as an audience *and* not worthy of adult audiences or literary ambitions.

Comix expanded alongside the civil rights, feminist, and gay liberation movements. They are graphic in the colloquial sense as well—I once burst from my office upon hearing an administrative assistant telling a student my graphic novels course would cover "novels with graphic sex and violence." But, in my attempt to correct the record, I had to concede there would be sex and violence—we would be reading Art Spiegelman, Alison Bechdel, and Los Bros Hernandez, along with more fantastical texts by Alan Moore,

Neil Gaiman, Frank Miller, Kelly Sue DeConnick, and Bryan K. Vaughan. "That just isn't the meaning of the term *graphic* in *graphic novels*" I added feebly. There would be gore, haunting images of hanged mice wearing Stars of David, and human bodies rent asunder. Nevertheless, the term "graphic" is more sophisticated pun than literal description.

Luminaries of comix, such as Robbins, who established *Wimmen's Comix* along with the Wimmen's Comix Collective, and Spiegelman, welcomed and cultivated writers and artists who could not create within mainstream comics under the CCA. When Spiegelman's *Maus* tore the veil between underground comix and mainstream publishing, it brought the underground above surface and disturbed established categories. *Maus* won a Pulitzer Prize in 1992 but in a special category,[3] so as not to open the door to other texts that might follow *Maus* through the rent in the fabric of literature.

II. I CAN'T UNSEE THAT!

Why did *Maus* break through where others could not? Despite Wertham's testimony that fantastical settings don't matter, truth does matter, and *Maus* offered a nonfiction narrative about a major historical event. Comix often deal with personal narratives or dark realities, but the historical bent of *Maus* allowed the establishment to see value in the medium, and in its relationship to the Holocaust and its aftermath, where the devastating violence is central to what we want a global citizenry to remember and learn. Yet *Maus*'s violence is also memorial—Spiegelman acts as mediator between his father's firsthand experience of violence and the reader's experience of that violence. Spiegelman captures a history we are afraid of losing as those who experienced it pass away of old age. Published around the time the youngest of WWII veterans neared their seventies, *Maus* acts as testament to a time of cultural anxiety, to a fear that the loss of survivors would mean a cultural loss of the Holocaust as warning; that *never again* could be possible again once the survivor generation passed away.

Regardless of the mediated storytelling in the text of *Maus*, the graphic form often implies direct storytelling through images. Vladek may *tell* the story to Art, whose perspective influences readers, but the violent images typically place the reader in Vladek's perspective. Moments when Vladek kills a surrendering soldier (48) or faces the violence of forced marches, camps, and transport trains (*Maus II*, 82–88) are drawn from Vladek's perspective, not from Art's. Spiegelman visually removes himself in these times to give the impression that the audience is receiving Vladek's story firsthand. The power of images is undeniable and yet graphic literature is held paradoxically suspect as not sophisticated enough to hold literary value and as a potential danger precisely because it *shows* us what we would rather be left to the imagination. The core iconography of *Maus* is taken directly from propaganda of the Third Reich in which Jewish people were frequently portrayed as vermin infesting the nation. Spiegelman's iconography also references international slang and slurs. These images could easily be misinterpreted, but Spiegelman takes dehumanized imagery typically associated with insults and humanizes it. Just after Vladek first encounters a Nazi flag and the violence that will become the Holocaust, we see a scene of idyllic international and interethnic socializing and dancing between German cats, French frogs, Polish pigs, American dogs and Jewish mice in *Maus I* (35); in *Maus II* Spiegelman depicts a blended family of a German (cat) wife, Jewish (mouse) husband, and children with mouse ears and cat stripes who help Vladek after the war (131). In both scenarios, Spiegelman simply allows the animal imagery to convey another level of story.

Violence—active and implied—factors into humanizing the animal imagery as well. In *Maus I*, we see the cry of a newborn Richieu—Spiegelman's brother—as a distinctly rodential open mouth provoking empathy (30). The mouth repeats a few pages later with a mouse being beaten to death, which is captioned, "The police came to his house and no one heard again from him" (33). This facial expression becomes a symbol of violence—nearly subliminally—as it repeats throughout, most notably on the faces of mice left hanging "to make an **example**" (83–84). The cry, which begins in innocence, becomes fully symbolic of paralyzing fear and ubiquitous violence. When this facial expression appears on Spiegelman's grandfather behind a window, we hardly need his anguish explained (115). The cry becomes more actively violent in *Maus II*—for instance the cover for "Chapter Two: Auschwitz (Time Flies)" where it appears on mice engulfed in flames and surrounded by flies (39). It is clear from the layout that the screams are from the past in Auschwitz and the flies are of the present, connecting death images of the Holocaust to the writer and reader's present.

Maus may allow us to see graphic texts as academically and literarily legitimate, but it is an ongoing battle. The German government had to be convinced the text was "a serious [historical] work" in order to justify publishing it in the face of laws against displaying the swastika; in 2015 *Maus* was pulled off Russian store shelves in response to a similar law (Gambino). In 2022, a ban of *Maus* by a school district in Tennessee (by unanimous vote) caused a national uproar—and greatly increased sales (Kasakove). Recently one of my students was accosted in the campus bookstore because of the swastika on the cover. *Images have power*—and in many ways the power of *Maus* is that the images show us violence and cause us pain for a positive purpose and in a way that text without graphics could not accomplish.

III. SURVIVING CHILDHOOD

The next few texts that gain acceptance by exploiting the fissure created by *Maus* share the nonfiction, biographical narrative component: Marjane Satrapi's *Persepolis* and Bechdel's *Fun Home*. Much later, Congressman John Lewis, Andrew Aydin, and Nate Powell's *March* trilogy reinvigorates the graphic memoir, pushing anew the boundaries of violence use and demonstrating concretely the need for depictions of violence.

Persepolis recounts a ten-year-old's blunt and brutal understanding of revolution—which quickly turns to barbarism—as her parents discuss the events of the evening:

> The doors had been locked from the outside a few minutes before the fire.
> The police were there.
> They forbade people to rescue those locked inside.
> Then they attacked them. (14)

Satrapi's artwork is gruesome—the police club those outside trying to help, while in the next frame the dying theatregoers appear as screaming white skulls whose bodies turn to flame as they try to flee—yet this is bookended by domestic images of her parents talking in bed, heads on soft pillows and comforter pulled up (14–15). Satrapi barges in demanding to accompany them to a protest, and her father explains, "It is very dangerous. They shoot people" (17). In some passages, Satrapi's text speaks of violence, but the imagery is domestic, as when her mother tells of her own father's torture and imprisonment: "Sometimes they put him in a cell filled with water for hours. / I remember when I was a small girl . . . / . . . every time there was a knock on the door I thought they were coming to take my father to prison" (24). In these three panels we see a horrified Satrapi listening to her mother, a sad-faced mother telling the story, followed by the mother as a child frightened from her dolls by a knock at the door.

Satrapi does also depict horrific violence. Images of men being tortured (whipped, urinated on, burned with irons) are directly shown to readers as the child listens to political prisoners reminisce about being tortured and the dismemberment of a friend—"My parents were so shocked . . . that they forgot to spare me this experience" (51–52). One of the most affecting panels in *Persepolis* is distinctly violent—showing young boys thrown in the air by explosions—but visually stylized. The image accompanies the moment Satrapi realizes authorities manipulate people—"The Key to Paradise was for poor people. Thousands of young kids, promised a better life, exploded on the minefields with their keys around their necks" (102)—and is illustrated with a stark silhouette that obscures individualized details of the dying boys but for the Keys to Paradise thrown out from their chests to convey the violence of the blast. Most of the CCA code regarding violence is violated in *Persepolis*.

More recent autobiographical texts such as the *March* trilogy shows us exactly why violence is needed.[4] *March* is unswerving in its depictions of violence during the civil rights era. Lewis's memoir is ostensibly *about* violence and serves as a history of the violence perpetually surrounding the student nonviolent resistance movement. Although the books progress from childhood to adulthood, they are not linear; we see—even before the title—marchers confronted by police brutality on Edmund Pettus Bridge. Even in *Book One*, originally marketed to middle school readers, the story and art do not shy away from violence—we see marchers beaten (8–9), Emmett Till's murdered body (57), and a brutal attack on a lunch counter sit-in while the police do nothing then arrest the victims (101–3). Unlike the other texts I've discussed here, *March* is unquestionably intended for young audiences (currently marketed to grades eight through twelve); it is crucial to acknowledge violence serves a constructive purpose even for young readers. Without seeing violence, the story is whitewashed and the power of nonviolent protest in the face of a violent establishment is lost.

These texts offer the real, lived experiences of violence often at the hands of—or at least condoned by—established authority, defined in CCA rule three as "Policemen, judges, Government officials and respected institutions" (quoted in Nyberg 166). Although these works all violate the CCA, their value as literature or cultural record—much like *Maus*—is more easily argued despite the violence. The violence is true as well as clearly depicted in service of a cause.

IV: MUTATION-AS-METAPHOR

Violence in service of fictional storylines potentially serves the same purpose as those we seem to accept more willingly in nonfiction. Contemporary neuroscience indicates that reading fiction improves our ability to function in the world. After demonstrating "significant increases in connectivity" in the brain after reading fiction (Berns et al.), Dodell-Feder and Tamir suggest that "readers may make good citizens because fiction reading is associated with better social cognition [and when] compared to nonfiction reading and no reading, fiction reading leads to a small, statistically significant improvement in social-cognitive performance" (1713). Scientific conclusions aside, it seems obvious from a humanities perspective reading about varied backgrounds and obstacles makes readers more adaptable to new people and situations; the nonfiction graphic memoir may have opened the door, but the superheroes Wertham and Congress feared also have the potential to present purposeful violence.

After Gaines republished the science fiction story "Judgment Day" in 1956, the next instance of mainstream comics standing up to the CCA was not until 1971, when Stan Lee, at the request of the US Health, Education, and Welfare Department (now HHS), wrote a Spider-Man arc about drug abuse. With a government agency backing him, Lee was not too far out on a limb to publish without CCA approval; however, it is notable that it took fifteen years for a second instance of comic creators defying the CCA overtly. Additionally, a thread of clear violations of the code by Lee presumably went under the radar of the CCA. They did not deny approval to *X-Men*, first published in 1963, which clearly violates the rule "to avoid references to physical afflictions or deformities" (quoted in Nyberg 167). What a double-edged sword! On the one hand, this situation illustrates bias in application of the code toward silencing potential social unrest; on the other that biased application of the code allowed for the birth of a comics universe that deals subversively with many real-world issues under the cover of mutation-as-metaphor.

And what of superheroes hiding their vigilantism behind a secret identity? Surely most superheroes "create sympathy for the criminal"; as criminal vigilantes they also violate the rule that "criminals shall not be presented so as to be rendered glamorous or to occupy a position which creates a desire for emulation" (quoted in Nyberg 166). Wertham was concerned about superheroes and classified them as criminals, also arguing that they promoted homosexuality—but the CCA selectively applied standards did not appear to identify vigilantism as crime. Nor did the CCA seem to worry that "all characters shall be depicted in dress reasonably acceptable to society" (quoted in Nyberg 167). If one is straight, white, male, and part of the power structure, it is probably okay to wear tights and beat people up. Thus, violence for the cause has always been allowed, but only if that cause supports the establishment.

Artists and writers were always creating adult fictional comics content. Alan Moore's *V for Vendetta*—with delayed-but-eventual recognition of literary merit—is an obvious example. *V* began publication in 1981 in *Warrior*, an alternative British magazine, but was unfinished when *Warrior* folded. Moore's introduction to the first full run indicates how relevant the violence of his created world was:

> It's 1988 now.... and the tabloid press are circulating the idea of concentration camps for persons with AIDS. The new riot police wear black visors, as do their horses, and their vans have rotating video cameras mounted on top. The government has expressed a desire to eradicate homosexuality, even as an abstract concept, and one can only speculate as to which minority will be the next legislated against. (6)[5]

While created outside the CCA-regulated system, Moore's work generally, and *V for Vendetta* particularly, illustrates many of the problems with that system.

V is consistently and excessively violent—by the second page, potential protagonist sixteen-year-old Evey makes her first awkward attempt at prostitution; by the third, police attempt to rape her; by the fourth, tear gas is deployed; by the fifth, a man blows up; by the sixth, government buildings blow up with Evey fearfully saying, "That's against the law! They'll kill you" (10–14). The pace of violence hardly slows from there, as we witness a criminal protagonist, kidnapping, torture, pedophilia, all manner of government abuse, and murder. It violates nearly every element of the CCA, but it never once seems gratuitous because the violence of *V* is central to the content and meaning. In this and other Moore works, the *cause* is a broader fight against authoritarianism or, more precisely, illuminating the dangers of not standing up when anyone is marginalized or subjugated by an established authority.

Moore's *Watchmen* also seeks to illuminate the tendency to glorify authority through revealing cultural issues with superheroes. Violence is used to expose our willful blindness to the ramifications of power—from specific violence such as rape (ch. II. 6–7) to broader world ending apocalypse (ch. IX. 10).[6] Where *Watchmen* shows us the dangers of accrued power and the lack of empathy accompanying power, Miller's *The Dark Knight Returns* asks us to question at what point *saving* others becomes an ethical issue and recontextualizes Superman as blindly following established authority (118–20, 185–98). Once we see this ignoble Superman, we inevitably crave a book like Mark Millar's *Red Son* showing a Superman following a different authority than the "American Way." *Red Son* exposes Superman's problematic patriotism by imagining what happens if he lands and is raised in Russia instead of the US. His ethic has not changed, but his power now serves totalitarianism as he attempts to kill off dissent to maintain peace and order, as Superman explains:

> Barely a decision was made across the length and breadth of the Soviet Union without my permission in some form or another. The population was largely grateful and obedient but the freedom fighters, inspired by the death of Batman, remained something of a problem. My desire for order and perfection was matched only by their dreams of violence and chaos. I offered them Utopia, but they fought for the right to live in Hell. (Millar 101)

The final frame of this speech depicts a spray-painted Batman emblem across a city building indicating that the resistance movement survives. The "violence and chaos" Superman speaks of is the struggle for freedom in the face of authoritarianism, and this Superman has no doubt about his proper role in suppressing resistance. Typical superheroes function much like capricious Greek Gods. Whereas Wertham warned of precode comics creating ethical and moral confusion and crime before the Senate Subcommittee, traditional CCA era superhero comics engendered submission to authority, their actions just had to be moved to a different context to reveal this. The skewed superhero tales of Moore and others attempt to expose how traditional superhero narratives cultivate readers' desire to be saved, to be ruled, and to sacrifice individual freedoms.

V. EMBRACING NONCOMPLIANCE

The series *Bitch Planet* takes place in an utterly imaginary realm of an off-world penal colony and is in that way nearly the opposite of *Maus* as historically significant memoir; yet it ends up being prophetic and culturally relevant. As writer and cocreator, Kelly Sue DeConnick said in a recent interview: "We weren't really trying to be a political warning. . . . Then the world went to hell in a handbasket" (quoted in Abad-Santos). What DeConnick and cocreator Valentine De Landro *were* trying to do, she goes on to say, was create a comic modeled after exploitation films "without being exploitative . . . to see if we could do these things . . . from a feminist perspective." The look of *Bitch Planet* has much in common with visual trappings associated with mainstream comics of the sixties and seventies—from Ben-Day dots to the structure of stylized mail-order advertisements. The propaganda and sloganeering associated with this nostalgia acts as an assault on the main characters. This nostalgia visually represents a traditional view of gender roles, gender identity and compliance to the patriarchal protectorate. As part of the larger paratext, several mock ad pages at the outset of the series are entitled "Hey Kids, Patriarchy!" These are gradually replaced by one-time headings such as "Welcome to Womanhood. Welcome to Compliance!" (*Book Two*, no. 6) and "Put It on Your Face: Misandry Cosmetics" (*Book Two*, no. 7). Ad pages feature coded missed connection personals and mail-order sales—in one ad we see "diet parasites," a popular media topic in the 1970s (*Book One*, no. 3); in another a pop-art wife (with husband reading the newspaper in the background) is told "What Every Girl Should Know: Your vagina is disgusting," while a different advert on the same page provides a drawing of a woman with victory rolls hairstyle promoting *Agreenex* pills which the small print indicates "[won't] change your circumstances, but it **keeps you from caring**. Because without thoughts, feeling or inconvenient opinions, you're **more fun to be around**" (*Book One*, no. 4). Through all these there is an undercurrent of unseen violence that complements and complicates the express violence within the storyline. By including this paratext, DeConnick and De Landro violate even the advertising rules of the CCA. Rule breaking is part of the point and *Bitch Planet* is relentlessly and clearly on a mission of empowerment, justice, and equality. The kick-ass protagonists are women labeled "non-compliant" (NC)—reasons for which range from turning down a date, talking back to a man, holding a position of power, to having a positive self-image when others think you should want to be thinner, or just being married to a man who prefers his mistress.

In the nonprison world, pink holographic women represent salespeople, secretaries, and peppy newscasters. On Bitch Planet, male representatives of the protectorate monitor women through surveillance, and the women instead interact with a monstrous pink hologram that fuses the virgin/whore dichotomy in the form of a nun's headdress and an over-sexualized, corseted body. Women held captive in the setting of a male-run prison provide the iconography of sexploitation and girls-in-prison films, which then become tools for DeConnick's feminist narrative. Within this world, The Fathers of the Protectorate "believe that participation in sports culture is a healthy channel for what could otherwise be a destructive impulse" and so broadcast Megaton competitions (*Book One*, no. 2). The game as explained in the comic is based on a violent, medieval Italian proto-football, *Calcio Fiorentino*,[7] which incorporates one-on-one combat; however, in *Bitch Planet*'s variation of the game, spectacle and showmanship are encouraged and a team may have any number of members as long as their combined weight is under a ton (*Book One*, no. 4). Kam, a former professional athlete pressured by threats to her family into leading the first NC team, provides the imagery of kung-fu films along with some imagery associated with blaxploitation and sexploitation films. In the first issue she immediately puts her fighting skills to use in the defense of others, and eventually readers encounter a shower scene featuring Kam that leads to a prison riot. The riot expands the world of the main characters; references throughout the first story arc suggest the existence of "gender traitors" who, in the second arc, are revealed to occupy another portion of the planet designed to imprison trans women.

Bitch Planet manages to be elevating despite being a violent, dystopian hellscape in which women who dare to show self-respect or critical thought are trapped. Heroes are established and then killed off—giving and taking away hope from the audience. But it is observing the fight and the small victories—which of course do not lead to escape or reestablishing the world order—along with a wickedly sarcastic sense of humor that generate hope in the face of hopelessness. Because *you can't jail the revolution.*

VI. OVERTHROW THE PROTECTORATE

Protecting children from violence and moral decrepitude is a common means of subjugating adults as well. Like *Bitch Planet*'s Fathers of the Protectorate, the Senate Subcommittee on Juvenile Delinquency and CCA believed they should have complete authority to determine what is appropriate. They are every bit the overbearing patriarchy silencing independent thought in *Bitch Planet*, the fascist Norsefire government of *V for Vendetta*, the police brutally beating nonviolent protesters of the *March* trilogy. This is hyperbolic, but I contend that it is also true. An examination of the code's application leaves no doubt that suppressing marginalized voices and quelling protest was at play in how the CCA applied rules against violence in comic books.

We live in a violent and unjust world. Censoring violence can silence those against whom violence and injustice are directed. Violence in comics not only gives voice to the marginalized, but also provides paths forward and generates a useful resistance in the reader—one that makes readers struggle or question in a way productive to the story and to real-world growth. Underground comix and independent creators allowed violence for a cause and amplified marginalized voices during the repressive years when the CCA dominated mainstream comics. Violent fictional worlds frequently speak to readers specifically because of how they illuminate the social justice failings in our own world. Very often the use of violence also functions as an entrance point to the literary heft of the text—a point at which the reader is confronted with self-reflection or layers of implications. We have been able to see this more easily in graphic nonfiction and admit those texts into the academic canon (respectability!) well before we could see how the same issues at play in these nonfiction texts may equally be functioning in fictional texts too.

Notes

1. Reprinted in *Incredible Science Fiction* 33 (Feb. 1956).

2. Wertham is remembered for crusading against comics but is not so one-dimensional. He worked with destitute patients and fought segregation—see "Psychiatry and the Prevention of Sex Crimes" (1938) and "Psychiatric Observations on Abolition of School Segregation" (1953). He likewise addressed Nazi doctors harming children (*A Sign for Cain*, 1966) and even applauded fanzines (*The World of Fanzines*, 1973).

Also notable is Christopher Pizzino's claim that Wertham—although "strongly biased" and an "anticomics crusader"—acts as "a key early theorist of the medium" because "for most of the twentieth century, contempt for comics trumped sincere scholarly curiosity about them" and Wertham at least entered into "serious inquiry of a kind" in his treatment of the medium (18).

Many of Wertham's views are abhorrent, however, such as his assertion that comics lead to "10, 11, 12, 13-year-old girls prostituting themselves to adults" (Senate Subcommittee 12:44–13:05). In introducing himself to the Senate, Wertham jokes about his research career commencing with "brain syphilis [which] came in good stead when I later on studied comic books" (2:37–2:50). But even in his zeal, he defends comics creators when a senator alleges they must be perverse (16:20–17:45).

3. According to Thomas Doherty, the Pulitzer committee was "befuddled by a project whose merit they could not deny but whose medium they could not quite categorize" (69). While *Maus II* begins with a meta-discussion of reality—"in real life you'd **never** have let me talk this long without interrupting" (16)—Spiegelman protested the *New York Times Book Review* categorizing *Maus* as fiction: "If your list were divided into literature and non-literature, I could gracefully accept the compliment as intended, but to the extent that 'fiction' indicates a work isn't factual, I feel a bit queasy" (quoted in Doherty 69). *Maus* moved to the nonfiction list.

4. A strong example related to gender is Una's *Becoming Unbecoming* (Arsenal Pulp, 2016), a memoir addressing a serial killer, sexual assault, and repercussions when authorities don't listen to or trust women's voices.

5. The same year, Moore published *AARGH!* (*Artists Against Rampant Government Homophobia!*), an anthology protesting Clause 28—UK antigay legislation outlawing "promotion of homosexuality." The international contributors include underground, alternative and mainstream creators such as Art Spiegelman, Neil Gaiman, Los Bros Hernandez, and Frank Miller.

Moore is not alone in giving voice to the marginalized in fictional comics of this time. Gaiman's *The Sandman* story arc, *A Game of You* (1991–1992), is provocative in how it uses violence to challenge sex and gender biases of its time—facing a backlash then for featuring a lesbian couple and a trans woman as protagonists but problematic now as views on sexuality and gender identity have evolved. Yet the violence and prejudice (as well as the love and friendship) characters encounter are realistic despite being in a fantasy comic.

6. HBO's *Watchmen* (2019) takes place in a future based on the graphic novel and addresses race, authority, and silencing in a way relevant to my position regarding violence. The focus on white supremacy makes its purpose more explicit than the graphic novel.

7. Benito Mussolini revived the medieval *Calcio Fiorentino* in 1930.

Works Cited

Abad-Santos, Alex. "Bitch Planet Has Always Been Absurd. But in 2017, It Reads Like a Warning: A Chat with Co-Creator Kelly Sue DeConnick." *Vox*, Feb. 8, 2017. vox.com/culture/2017/2/8/14480086/bitch-planet-interview-deconnick.

Bechdel, Alison. *Fun Home: A Family Tragicomic*. Mariner-Houghton Mifflin, 2006.

Berns, Gregory S., Kristina Blaine, Michael J. Prietula, and Brandon E. Pye. "Short- and Long-Term Effects of a Novel on Connectivity in the Brain." *Brain Connectivity* 3, no. 6 (2013): 590–600.

Bradbury, Ray. Letter. "Cosmic Correspondence." *Weird Fantasy* 20, EC Comics. July–August 1953. "JUDGEMENT DAY (EC, 1953)." Imgur. holyicon, June 21, 2015. imgur.com/gallery/RIcAF.

DeConnick, Kelly Sue, and Valentine De Landro. *Bitch Planet. Book One: Extraordinary Machine*. Portland: Image Comics, 2015.

DeConnick, Kelly Sue, and Valentine De Landro. *Bitch Planet. Book Two: You Can't Jail the Revolution*. Portland: Image Comics, 2017.

Dodell-Feder, David, and Diana I. Tamir. "Fiction Reading Has a Small Positive Impact on Social Cognition: A Meta-Analysis." *Journal of Experimental Psychology* 147, no. 11, (2018): 1713–27.

Doherty, Thomas. "Art Spiegelman's *Maus*: Graphic Art and the Holocaust." *American Literature* 68, no. 1 (1996): 69–84.

Feldstein, Al, and Joe Orlando. "Judgment Day." *Weird Fantasy* 18, EC Comics. April 1953. "JUDGEMENT DAY (EC, 1953)." Imgur. holyicon, June 21, 2015, imgur.com/gallery/RIcAF.

Finkelstein, Avram. *Silence = Death*. San Francisco Museum of Modern Art, San Francisco, 1986.

Gaiman, Neil. *The Sandman. Volume 5: A Game of You*. Preface by Samuel R. Delany. New York: DC-Vertigo, 1993.

Gambino, Lauren. "Art Spiegelman Warns of 'Dangerous' Outcome as Russian Shops Ban *Maus*." *The Guardian*. April 28, 2015. www.theguardian.com/books/2015/apr/28/art-spiegelman-russia-maus-bookstores-holocaust.

Gomez, Betsy. Editor's Note. *She Changed Comics: The Untold Story of the Women Who Changed Free Expression in Comics*. Berkeley: CBLDF-Image, 2016.

Kasakove, Sophie. "The Fight Over *Maus* Is Part of a Bigger Cultural Battle in Tennessee." *New York Times*, March 4, 2022. https://www.nytimes.com/2022/03/04/us/maus-banned-books-tennessee.html.

Lewis, John, Andrew Aydin, and Nate Powell. *March Trilogy*. Marietta, GA: Top Shelf, 2016.
Miller, Frank. *Batman: The Dark Knight Returns*. 1986. Burbank: DC Comics, 2002.
Millar, Mark. *Superman: Red Son*. Burbank: DC Comics, 2003.
Moore, Alan, ed. *AARGH! (Artists Against Rampant Government Homophobia!)*. Mad Love, 1988.
Moore, Alan, and Dave Gibbons. *Watchmen*. Burbank: DC Comics, 1987.
Moore, Alan, and David Lloyd. *V for Vendetta*. Burbank: DC Comics, 1990.
Nyberg, Amy Kiste. *Seal of Approval: The Origins and History of the Comics Code*. Jackson: University Press of Mississippi, 1998.
Pizzino, Christopher. "On Violation: Comic Books, Delinquency, Phenomenology." In *Critical Directions in Comics Studies*, edited by Thomas Giddens, 13–34. Jackson: University Press of Mississippi, 2020.
Robbins, Trina. *Pretty in Ink: North American Women Cartoonists, 1896–2013*. Seattle: Fantagraphics, 2013.
Satrapi, Marjane. *Persepolis: The Story of a Childhood*. Paris: L'Association, 2000. Translated by Blake Ferris and Mattias Ripa (New York: Pantheon, 2003).
Senate Subcommittee on Juvenile Delinquency. "Subcommittee to Investigate Juvenile Delinquency and Comic Books Afternoon Session," testimony from Fredric Wertham and William Gaines recorded April 21, 1954. NYC Municipal Archives, WNYC Collection / The NYPR Archive Collections. wnyc.org/story/subcommittee-to-investigate-juvenile-delinquency-and-comic-books-afternoon-session/.
Spiegelman, Art. *Maus I: My Father Bleeds History*. New York: Pantheon, 1986.
Spiegelman, Art. *Maus II: And Here My Troubles Began*. New York: Pantheon, 1991.
Von Bernewitz, Fred, and Grant Geissman. *Tales of Terror: The EC Companion*. Seattle: Fantagraphics, 2000.
Watchmen. Created by Damon Lindelof. Season 1. HBO, 2019.
Wimmen's Comix Collective. *The Complete Wimmen's Comix*. 1970–1992. Seattle: Fantagraphics, 2016.

ACKNOWLEDGMENTS

This project is a long time in the making, and we are deeply thankful to everyone involved. *BOOM! SPLAT! Comics and Violence* was first conceptualized at a Society for the Study of Southern Literature conference, when the late great M. Thomas Inge happened to overhear our conversation and enthusiastically encouraged us to move forward with the project—we are certain that without his initial push and excitement, you wouldn't be holding this book in your hands. Suffice it to say, it's been a journey to get here, and there are many people to whom we would like to express our gratitude.

Jim would like to thank Katie, Finn, and Irene for their unwavering support and positivity. He would also like to acknowledge the faculty at Indiana University Kokomo for their helpful suggestions and encouragement. He is grateful to Jo for her knowledge, insight, and tenacity (and for her being the voice of reason and calming his anxieties about the project). And, of course, thank you to our contributors!

Jo is immensely grateful to her partner, Colin, and their child, August—thank you so much for your patience and loving kindness. She would also like to thank Addie Tsai, TJ Tallie, Daniel Davis, Don and Beth Davis, Anna Hinton, Devin Garofalo, Priscilla Ybarra, Aja Martinez, Jacque Vanhoutte, John Edward Martin, Maia Butler, Megan Feifer, Steve Cobb, Andy Kunka, Vinny Haddad, and all the contributors to this volume for the (material, emotional, intellectual) support in bringing this volume to completion. She would *especially* like to thank her coeditor, Jim, for his grace, steadfastness, and helpfulness—this project would never have been realized without you! Finally, Jo would like to thank the English Department at the University of North Texas for providing her with a semester off from teaching, which made possible the final stages of editing and writing the collection.

ABOUT THE CONTRIBUTORS

Lawrence Abrams is a doctoral candidate in history at the University of California, Davis, and a teacher with Portland Public Schools in Oregon. He is a specialist in British imperial history, interactions between social and educational systems with the military, and comics media. His research explores ideas of union and changing modes for the expression of Scottish identity in political, military, and cultural arenas. He is also working on projects investigating the relationship between comics and national identity in an international and postcolonial context in the activist comic years since 1970. He is the coeditor of *Historians without Borders: New Studies in Multidisciplinary History* (Routledge, 2019).

Diana Álvarez Amell is associate professor of Spanish at Seton Hall University. She has a PhD from Cornell University. Her areas of interest are Latin American literature and cultural and visual narratives. Her work focuses on the representational constructions in fiction. Her most recent book *Tres Novelas* is an edited edition of three early novels by Cirilo Villaverde. She has also published *El discurso de los prólogos del Siglo de Oro: la retórica de la representación*. She is a contributing editor of the Hispanic Division of the Library of Congress and a literary translator. Her articles have been published in American and international academic as well as in literary journals. Her article "El diadema sobre los pergaminos. La importancia de la poesía de José Triana" appeared in *Justicia para todos/Justiça para todos/Justice for All* in 2022.

Partha Bhattacharjee is assistant professor of English at SRM University *AP*, Andhra Pradesh, India. He earned his doctoral degree from the Department of Humanities and Social Sciences, IIT Patna, under the supervision of Dr. Priyanka Tripathi, associate professor of English. Prior to that, he pursued MPhil and MA degrees in English from the University of Burdwan, India. Apart from three book chapters in edited volumes, *Tintin in Tibet by Herge:*

A Critical Companion (2021), *The Routledge Handbook of Translation and Activism* (2020), and *Performativity, Cultural Construction, and the Graphic Narrative* (*Routledge Advances in Comics Studies*, UK) (2019), he has had his articles published in reputed journals such as *Journal of Visual Communication in Medicine* (Taylor & Francis, Q1), *Studies in Comics* (Q2), *Journal of International Women's Studies*, *Journal of Gender Studies* (Taylor & Francis, Q1), *Journal of Graphic Novels and Comics* (Taylor & Francis, Q1), *The Translator* (Taylor & Francis Q1), *IUP Journal of English Studies* (Q3), and *Atlantic Literary Review*, to name a few. He has also reviewed two books for reputed journals. He serves as an editorial board member for the *Journal of International Women's Studies* (Q3).

Natalja Chestopalova is a researcher, writer, and multimedia producer at OCAD University. Her work focuses on immersive installations and multimodality in the graphic novel medium, animation of archives and museum collections, and blockchain solutions for art and site-responsive projects. Natalja's publications have been featured in *Collections: A Journal for Museum and Archives Professionals*, *Canadian Journal of Communication*, and *Dialogue*; latest book chapters can be found in *The Comics of Alison Bechdel: From the Outside In*; *Who's Laughing Now? Feminist Perspectives on Humour and Laughter*; and *Television Series as Literature*.

Jim Coby is assistant professor of English at Indiana University Kokomo. He is currently coediting *Conversations with Stephen Graham Jones* and has previously published or has work forthcoming in *South Central Review*, *Rocky Mountain Review of Language and Literature*, *North Carolina Literary Review*, *Clues: A Journal of Detection*, *Supernatural Studies*, and others.

Rita Costello holds creative writing and English degrees from Bowling Green State University, Wichita State University, and the University of Louisiana at Lafayette. Originally from New York state, she has also lived in the Midwest, the South, and in Central China. Currently, she serves as assistant department head of English and Foreign Languages as well as the program director of Women and Gender Studies at McNeese State University, where she teaches courses on the graphic novel, science fiction and fantasy, drama, poetry, hybridity, women and gender studies, and more. Recent presentations on related topics include "Desirable Difficulties: A Pedagogy of Graphic Texts and Visual Rhetoric," "In the Gutter and the Gallery: When Shifting Space Alters Everything," "Moving the Margins: Creating Physical Space for the Other in Mainstream Comics and Graphic Novels," "The Bureaucratic

Nightmare: From *The Memorandum* to *Bitch Planet*," and "Time (and Time Again): Creating Credibility through Visual Manipulations of Time and Memory in Graphic Memoir." She is coeditor of the LGBTQ+ poetry anthology *Bend Don't Shatter*—and, with Asimov's "any book worth banning is a book worth reading" in mind, felt a spark of satisfaction when the old book turned up on the list of 850 books banned by Texas in 2021. Her creative work has appeared in journals such as *Under the Sun, Glimmer Train, ACM, Chattahoochee Review, Eastwesterly Review*, and *Baltimore Review*. A personal and professional highpoint was the opportunity to meet and speak with Congressman John Lewis when asked to present at a National Book Awards Festival event celebrating *The March Trilogy*.

Sam Cowling is associate professor in the department of philosophy at Denison University. He is the coauthor of *Philosophy of Comics* (Bloomsbury, 2022) with Wesley D. Cray and *Abstract Entities* (Routledge, 2017). Dr. Cowling's research focuses on metaphysics and the philosophy of comics. He has published articles in *Analysis, American Philosophical Quarterly, Australasian Journal of Philosophy, Inks, Philosophical Studies, Philosophical Quarterly*, and the *Stanford Encyclopedia of Philosophy*.

Joanna Davis-McElligatt is assistant professor of Black literary and cultural studies at the University of North Texas, where she is affiliate faculty in women's and gender studies, and LGBTQ studies. She is at work on her first monograph, entitled *Black Aliens: Navigating Narrative Spacetime in Afrodiasporic Speculative Fiction*. She is the coeditor of five volumes: *Narratives of Marginalized Identities in Higher Education: Inside and Outside the Academy* (Routledge, 2019), *Narrating History, Home, and Dyaspora: Critical Essays on Edwidge Danticat* (University Press of Mississippi, 2022), *Afrosouthernfuturism* (in progress), and *Transgressive Teaching and Learning: Critical Essays on bell hooks' Engaged Pedagogy* (in progress). Her scholarly work appears or is forthcoming in *south: a scholarly journal, Mississippi Quarterly, The New William Faulkner Studies* (Cambridge University Press, 2022), *The Cambridge Companion to the American Graphic Novel* (forthcoming, Cambridge University Press), *A History of the Literature of the U.S. South* (Cambridge University Press, 2021), *Routledge Companion to Literature of the U.S. South* (Routledge 2022), and *Small Screen Souths: Region, Identity, and the Cultural Politics of Television* (LSU Press, 2017), among other places. Her work on comics has appeared in the *Comics Journal, Snapshots: Teaching Love and Rockets* (2023), *Graphic Novels for Children and Young Adults* (University Press of Mississippi, 2017), and *The Comics of Chris Ware: Drawing Is a Way* *of Thinking* (University Press of Mississippi, 2010). She is the illustrator for *Educating for Social Justice: Field Notes from Rural Communities* (Brill/Sense, 2020). In 2024, she will serve as president of the Comics Studies Society.

Elisabetta Di Minico is a UNA4CAREER postdoctoral researcher with a project on the "Enmity of Otherness" at the Complutense University of Madrid (Faculty of Political Science and Sociology). Her studies focus on the relation between fiction and history. She deals primarily with dystopia, control, otherness, and violence (racial and gendered). She uses novels, comics, movies, and TV series to provocatively analyze the real "bad places" of contemporary society on a historical and sociological level. With a PhD *cum laude* in contemporary history from the University of Barcelona, she also teaches comic history at IULM-Free University of Language and Communication of Milan and is part of the HISTOPIA research group. Among her publications stand out the monograph *Il futuro in bilico* (Meltemi, 2018), the chapters "Utopía y distopía del cuerpo femenino" (in *Lugares de utopía. Tiempos, espacios y estrías*, Libros Polifemo, 2019), "X-Men Saga and the Dystopian Otherness: Race, Identity, Repression and Inclusiveness in the Mutant World" (in *Utopia and Dystopia in the Age of Trump*, Fairleigh Dickinson University Press, 2019), and the articles "Entre el malson i la realitat. Reflexions distòpiques sobre la societat contemporània" (in *Quaderns de Filosofia* 7/2, 2020), "Spatial, Linguistic and Psycho-Physical Domination of Women in Dystopia: *Swastika Night*, *Woman on the Edge of Time* and *The Handmaid's Tale*" (in *Humanities* 8, 2019), and "*Ex-Machina* and the Feminine Body Through Human and Posthuman Dystopia" (in *Ekphrasis. Images, Cinema, Theatre, Media* 1/17, 2017).

Kiera M. Gaswint graduated from Bowling Green State University with her master's degree in literary and textual studies in May 2018. Kiera's research activities include gender representations in popular media such as comics, film, and television. Her recent publications include her thesis, "A Comparative Study of Women's Aggression," and a chapter titled "'There Must Always Be a Thor': Marvel's *Thor the Goddess of Thunder* and the Disruption of Heroic Masculinities," published in *Superheroes and Masculinity*.

Vincent Haddad is associate professor of English and the coordinator of interdisciplinary studies at Central State University. He is currently writing his first book, *Repping the D: How Black Writers Transformed the Detroit Genre after 2008* (Lever Press). He was recognized with the 2022 Comics Studies Society Article Prize for his article "Detroit vs. Everybody (Including

Superheroes)." His academic scholarship on comics has appeared or is forthcoming in *Inks*, *College Literature*, and *ImageTexT*, as well as several edited collections. His public scholarship on comics has appeared in *Middle Spaces*, *Los Angeles Review of Books*, *The Rambling*, and *Public Books*.

Kaleb Knoblauch is a PhD candidate at the University of California, Davis, where he specializes in modern Breton history. His research includes identity formation and its mediation in popular culture, francophone and Breton comics, and the history of superhero comics. He has taught secondary and university history courses in European, world, and American history. He is the coeditor, with Lawrence Abrams, of *Historians without Borders: New Studies in Multidisciplinary History* (Routledge, 2019).

Christina M. Knopf is professor and presentation-skills coordinator in the Communication and Media Studies Department at the State University of New York (SUNY), Cortland. Dr. Knopf is the author of *Politics in the Gutters: American Politicians and Elections in Comic Book Media* (University Press of Mississippi, 2021) and *The Comic Art of War: A Critical Study of Military Cartoons, 1805–2014* (McFarland, 2015). Her work on military culture, political communication, and the popular arts also appears in numerous edited volumes and journals, such as *NANO*, *Military Sociology: An Annual Review*, *Space Power Journal*, and *Unbound*. She is a John P. Wilson Fellow of the New York State Communication Association, a past president of the New York State Communication Association, and a Distinguished Research Fellow of the Eastern Communication Association. Dr. Knopf is a coeditor of the Routledge Advances in Comics Studies series and serves on the editorial board of the *Home Front Studies* journal. She holds a PhD from the University at Albany, concentrating in cultural sociology and political communication.

Leah Milne is the author of *Novel Subjects: Authorship as Radical Self-Care in Multiethnic American Narratives* (University of Iowa Press), which won the Midwest Modern Language Association Book Award in 2021. *Novel Subjects* examines multiculturalism and self-care in metafictional works by authors such as Carmen Maria Machado, Ruth Ozeki, Toni Morrison, and Louise Erdrich. Milne is an associate professor of English at the University of Indianapolis, where she teaches courses on multicultural, postcolonial, and young adult literature and directs the English graduate program. Her scholarly work has been published in journals such as *The Journal of American Culture*, *African American Review*, and *MELUS*. Her op-eds have been published in *Newsweek*, *The Hill*, and *Ms. Magazine*.

Jacob Murel currently holds a postdoctoral research position at Northeastern University in Boston. Much of his research has focused on digital methods and approaches to analyzing the visual and textual features of comics. His work has appeared in *ImageText*, *Digital Scholarship in the Humanities*, and *INKS: The Journal of the Comics Studies Society*, among other venues.

Priyanka Tripathi is associate professor of English and head of the Department of Humanities and Social Sciences at the Indian Institute of Technology Patna. She is also the coexecutive editor of *Journal of International Women's Studies* (published by Bridgewater State University). She has been awarded a visiting research fellowship (2022–23) by IASH, University of Edinburgh, for her project titled "Optimizing Caste Intersectionality: A Decolonial Reading of Gender-Based Violence in Select Subaltern Fiction in India." She has published extensively and received several grants: JIWS fellowship 2021–22 (Bridgewater State University), Shastri Conference and Lecture Series Grant (SCLSG) 2021–22, Post-Colonial Association grant 2020–21, CIIL conference grant 2020, amongst others. She has also worked on several government-sponsored projects related to gender issues. Her forthcoming monograph with Bloomsbury is titled *The Gendered War: Evaluating Feminist Ethnographic Narratives of the 1971 War of Bangladesh*. She works in the areas of gender studies, South Asian fiction, GeoHumanities, and graphic novels.

Steven S. Vrooman is professor of communication at Texas Lutheran University and chair of the Department of Communication, Cultures, English and World Languages. He teaches on popular culture, rhetoric, gaming, social media, and data analytics. His research has included work on fandom, nerd culture, comics, horror film, reality television, and internet cultures, as well as leadership and pedagogy. He is the author of *The Zombie Guide to Public Speaking*.

INDEX

adolescence, 8, 142, 157, 165–66, 167, 169
Africa, 192
African Americans, 91–92, 173, 177, 180, 194, 213
aggression, 46, 63, 106, 110, 117–19, 120–21, 122–27, 128–29, 136, 144, 146, 153–54, 155, 156
archives, 11, 56, 57–58, 60, 62–64, 66, 67, 167, 173, 186
Aristotle, 23
Armada, Santiago. *See* Chago
Australia, 34–35
autobiography, 11, 56, 67, 106, 161–62, 164, 169, 218
autographics, 14, 58–61, 64–65, 67, 161–69
Aydin, Andrew, 14, 186, 187, 188–89, 217

Bairnsfather, Bruce, 34–35
Barry, Lynda, 162
Barthes, Roland, 59, 109, 112
Batman (character), 104, 123, 133, 137, 143, 221
biography, 36, 217
Bitch Planet (comics), 221–23
Black (graphic novel), 173, 176–78, 180
Black Lives Matter, 14, 173, 177, 179, 183, 193
Blackness, 4, 12, 83–85, 89–90, 91–96, 117, 136, 173, 174–79, 180–81, 182–83, 187, 190, 192–93, 199, 213
bodies, 4, 89–91, 93, 95, 103, 106, 110, 119, 121–22, 126, 129, 134, 139–41, 144, 145, 147n4, 152, 161–63, 166, 167, 168, 170n1, 181, 198–99, 200, 201, 202, 204, 206, 208, 218, 222
Bronze Age of Comics, 138, 143

Calvin and Hobbes (comic strip), 71–81
Canada, 34, 64
Captain Marvel (DC character), 123, 135, 147
Captain Marvel (Marvel character), 13, 117, 119, 122–25, 128–29, 136, 147
caricature, 24, 45, 48, 88–89, 179
cartoons, 6–15, 34–36, 38, 44–54, 71, 72, 81, 85, 87–88, 97, 135, 173, 175, 176, 177, 178–79, 180–81, 182–83, 186
censorship, 44, 48, 51–53, 202, 212–14, 223
Central Intelligence Agency (CIA), 45, 196, 206, 208
Chago, 11, 44, 47–48, 50–53
childhood, 47, 49, 63, 66, 105, 145, 161, 163–65, 166, 169, 185, 188, 198, 200, 204, 213, 217
Chute, Hillary, 15, 35, 39, 104–6, 151, 167, 186
Clowes, Daniel, 12, 100–102, 111–12
cognition, 5, 62, 66–67, 135, 219
Cohn, Neil, 71–75
Cold War, 46–47
comedy. *See* humor
comic and newspaper strips, 3, 12, 34, 45, 48–49, 52, 71–72, 73–75, 77–78, 79–81, 83–84, 135, 149, 167
comics: anthology, 33–34, 38, 224; closure, 9, 61, 76–77, 174, 201; color, 8, 33, 37, 40, 83–97, 163, 187; grammar, 85–86, 87–89, 103, 111; gutter, 58, 76–78, 108–9, 164, 174–75, 186, 188, 191, 198; icon, 12, 71, 89, 162, 216, 222; ink, 36, 39, 83, 89, 139; montage, 102–3, 108–10; onomatopoeia, 3, 74, 198, 200–201, 203, 205, 207; word

235

balloon, 7–9, 38, 58, 61, 63, 66, 108–10, 169, 188
Comics Code Authority, 9, 15, 30n5, 176, 212–14, 218–23. *See also* Wertham, Frederic
Crenshaw, Kimberlé, 4–5
Crowley Jack, Dana, 117–18, 119, 120–21, 122, 126–27

Dark Horse Comics, 84
DC Comics, 3, 13, 20–21, 83, 123, 133, 147–48, 203
death, 3–4, 6, 9–10, 35–36, 37, 38, 39, 40, 52, 63, 76, 85, 95–96, 105, 110, 120–22, 137, 142–43, 152, 156, 168, 173–74, 177, 180–83, 185, 192–94, 198, 205–6, 216–18, 221
decolonization, 11, 56, 57, 58, 59, 60, 61, 62, 64–65
DeConnick, Kelly Sue, 136, 215, 221–22
Derrida, Jacques, 101–2, 106, 112
Downie, Gord, 11, 57–58, 63–64, 65, 66–67

Eco, Umberto, 49
Eisner, Will, 7, 85
ethics, 6, 10, 21, 22–24, 25, 27, 28, 29, 30, 56–59, 61–62, 65–67, 87, 174, 176, 178, 186, 220–21
Evans, Kate, 11, 57, 58, 59, 62–63, 65–67

feminism, 4, 111, 133–34, 135, 136–38, 146–47, 179, 214, 221–22
film, 3, 9, 46, 48, 84, 106, 108, 117, 150, 166, 176, 221–23
Foucault, Michel, 100

Gaines, William, 213, 219
Gardner, Jared, 58
gender, 4, 46, 86, 101, 107, 117, 118–19, 120, 121, 122, 124, 125–26, 127–28, 129, 132–33, 134, 136, 137, 138–39, 141, 142, 144, 146, 179–80, 196, 199–200, 214, 222–23
Genius (graphic novel), 173, 179–81
Gerads, Mitch, 15, 196–97, 199–201, 203–4, 207
Golden Age of Comics, 137

graphic novels, 11, 14, 33–34, 36, 56–58, 59–63, 65, 67, 83, 106–7, 109, 173, 182, 185, 188, 198, 214–15
Groensteen, Thierry, 10, 81

Hernandez, Gilbert, 106, 214
Holocaust, 215–16
horror, 3, 8–9
Hulk (character), 119, 121–22, 129
humor, 34–36, 40, 45, 47, 49–51, 72, 80–81, 133, 201, 223

I Am Alfonso Jones (graphic novel), 173, 182–83
Indigeneity, 63–64, 117
Infantino, Carmine, 20–21
Inge, M. Thomas, 151, 227
Iraq, 196–208
irony, 21, 34, 39–40, 46, 101, 138, 179, 196, 201

King, Tom, 15, 196–97, 199–201, 203–4, 207–8
King, Martin Luther, Jr., 177, 188–89, 191, 193–94
Kirby, Jack, 101, 147–48
Ku Klux Klan, 192–93

Lee, Stan, 15, 147–48, 219
Lemire, Jeff, 11, 57–59, 62, 63–64, 65, 66–67
Lewis, John, 14, 185–89, 190–94, 217–18

MAD (magazine), 45–47, 50–51
Malcolm X, 192
Marston, William Moulton, 133, 137, 147
Marvel Cinematic Universe, 117
Marvel Comics, 3, 13, 119–20, 123, 129, 133, 135, 147–48, 176
McCloud, Scott, 9, 12, 61, 76–78, 101, 102–4, 105–6, 112, 186, 210
memoir, 14, 161, 163, 186, 194, 217, 218, 219, 221
memorialization, 11, 32, 41, 56, 62, 198, 215
memory, 11, 14, 32–33, 35–37, 38, 39, 40–41, 56–57, 63, 67, 103–4, 125, 141, 164, 169, 174
military, 20, 33, 39, 44, 47–48, 58, 147, 179, 181, 197, 203, 206

Millar, Mark, 141, 220–21
Modern Age of Comics, 138
Moore, Alan, 15, 104, 143, 214, 219–21, 224

New Criticism, 100
New Journalism, 59–60, 65
New Zealand, 34
nonfiction comics, 36, 56, 57–58, 59, 60, 62, 64–65, 66, 67, 215, 217–19, 224. *See also* autobiography; memoir
nonlinear storytelling, 163, 165, 187
nonviolence, 10, 14, 19, 26–28, 104, 107, 180, 185, 188–89, 191–92, 193, 194, 218, 223. *See also* pacifism
nostalgia, 38, 40, 221–22

onomatopoeia, 3, 74, 198, 200–201, 203, 205, 207

pacifism, 10, 19, 25, 27–28, 207. *See also* nonviolence
pain, 6–7, 11, 35–37, 53, 65, 79, 95, 124, 142–43, 154, 163, 164–65, 167, 169, 173, 175, 208, 217
patriarchy, 128, 133, 134, 136–37, 140, 141, 142, 144, 146, 147n1, 222–23
photography, 14, 36, 60, 90–92, 95, 142, 173–74, 186, 200
Polak, Kate, 174–75, 178, 180, 186
Postema, Barbara, 58–59, 78, 81
Powell, Nate, 14, 187–89, 192–93, 217
Prohías, Antonio, 11, 44–47, 49, 51, 53
psychology, 3, 5–8, 13, 28, 40, 44–45, 49, 63, 103, 126, 133–34, 136, 141, 143, 145, 148, 151, 154, 156–57, 161, 163, 165–66, 169–70, 175, 198–99, 204–5, 208

race: difference, 83–84, 86, 88–89, 92, 94, 97, 175, 178, 194; inequality, 93, 176; phenotype, 12, 83–85, 89–92, 93, 94, 96; racecraft, 86–88, 90
rage, 38, 120–22, 128–29, 146, 190
Rand, Ayn, 22–24
rationalism, 24–25, 52
refugees, 11, 57, 59–61, 63, 65–66
Robbins, Trina, 214–15

Sacco, Joe, 11, 56–57, 58, 59, 60–62, 63, 65–67, 72
satire, 35, 46, 140
Satrapi, Marjane, 15, 217–18
science fiction, 9, 111, 219
semiotics, 7, 12, 47, 59, 61, 65, 72, 88, 101–2, 103, 104, 105, 112, 162
sentimentalism, 24
sexuality, 52, 108, 119, 132, 133–34, 135–37, 138, 139, 140–41, 142, 143–44, 145–46, 147n1, 162, 164–65, 166, 167–68, 212–14, 224–25
She-Hulk (character), 13, 117, 119–22, 125, 126, 127, 128–29
Shendruk, Amanda, 132–33, 138–39
Silver Age of Comics, 138, 141, 143
Skeates, Steve, 19, 20–21, 22, 23, 26–27
Spiegelman, Art, 15, 51, 87–89, 214–16, 224
Spy vs. Spy (comic), 11, 46–47
structuralism, 100–103, 106, 112
Student Nonviolent Coordinating Committee (SNCC), 189–90, 193, 218
Supergirl (character), 119, 123, 135
superheroes, 3, 10–11, 13–14, 19–21, 28, 29–30, 56, 72, 105, 117, 118–19, 120, 122–23, 125–26, 127, 128, 129n2, 132, 133–36, 137, 138–40, 141–44, 146, 147n1, 147nn3–4, 148nn5–6, 173, 175–76, 177–78, 181–82, 187–88, 194, 213, 219–20, 221
Superman (character), 9, 49, 104, 119, 123, 137, 141, 220–21

television, 56, 103, 110, 158, 166, 174, 177, 187, 193–94, 202
Tilley, Carol L., 8
Töpffer, Rodolphe, 3, 9, 87–89
trauma, 6, 11, 13–14, 35, 38–39, 56–57, 59–60, 61, 62–63, 64, 66, 106, 120–22, 141–42, 145–46, 156–57, 161, 162–65, 166, 167–69, 174–75, 179, 201

underground comix, 214–15, 223
United Kingdom, 10, 33, 65

Vertigo Comics, 83

victims and victimization, 14, 53, 57–58, 62, 95, 108, 110, 141, 144–46, 155, 169, 173–74, 177, 182–83, 198–200, 209, 218

Vietnam, 20, 143

violence: aesthetics, 5, 7, 14, 30, 32, 36, 40, 133; affect, 5–6, 24, 58, 60–63, 65–66, 67, 87–88, 153, 161, 163, 218; collective, 3–5, 12, 39–41, 198; emotional, 3, 6–7, 26, 38, 62, 72, 122, 126–27, 198, 203, 207; gendered, 4, 102, 121, 196, 199–200; ideological, 3, 5, 7, 47, 49–51; individual, 4–5, 11, 57–59, 63–64, 76, 78–79, 118, 144, 201, 207; physical, 3–6, 11–13, 26–28, 38, 40, 44, 63, 71–76, 78–82, 87, 106, 117, 121–22, 124, 125–28, 132–33, 136, 154, 156–57, 159, 161, 163, 166, 169, 170n1, 197–99, 219; police, 26, 66, 86, 173, 175–77, 179, 180–81, 182, 183, 187, 192–93, 196, 212, 216–18, 220, 223; racial, 4, 14–15, 58, 59–60, 66, 85, 86, 89, 90–91, 92, 94, 95, 96–97, 173–75, 176, 177–79, 180–83, 196, 199; self-harm, 4, 198, 200, 203; sexual, 63, 133, 142–46, 161–62, 164, 174, 198–201, 220

Wertham, Frederic, 3, 8, 150, 213, 219, 221, 224. *See also* Comics Code Authority

white supremacy, 85–86, 88, 89, 90–91, 92, 94, 95, 97, 225

whiteness, 84, 89, 91–92

witnesses and witnessing, 7, 8, 12, 26, 39, 47, 56–58, 62, 67, 78, 90, 95, 121, 138, 147, 157–59, 162, 165, 179, 186, 188, 190, 202, 213, 220

Wonder Woman (character), 119, 133–34, 137, 143, 147

World Health Organization, 3, 197

World War I, 10, 32–33, 36, 39–40

World War II, 36, 134, 147, 200

X-Men (comics), 133–37, 219

X-23 (character), 117, 119, 126–29

Printed in the USA
CPSIA information can be obtained
at www.ICGtesting.com
JSHW021550030224
56306JS00005B/10